THE MYSTERIOUS NUMBERS OF THE HEBREW KINGS

Edwin R. Thiele

THE MYSTERIOUS NUMBERS OF THE HEBREW KINGS

New Revised Edition

kregel
PUBLICATIONS

Grand Rapids, MI 49501

The Mysterious Numbers of the Hebrew Kings
by Edwin R. Thiele.

Copyright © 1983 by The Zondervan Corporation.

This edition issued by special arrangement with
Zondervan Publishing House, Grand Rapids, Michigan,
U.S.A. in 1994 by Kregel Publications, a division of
Kregel, Inc., P.O. Box 2607, Grand Rapids, MI 49501.
Kregel Publications provides trusted, biblical publica-
tions for Christian growth and service. Your comments
and suggestions are valued.

Cover design: Alan G. Hartman

Library of Congress Cataloging-in-Publication Data
Thiele, Edwin Richard, 1895–1986.
  The mysterious numbers of the Hebrew kings / by
Edwin R. Thiele.
      p.   cm.
Previously published: Grand Rapids, MI,: Zondervan,
c1983.
Includes bibliographical references and indexes.
  1. Bible. O.T. Kings—Chronology. 2. Bible. O.T.
Chronicles—Chronology. 3. Chronology, Jewish.
4. Jews—History—953–586 b.c.—Chronology. I. Title.
BS1335.5,T48   1994   222'.5095—dc20   94-25569
                                            CIP

ISBN 0-8254-3825-x

    1 2 3 4 5 6 Printing / Year 98 97 96 95 94

Printed in the United States of America

Contents

Appendixes

List of Charts of Reigns and Map

List of Diagrams

Lists

DATES OF THE RULERS OF JUDAH AND ISRAEL

JUDAH	B.C.	ISRAEL	B.C.
Rehoboam	930–913	Jeroboam I	930–909
Abijah	913–910	Nadab	909–908
Asa	910–869	Baasha	908–886
Jehoshaphat		Elah	886–885
coregent	872–869	Zimri	885
Jehoshaphat		Tibni	885–880
total reign	872–848	Omri	885–874
Jehoram		Ahab	874–853
coregent	853–848	Ahaziah	853–852
Jehoram		Joram	852–841
total reign	853–841	Jehu	841–814
Ahaziah	841	Jehoahaz	814–798
Athaliah	841–835	Jehoash	798–782
Joash	835–796	Jeroboam II	
Amaziah	796–767	coregency	793–782
Azariah (Uzziah)		Jeroboam II	
overlap with Amaziah	792–767	total reign	793–753
Azariah (Uzziah)		Zechariah	753
total reign	792–740	Shallum	752
Jotham		Menahem	752–742
coregency	750–740	Pekah	752–732
Jotham		Pekahiah	742–740
official reign	750–735	Hoshea	732–723
Jotham			
total years	750–732		
Ahaz			
overlap with Jotham	735–732		
Ahaz			
official years	732–715		
Hezekiah	715–686		
Manasseh			
coregent	696–686		
Manasseh			
total reign	696–642		
Amon	642–640		
Josiah	640–609		
Jehoahaz	609		
Jehoiakim	609–598		
Jehoiachin	598–597		
Zedekiah	597–586		

THE DATA AND DATES OF THE RULERS OF JUDAH AND ISRAEL IN THEIR ORDER OF SEQUENCE

No.	Reference	Ruler	Kingdom	Synchronism	Length	Notes	Dates
1.	1 K 12:1-24; 14:21-31	Rehoboam	Judah		17 years		930–913
2.	1 K 12:25–14:20	Jeroboam I	Israel		22 years		930–909
3.	1 K 15:1-8	Abijah	Judah	18th of Jeroboam	3 years		913–910
4.	1 K 15:9-24	Asa	Judah	20th of Jeroboam	41 years		910–869
5.	1 K 15:25-31	Nadab	Israel	2d of Asa	2 years		909–908
6.	1 K 15:32–16:7	Baasha	Israel	3d of Asa	24 years		908–886
7.	1 K 16:8-14	Elah	Israel	26th of Asa	2 years		886–885
8.	1 K 16:15-20	Zimri	Israel	27th of Asa	7 days		885
9.	1 K 16:21, 22	Tibni	Israel			Rival of Omri	885–880
10.	1 K 16:23-28	Omri	Israel			Rival of Tibni	885–880
					12 years	total reign	885–874
				27th of Asa		made king by the people	885
				31st of Asa		beginning of sole reign	880
						official reign	880–874
11.	1 K 16:29–22:40	Ahab	Israel	38th of Asa	22 years		874–853
12.	1 K 22:41-50	Jehoshaphat	Judah		25 years	coregency with Asa	872–869
						official reign	872–848
				4th of Ahab		beginning of sole reign	869
						Jehoram Jehoshaphat's regent	853–848
13.	1 K 22:51–2 K 1:18	Ahaziah	Israel	17th of Jehoshaphat	2 years		853–852
14.	2 K 1:17	Joram	Israel	2d of Jehoram			852
	2 K 3:1–8:15			18th of Jehoshaphat	12 years		852–841
15.	2 K 8:16-24	Jehoram	Judah	5th of Joram	8 years	coregency with Jehoshaphat	853–848
						sole reign	848–841
						beginning of sole reign	848
						official reign	848–841
16.	2 K 8:25-29	Ahaziah	Judah	12th of Joram	1 year	nonaccession-year reckoning	841
	2 K 9:29			11th of Joram		accession-year reckoning	841

17.	2 K 9:30–10:36	Jehu	Israel		28 years		841–814
18.	2 K 11:1-21	Athaliah	Judah		7 years		841–835
19.	2 K 12:1-21	Joash	Judah	7th of Jehu	40 years		835–796
20.	2 K 13:1-9	Jehoahaz	Israel	23d of Joash	17 years		814–798
21.	2 K 13:10-25	Jehoash	Israel	37th of Joash	16 years		798–782
22.	2 K 14:1-22	Amaziah	Judah	2d of Jehoash	29 years		796–767
						overlap with Azariah (Uzziah)	792–767
						coregency with Jehoash	793–782
23.	2 K 14:23-29	Jeroboam II	Israel	15th of Amaziah	41 years	total reign	793–753
						beginning of sole reign	782
						overlap with Amaziah	792–767
24.	2 K 15:1-7	Azariah (Uzziah)	Judah	27th of Jeroboam	52 years	total reign	792–740
						beginning of sole reign	767
25.	2 K 15:8-12	Zechariah	Israel	38th of Azariah	6 months		753
26.	2 K 15:13-15	Shallum	Israel	39th of Azariah	1 month		752
27.	2 K 15:16-22	Menahem	Israel	39th of Azariah	10 years	ruled in Samaria	752–742
28.	2 K 15:23-26	Pekahiah	Israel	50th of Azariah	2 years		742–740
29.	2 K 15:27-31	Pekah	Israel	52d of Azariah	20 years	in Gilead; overlapping years	752–740
						total reign	752–732
30.	2 K 15:32-38	Jotham	Judah	2d of Pekah	16 years	beginning of sole reign	740
						coregency with Azariah	750–740
						official reign	750–735
	2 K 15:30					reign to his 20th year	750–732
						beginning of coregency	750
31.	2 K 16:1-20	Ahaz	Judah	17th of Pekah	16 years	total reign	735–715
							735
32.	2 K 15:30	Hoshea	Israel	12th of Ahaz*	9 years	from 20th of Jotham	732–715
							732–723
33.	2 K 18:1–20:21	Hezekiah	Judah	3d of Hoshea*	29 years	20th of Jotham	732
							715–686

No.	Reference	Name	Kingdom	Length	coregent with Hezekiah	total reign
34.	2 K 21:1-18	Manasseh	Judah	55 years	696–686	696–642
35.	2 K 21:19-26	Amon	Judah	2 years		642–640
36.	2 K 22:1–23:30	Josiah	Judah	31 years		640–609
37.	2 K 23:31-33	Jehoahaz	Judah	3 months		609
38.	2 K 23:34–24:7	Jehoiakim	Judah	11 years		609–598
39.	2 K 24:8-17	Jehoiachin	Judah	3 months		598–597
40.	2 K 24:18–25:26	Zedekiah	Judah	11 years		597–586

*These data arise when the reign of Hoshea is thrown twelve years in advance of its historical position.

The references in Kings for the various rulers, given in the first column in their order of sequence, present the reigns in accord with the sequence in which they began. But Pekahiah, number 28, is not in accord with this sequence, for he began in 742, and thus should have followed Pekah and Jotham, numbers 29 and 30, who began in 752 and 750 respectively.

Two systems of reckoning were used for the Hebrew kings, accession-year reckoning (postdating), and non-accession-year reckoning (antedating). Since in the latter system the year in which a ruler began is termed his first official year, that year is counted twice, for it is also the last year of the previous ruler. Thus in a country where this system is used, one year must always be deducted from the official total of every reign in order to secure actual years. Totals according to accession-year reckoning, however, equal actual totals. Judah used accession-year reckoning from Rehoboam to Jehoshaphat, non-accession year reckoning from Jehoram to Joash, and accession-year reckoning again from Amaziah to Zedekiah. Israel used nonaccession-year reckoning from Jeroboam to Jehoahaz, and accession-year reckoning from Jehoash to Hoshea. The dates here given are in accord with the use of these systems.

Since regnal years in Judah began with Tishri in the fall, and in Israel with Nisan in the spring, Hebrew regnal years always overlapped two January years, and for this reason a dual symbol such as 931/930 would be more accurate than the single date 930 here used. In the interests of simplicity, however, single dates are here given.

Preface

For more than two thousand years Hebrew chronology has been a serious problem for Old Testament scholars. Every effort to weave the chronological data of the kings of Israel and Judah into some sort of harmonious scheme seemed doomed to failure. The numbers for the one kingdom could not, it seemed, be made to agree with the numbers of the other. The data concerning the synchronisms appeared in hopeless contradiction with the data as to the lengths of reign. Dates established by the biblical numbers seemed to be constantly out of line with the dates of Israel's neighbors.

All through the ages, however, the unexplained mysteries of Hebrew chronology have strangely intrigued biblical scholars. Baffled and bewildered though they often were, they did not give up the attempt to solve the vexing problems of Old Testament chronology. The mysterious numbers of the kings must at length be made to reveal their secrets. The frequency with which studies on this subject have continued to appear is indicative of the sustained interest in this problem and of the unceasing urge to bring it to a solution.

As long as Old Testament study remains the serious subject that it is, and as long as chronology retains so vital a place in this field of study, efforts to solve the seemingly inscrutable riddle of Hebrew chronology will be in order. This is outstandingly so in the periods of the monarchies of Israel and Judah when many of the writings of the Old Testament came into being and when Hebrew history was so closely in touch with the stirring events of the ancient East.

The establishment of the correct chronology of a nation is always a matter of some importance, and in the case of the Hebrews—in view of the important role they have played in world events throughout the ages—this is particularly true.

The greatest drawback in the study of Old Testament chronology has been, and still remains, a tendency to hold to certain preconceived opinions without first endeavoring to ascertain just what the Hebrews did in the matter of chronological procedure. Altogether too often we formulate our own conclusions as to what they did, or should have done. Then, without sufficient evidence, we endeavor to produce chronological schemes in accord with our own

15

predetermined ideas, only to be led into impossible impasses and hopeless confusion. Instead of such a priori methods, we must approach the work of the ancient Hebrew chronologists with an open mind, examining fairly and objectively what they did, and, on the basis of the facts, build our interpretation of the data they have left for us. The only basis for a sound chronology of the period to be discussed is a completely unbiased use of the biblical statements in the light of all other knowledge we can bring to bear on this problem, notably the history and chronology of the ancient Near East.

The problem is one with which I wrestled long before vague outlines of a solution began to crystallize in my mind. At first I went on the natural supposition that Israel and Judah had alike used identical chronological methods and had begun their regnal years at the same time. But I could reach no satisfactory results. At length further study revealed clues and hints of a far different situation, which I have set forth in detail in the pages of this study. These proved to be the key that opened the way for further advance. But there remained hosts of knotty questions that had to be undertaken in succession; and only slowly and through constant recriticism of my results have I been able to arrive at the conclusions that I now present to Old Testament scholars and the Bible reading public. Those who are familiar with my preliminary study[1] will be in a position to observe that the main lines of my position as then attained have stood up under the criticism that I have since given it. Yet at several points I have advanced beyond my original results and have, I believe, succeeded in throwing further light on this complex but very important issue.

All the early work was necessarily explorative. I did not decide a priori that either the data regarding the synchronisms or the lengths of reign must necessarily be late and probably largely in error. Instead, I made an attempt to ascertain whether there might exist some method of chronological procedure whereby the numbers that seemed so obviously and hopelessly contradictory could be fitted together into a harmonious pattern of reigns. It was known beforehand that any reconstructed pattern of the Hebrew kings must, if it was to be indeed the original arrangement of reigns, be in complete agreement with every fixed date in Near Eastern history at which exact contact with Hebrew history could be established; hence no dates were used in the early pattern that I produced. In this way I eliminated the inclination, as certain fairly well established dates in Hebrew history were being approached, to endeavor to modify the pattern one way or another to cause it to conform to preconceived ideas of what it ought to be at those points. The completed pattern, when tested by the ascertained dates of synchronisms with Near Eastern history, thus provided its own fairest and severest test as to accuracy and fidelity. Thus as the pattern was being developed there was no knowledge of the date B.C. of any event or king. Nor were figures used to give an indication of the overall passage of time. To have inserted such numbers would have been extremely simple, for the pattern being developed showed the years of reign for all kings of Israel and Judah as they interlinked with each other; but the use of such numbers might again have resulted in an effort at adjustments as certain strategic points were

---

[1]Edwin R. Thiele, "The Chronology of the Kings of Judah and Israel," *Journal of Near Eastern Studies* 3 (1944): 137–86.

reached. The aim was to produce a system, if possible, in which the reigns of the kings were arranged in harmony with the data on both the synchronisms and the lengths of reign. Then, on the completion of such a pattern, I meant to test the results by a comparison with the established dates of contemporary history.

Thus the pattern to be set forth in this volume began with the reigns of Rehoboam and Jeroboam and was carried on to Hezekiah and Hoshea without knowledge as to the overall passage of time involved. The supreme test as to the correctness of this pattern was to come at the end by a comparison with the dates of contemporary events. Not until the preliminary pattern had been completed from Rehoboam to Hezekiah inclusive, and from Jeroboam to Hoshea, was an effort made to supply dates for the reigns of the kings.

In the pattern as it then existed, there was a harmonious arrangement of reigns according to the data of Kings for both the synchronisms and the lengths of reign except for the two synchronisms of 2 Kings 15:32 and 16:1, that is, for the accessions of Jotham and Ahaz. On the pattern as it then stood, Hoshea came to the throne in a year that was both the twentieth year of Jotham and the twelfth year of Ahaz, according to the synchronisms of 2 Kings 15:30 and 17:1; and Hezekiah began to reign in the third year of Hoshea, in harmony with 2 Kings 18:1. Jotham, however, on that pattern came to the throne in the same year as did Pekah in Israel, the year of Azariah's death, and not in Pekah's second year as called for by the synchronism of 2 Kings 15:32. Ahaz began his reign in the eighth instead of the seventeenth year of Pekah as called for by the synchronism of 2 Kings 16:1. Except for these latter two synchronisms, my arrangement was in agreement with all the data of Kings.

It was at this stage that the first endeavor was made to introduce absolute dates into the overall pattern of reigns and to test the results. The earliest known synchronisms between Hebrew and Assyrian history were the battle of Qarqar in the sixth year of Shalmaneser III at which Ahab fought in his last year, according to my arrangement of reigns, and Jehu's payment of tribute to Shalmaneser III in the latter's eighteenth year, which was the year of Jehu's accession. According to the pattern of Assyrian chronology I then followed, 854 was the date for the battle of Qarqar and 842 was the eighteenth year of Shalmaneser III. On that basis Ahab's death occurred in 854 and the year of Jehu's accession was 842. From these two basic dates, other dates were supplied back to the time of the disruption and down to the reigns of Hoshea and Hezekiah.

To my surprise and dismay the fourteenth year of Hezekiah on this pattern turned out to be 702 instead of 701, as should have been the case by a comparison with Assyrian chronology. The last year of Hoshea and the fall of Samaria was 711. A careful review of the pattern from beginning to end indicated that if the data then followed were to remain the basis of the arrangement of reigns, no adjustment for the reign of any king of either Judah or Israel was possible. A careful investigation into the exact dates of Assyrian history, however, revealed the unexpected evidence that 853 rather than 854 was the correct date for Qarqar and that 841 rather than 842 was the true date for the eighteenth year of Shalmaneser III. With such an adjustment for the dates of Ahab and Jehu, the fourteenth year of Hezekiah was found to be 701 instead of 702, a date that was absolutely correct as evidenced by Assyrian chronology. But the date for the fall of Samaria then became 710, some twelve years after the city fell according to Sargon's claims.

The next step was a careful study of the synchronistic data of 2 Kings 15 and 16 in connection with the data of 2 Kings 17 and 18. This resulted in a pattern in which harmony was secured for the synchronisms of 2 Kings 15:32 and 16:1, providing the date 723/22 for the last year of Hoshea and Samaria's fall and for the still more surprising results in chapters 6 and 9 of this volume.

Let it be repeated that the pattern of reigns set forth in the present book is not the product of certain arbitrary adjustments to secure a series of predetermined results. Rather, it resulted from a quest to ascertain whether or not the numbers now found in Kings could be brought together into some harmonious arrangement of reigns, and whether or not such an arrangement once produced was in harmony with the established dates of Near Eastern history.

In this study an endeavor has been made to keep in mind all readers who might be interested in the results achieved, whether laymen or ministers, students or teachers, undergraduates or graduates—any to whom the problems of Old Testament chronology might present an appeal.

For the results achieved, I am first and foremost indebted to my former teacher, Prof. William A. Irwin, head of the section of Old Testament in the Department of Oriental Languages and Literatures at the University of Chicago. To a large degree my interest in this present study was stimulated by Professor Irwin's keen analysis and presentation of Old Testament problems. It was in Professor Irwin's discussion of the chronological problems of the Hebrew kings that I first came to sense the need to bring order out of the prevailing chaos regarding the chronological data of the rulers of Judah and Israel. If there is anything in this volume that may contribute to the solution of this vexing problem, I owe it in large measure to the inspiration, instruction, and encouragement of Professor Irwin. To him I am also under obligation for a critical reading of this manuscript.

To Prof. George G. Cameron of the University of Michigan I am likewise indebted for much encouragement and many suggestions as well as for a reading of the manuscript. At times when the going was hard and it seemed as if certain aspects of the problem were beyond solution, Professor Cameron provided encouragement and inspiration that kept the quest under way. To him I will ever be grateful.

To Profs. Richard A. Parker of Brown University and Raymond A. Bowman and F. W. Geers of the University of Chicago, I likewise wish to express my gratitude for their suggestions and contributions.

If this volume may contribute in some small way to a better understanding of the Old Testament and the amazing story of Israel's religious experience so full of meaning for our own troubled day, I shall feel amply repaid for the effort put forth.

EDWIN R. THIELE

Berrien Springs, Michigan
7 February 1951

Preface to Second Edition

Twenty years have passed since my initial study of the chronology of the Hebrew kings was first set before students of the Bible and of the ancient Near Eastern world. The question I now face is, What have the intervening years done to the views expressed and the dates then set forth? Is the arrangement of reigns in accord with historical facts? Have my earlier views stood the test of time and of careful investigation? Or has positive evidence come to light against my conclusions? Is it correct, or still too early, to say that the outstanding chronological problems of the kings of Israel and Judah have been basically and finally solved? What are my own reactions today? Have I changed my views on any points or dates of major importance? In what areas have modifications been made, and what are the points calling for further study and clarification?

Few problems are ever so completely solved that no new light can be thrown on them by further investigation. The Hebrew kings will continue to remain a subject of study for years to come. But coming quickly to the major point, I must say that after reviewing all that is involved in this question and after having had the benefits of the reactions of scholars around the world, I am today more fully convinced than ever of the basic soundness of my early conclusions. No evidence has been forthcoming that has given me cause to change my views on any item of major importance. It is true, however, that new evidence has come to light that has made possible the fixing with certainty of a number of dates for which earlier evidence was inconclusive.

The discovery in the British Museum of certain Neo-Babylonian tablets covering the closing years of Nabopolassar and the opening year of Nebuchadnezzar has made possible the adjustment of one year in the closing dates of Josiah, Amon, and Manasseh, and the beginning date of Jehoiakim. An adjustment of a year has also been made for the beginning of Azariah's reign, which I now commence with an accession year rather than the first year of a coregency. Otherwise, my dates stand today as they did in my earlier presentations. I believe these dates are the final and absolute ones of the rulers of Israel and Judah.

In fact, many points now stand out much more clearly than during my first investigations. Of particular importance is the period involving the synchronisms of 2 Kings 17 and 18. My early views concerning those synchronisms were sound. Today I am in a position to provide biblical proof that they are right. I now understand much better their true significance, and I can see just how and when and why they came to be. These points will be presented in detail in chapters 6 and 9.

Another point that stands out more clearly today is how the documents containing the earliest contemporary records of the rulers of Israel and Judah, which later developed into the Books of Kings, first came into being. The question as to how they later were brought into the form in which we find them today will be the subject of chapter 10.

As my chronology has been discussed, responses for the most part have been favorable. More and more my chronological pattern of Hebrew history is finding acceptance, in whole or in part, in the scholarly world.

Criticisms fall into two main categories. On the one hand, certain members of liberal groups do not regard it possible for these numbers to have been handed down through so many years and so many hands "without often becoming corrupt." On the other, a few vigorously outspoken members of conservative groups view with horror any questions that may be raised concerning the absolute accuracy of any details in the Old Testament chronological data. Far apart though these two points of view may be, both rest on the same foundation of an a priori bias. Both categories have prejudged the questions at issue. Rather than permitting truth to be determined by objective investigation, both groups have pronounced a precursory judgment. Such, however, is not the attitude of true scholarship, nor is it in accord with biblical principles of religious faith and practice. Scholars impelled solely by a sincere desire for truth and an earnest effort to find it, and religious believers who find in God the very embodiment of truth and in the Hebrew Scriptures its most absolute expression, find little difficulty in putting aside early notions and accepting new light whenever and however it may come.

At times I am asked where my chronological scheme may find its greatest strength or weakness. Let me say without hesitation that the areas of greatest strength and certainty are precisely those areas where in the past the greatest difficulties and uncertainties were found. These are in the period of the divided monarchy for which there are four separate chronological yardsticks, all seemingly at constant odds with each other and with the years of contemporary history. It was long felt that these seemingly contradictory lines of measurement must be in error—one giving the years of the kings of Judah, another the years of the rulers of Israel, a third the synchronistic years of Israel with Judah, and the fourth the synchronisms of Judah with Israel. Systems of measure often vary from each other. Months or years among the ancients were not always the same. More letters are found in a line of pica type than of great primer, but fewer than of minion or nonpareil. Lines with paragraph indentations are shorter than those without. If printers, surveyors, and tailors must take into consideration the nature of the measuring instruments used and their specific methods of use, this is also true of those dealing with ancient chronology. Complex? Perhaps. But unreasonable or lacking in logic? Not at all.

When the nature of the biblical chronological yardsticks is once understood, the four instruments of measurement for the period of the divided monarchy are of the highest value in providing a sound chronology for the rulers involved. Like a jigsaw puzzle, these numbers fit together only at certain precise points and only in line with certain basic principles of chronological procedure. It was four years after I had begun a serious study of the chronological involvements of the Hebrew kings before I was able to work my way through the data for the first two or three kings of Israel and Judah. But then, having once discovered the various principles involved, in only a few weeks I made my way through to the end.

If the numbers in Kings are taken as they are, they call for certain arrangements of reigns not immediately apparent but basically inherent in the data themselves. In this volume all the data are considered, and all are allowed to have their individual bearings on the pattern produced. As I now look back on what had for so long appeared to be only an inextricable tangle of kings and lives and times, and view the clear and concise pattern of reigns for which the data call, I have no choice but to believe that this is indeed the correct restoration of ancient Hebrew history.

Let me once more call attention to the fact that in the production of the pattern here set forth, the original purpose was to secure an arrangement of reigns in harmony with the data themselves. Charts were prepared without dates of any kind to show the interrelationships of the rulers of Israel and Judah. Only at the end was there to be a check with the known years of ancient history. The results brought both surprise and delight, and it is these results that are here set forth.

At times it is said that the chronological pattern set forth here is highly complicated. That, however, is largely a matter of personal opinion. But even if complicated, would that constitute proof that the dates are wrong? The facts of history and science are often far from simple. Life is complicated but it must be lived. Chemistry and physics are highly complicated but their involved truths must be ascertained if they are to be of service to man. The great achievements of our age were not attained by appeals to simplicity.

The essential points of the chronological scheme we will present are in brief as follows: Judah began with the accession-year system, both for its own kings and its synchronisms with Israel. At a time of alliance and intermarriage with Israel, the system of Israel was adopted by Judah and was used through four reigns, after which Judah returned to its original system of reckoning. Regnal years in Judah began with the month of Tishri. In Israel the nonaccession-year system was used for the length of reign in Israel and the synchronisms with Judah. When Judah shifted back to the accession-year system, Israel also adopted that method. Regnal years in Israel began with the month of Nisan. In both Judah and Israel a number of coregencies occurred, and in Israel there were two instances of rival reigns.

After Israel had come to its end, the only chronological data were the lengths of reign of Judean kings. If chronological certainty here is to be ascertained, there must be checks with contemporary chronology. For the fourteenth year of Hezekiah, we have Sennacherib's third campaign in 701. There are no further precise contacts until 609 when Neco of Egypt marched through Megiddo on his way to the Euphrates. The intervening century is the period of greatest darkness and uncertainty. But even there the proven reliability of the data in earlier years provides confidence that in this area Judah's chronology continues to be sound.

Throughout the pages to follow we will deal with numbers and dates, with synchronisms and lengths of reign, and with regnal years commencing with Nisan or Tishri. We will also deal with various types of chronological reckoning, with coregencies and rival reigns, with Hebrews at peace or at war with each other and with their neighbors—with facts that may often appear dull and prosaic—or so small and distant as to play no significant part in our world. We must not, however, allow ourselves to become so absorbed with seemingly trifling minutiae that we lose sight of the greater issues. We are dealing with the bricks and stones, the mortar, timber, and clay that went into the building of one of the most important structures ever reared by man—the Hebrew state. This state not only had a tremendous influence in the days of David and Isaiah, and of Assyria and Babylon, but also on us three millennia later.

It is because of the timeless significance of the Hebrew people and their message of righteousness, truth, and God that we are discussing these facts. It is my hope that once this volume has been put aside and the difference between accession- and nonaccession-year reckoning has been forgotten, we may be in a better position to discern truth, chronological as well as theological and historical, and that we may recognize uprightness and justice and the things of God as matters of the highest significance to us and the world in which we dwell.

EDWIN R. THIELE

Berrien Springs, Michigan
September 1963

Preface to Third Edition

Thirty years after the publication of my solution to the problem of the mysterious numbers of the Hebrew kings comes a need for a new edition. Confused and erroneous though these numbers appeared to be, they have proven themselves to be remarkably accurate. The basic factors that brought about the solution stand out today more clearly than ever, and I will endeavor to present them here as simply as I can in dealing with admittedly complicated involvements.

I will discuss the Hebrew rulers one by one in the order of sequence in which their accounts appear in Kings. That order is important, for it is the order in which the editors of Kings believed the rulers to have commenced their reigns. Step by step I will build up the pattern that represents the original arrangement of years in which the Hebrews fitted into ancient history.

The basic principles of chronological recording followed in the original records should be clearly understood. Israel began with the nonaccession-year system and later shifted to accession-year reckoning. Judah began with the accession-year system and at a time of collaboration with Israel adopted its nonaccession-year method. Later both nations simultaneously shifted to accession-year reckoning and followed it to the end. Each nation used its own system in its synchronisms with the other nation. In Israel the regnal year began with the month of Nisan and in Judah it began with the month of Tishri. When these points are understood, order will begin to replace chaos in dealing with the regnal data.

Another point of major importance is what I have termed *dual dating*. This is discussed on page 55 of the present volume and should be carefully studied. This is the method used for the regnal data in five of the nine coregencies, or overlapping reigns, in Israel and Judah. More than anything else, the failure to understand dual dating has been responsible for the bewilderment that came in dealing with the numbers in Kings.

As I first completed my pattern of reigns, I faced problems of a single year with my date of 853 for the battle of Qarqar and 723 for Samaria's fall. The accepted date for Qarqar then was 854, a year earlier than my date; the accepted date for the fall of Samaria was 722, a year later than my date. However, in both these cases my pattern since proved to be accurate.

The year 701, when Sennacherib came against Jerusalem in the fourteenth year of Hezekiah, is a major anchor point in my pattern. That date cannot be changed. But neither can my pattern be adjusted anywhere along the line. This pattern calls for precisely 152 years from the death of Ahab to the fourteenth year of Hezekiah. And Assyrian chronology likewise calls for precisely 152 years from the battle of Qarqar in 853 to Sennacherib's attack on Hezekiah in 701. With my pattern correct at these points, I know it is also correct at all points in between.

This pattern I am again setting before students of the Bible and of the ancient Near East. It should be of value not only in setting forth the correct dates of the Hebrew kings, but also in throwing light on the correct years of neighboring nations with whom the Hebrews made precise contacts.

It is my hope that this presentation will serve to bring confidence in the biblical numbers of the Hebrew kings, in the God who placed them on their thrones, and in the principles of righteousness He expected them to uphold. This confidence, now so woefully lacking, is our primary need in our troubled and perplexed times. If we would restore confidence in God, we must restore confidence in the Bible—confidence that comes through an intelligent trust.

EDWIN R. THIELE

Angwin, California
April 1982

Introduction

It has been well said that chronology is the one sure basis of accurate historical knowledge. History, it is true, is much more than tables of dates and lists of events; these are merely annals, but history must set all in a coherent and meaningful structure of change and development. Nonetheless, to the extent that the historian is deprived of accurate dating, his results grow proportionately vague and uncertain. They become, one might say, a collection of mental antiquities, interesting and possibly beautiful, but nothing more than curios until touched by magic like that of the trained museologist who arranges his disparate pieces in a cultural sequence. When this is done, they tell to every chance observer a thrilling story of endeavor and achievement, and across the gulf of millennia we sense the toil and hopes and common routine through common days of men whom we greet as brothers and comrades in the age-long struggle for better things.

Into the *disjecta membra*, the museum pieces as it were, of events, the chronologist brings the illumination of time and sequence. And the former tales of "old forgotten, far off things, and battles long ago," mere entertainment to pique an idle mood, marshal in serried ranks and deploy against the circumstances and perplexities of the present. The matter is clarified by a contrast. An older history of Babylonia begins with the mention of three fragments of a vase of Utug, patesi of Kish, that were found on the mound of Nippur at "a great depth beneath the pavements of very early kings" and then moves on to Mesilim, who followed Utug at Kish, "though we do not know how great was the interval." This is not history, nor did the author suppose it to be. Fortunately, subsequent discoveries in the plain of Babylonia have reduced our ignorance and gone far in linking up available facts in a connected sequence. Nonetheless, it must be admitted that long stretches of history of the lands of the ancient East are yet dark ages. But the chronology of its later periods is definitely fixed, and investigations are steadily pushing farther back the limits of our precise knowledge. Isolated events can thus be fitted into the entire circumstance and movement of their time and can take on a relevance denied them as atomistic occurrences. They become historic.

There are still considerable periods of the life of ancient Israel where more light is needed. What can be written, for example, of the time from the work of Ezra to the rise of the tensions that eventuated in the Maccabean struggle? The period is historic, and the wider Orient events and their dates are well known. But for Jewish history we lack many facts. All we can affirm is that highly important developments were in process. When the veil of obscurity lifts, a very different Judaism meets the eyes. But we know next to nothing about the definite incidents and personal achievements that fit into the succession of the years. Very different is the problem of the time of the Judges, which is rich in dramatic and significant events. Yet, notwithstanding an increasing precision in the chronology of the greater political centers of that time, the Hebrew stories can be dated only in wide and sweeping generalizations. The incidents that gave rise to the Samson stories must have occurred, it is apparent, subsequent to the settlement of the Philistines on the coastal plain in the first decade of the twelfth century. The story of Micah and his idolatry and the migration of the Danites are dated by the same event. The attack on Gibeah is attested in the excavations at Tell el Ful; but it is seldom that archaeological dating, if devoid of written finds, can do more than indicate a period, a half or quarter century, or happily a decade. In this vague way one may attach a loose timing to most of the Judges stories. But that is the best we can do at present. Efforts to demonstrate an accurate chronology simply do not merit serious consideration. And so we cannot write the history of the time. Who knows, for example, whether the exploit of Ehud at Jericho preceded or followed that of Gideon at Mount Tabor, and whether there was a relation between them more intimate than mere sequence? Vague generalizations can be brought to bear on the question, but strict chronology defies us. Hence history is impossible.

Even when attention moves on to the times of David and Solomon we encounter a similar frustration. The events in the reign of David include rich personal episodes that are related by the world's first great historian. And for the time of Solomon, too, quite apart from the great royal enterprise in building, there are numerous hints and allusions that tantalize the historian with glimpses of significant movements. But we have no chronology, scarcely a scheme of sequences. We may labor to construct an outline of the major events of the time, but the inner motivation—a real understanding of that notable period—is at the best no more than vaguely discerned. At the worst it quite eludes us. If we could with reasonable certainty set one incident after another in its correct timing, we would have taken a major step toward grasping the policies of these two, Israel's grand monarchs.

To relieve such bafflement we turn to the record of the time from the disruption under Rehoboam until the extinction of the two rival kingdoms, the north in 723/22 and the south in 586 B.C. Every reader of the Bible knows that king after king is carefully dated according to the regnal years of his contemporary with lengths of reign given in each case, and occasionally further synchronisms as well are recorded. Clearly, the Hebrew historians had awakened to the importance of chronology; here at length we have something to serve well our purpose. The prospect seems limited only by the meager political content of the Books of Kings. The historians delay over the temple and other building by Solomon and include the famous stories of Elijah and Elisha and the colorful episodes of Jehu's revolt. Too often, however, they provide us with no more than a compact summary of a single strand of events through decades, at times half a century or more. The promise, whatever it may be, all too soon fades. Then the chronology of these books becomes a favorite source for those who would demonstrate the inaccuracy of the Bible. What can one say of a system that seemingly contradicts itself? The totals of the years of the kings in the sister kingdoms seem to diverge notably in the two precisely delimited periods provided by Jehu's revolt and the fall of Samaria. Through the first of these, the Judean kings would seem to have reigned less years than did the Israelite; in the second, the situation is reversed—and contemporary chronology seems to show that both are wrong! Surely this is the nadir of historicity. But here is yet another "blunder" that every tyro in biblical history seizes. Sometime in the ten-year reign of Menahem he paid tribute to Pul (Tiglath-Pileser) of Assyria (2 Kings 15:19). The date has commonly been given as 738 B.C., but Professor Thiele shows that it must be carried back to 743 or 742. This will then be approximately twenty years before the destruction of Samaria in 723/22. But into that period the biblical record compresses the balance of the reign of Menahem, the two years of Pekahiah, the twenty years of Pekah, and the nine of Hoshea—a total of thirty-one years apart from the unstated years of Menahem!

These are samples of the more glaring "errors" of the biblical records. As examination moves on to greater detail, the seeming inconsistencies multiply. Is it remarkable, then, that serious students have given up the problem in despair and concluded that the biblical chronology of the times of the kings is notable most of all for its undependability? It is thought to have value, to be able to serve as a guide; but its precision defies the student, a fact declared by the chaos of results revealed by a comparison of reputable histories of Israel. No serious student charges that the Hebrew historians were willfully dishonest; the problem, it is said, is merely that they evolved an inaccurate system. And we should realize their difficulties. Therefore, the explanation has been advocated that although a sense of need for dating was early and repeatedly manifested in the Orient, it was not until relatively late times that one was established that received wide recognition. Even then it never attained a status comparable with the chronology of the Christian era, which we are prone to accept, like the sunlight, as commonplace. The great cultures of the ancient East had long wrestled with the problems of chronology and had attained results of greater or lesser dependability. Thus the Assyrian system provided us with an absolute chronology, fixed by modern astronomical calculations. But the Hebrews—so the thinking goes—were one of the major peoples of the ancient world, and their chronology, like many other aspects of their culture, was inferior and owed what merits it may have possessed to borrowings from mighty neighbors.

Whatever the errors or excesses of this sort of reasoning, no one may dismiss it as merely an expression of the pettifogging criticism of a "modern" mood. Every serious student of the problem knows that the devout Jews who translated the Old Testament into Greek in the immediately pre-Christian centuries held a comparable view. They altered the dates given in the Hebrew text, apparently in an effort to smooth out the supposed inconsistencies. Josephus, writing in the first century of our era, did the same, though with results different from those of the Greek translation.

All this the reader will find in greater detail and lucidity in Professor Thiele's presentation. It has been of value, however, to delay over it here, for it provides a foil and background for his results. The astonishing fact is that he demonstrates conclusively the precise and dependable accuracy of Hebrew chronology of the times of the kingdoms. This, it is true, is no more than has long been claimed by students of the Bible who incline to traditional views, although it is well to observe that the support they claim from tradition is seriously qualified by the testimony of the Greek version and of Josephus, just now mentioned. Nonetheless, they accept the biblical figures as absolute and are willing to be forced thereby into positions that others consider a defiance of incontestable facts. The unique feature of Professor Thiele's work is that he has attained his results by the most rigid application of scholarly facts and methods. He has brought to bear on the problem all relevant knowledge of the history and chronology of the ancient Orient, plus whatever is provided by the most approved methods of biblical study. Having done so, he has shown that the seeming inconsistencies and mathematical contradictions no more than hinted at above really are nothing of the sort but are integral elements in a sound and accurate chronological system. He does admit, it is true, that something has happened to confuse the chronology through much of the latter half of the eighth century. What is one to do, for example, when the accession of Hezekiah is dated both in the sixth year before the fall of Samaria in 723/22 (2 Kings 18:10) and in the fourteenth before Sennacherib's invasion of Judah in 701 B.C. (2 Kings 18:13)? It is, too, a mark of his precision that he notes a seeming discrepancy in a matter of days between the accounts in 2 Kings and the Book of Jeremiah (2 Kings 25:8; cf. Jer. 52:12; 2 Kings 25:27; cf. Jer. 52:31), for which he is unable to offer a solution. Apart from these matters, the records are uncannily precise. The trouble has been that we did not know how to use them!

Professor Thiele himself declares the measure of his indebtedness to previous investigators. And it is obvious that, lacking a familiarity with all that has gone before, his results, however brilliant, would fall short of conviction. Every reader would say, "Summon also Hushai the Arkite, so we can hear what he has to say." Scholarship is a great cooperative endeavor in which each worker, standing as it were on the shoulders of all who have gone before, stretches up to grasp more than he or she can reach. And certainty—or such measure of certainty as is possible for our fallible human processes—emerges out of the conflict and seeming confusion where interpretation meets interpretation in mortal conflict, and truth is the only arbiter. Professor Thiele here learns from all who have preceded him, but at the same time gives battle to all comers. His fair interpretations along with the incisiveness of his criticisms—always reinforced with ascertained facts—will suffice to show the inadequacy of all other treatments of Israel's chronology. But then the validity of his own findings rests on the simple fact that they work! They take account of all the data provided by the biblical record and organize them in a system that is rational, consistent, and precise. His findings harmonize with all that is known of relevant chronology of the entire world of the Bible. Let us repeat for emphasis: the striking feature of Professor Thiele's illumination of this once insoluble riddle is its high scholarship and appeal only to scholarly considerations. It moves with the ease and certitude of the master among the facts and methods of historiography as it relates to the ancient Orient; it repudiates the special pleading that with shoddy devices has sought to make biblical chronology a world apart; at the same time it uses all the biblical data and except for the small strand of contradictory dates spoken of above, builds them, even the most inconsistent, into a unity that is convincing by virtue of its utter simplicity and reasonableness.

Yet this does not exhaust the contribution of Professor Thiele's study. Concerned though it may appear to be with mere mathematical calculations, dates, and calendrical systems, it actually reveals at many points inner motivation and circumstances of the political life of Israel for which, every historian realizes, our records are tantalizingly meager. The statement in 2 Kings 13:10 that Jehoash began to reign in Israel in the thirty-seventh year of Joash of Judah, a commonplace remark that most readers have probably passed over with little thought, provides for Professor Thiele's exact computations the clue to demonstrate that in this period the northern kingdom had revised its system of regnal dating. Further, this was a concession to the rising power of Assyria, which within the century was to sweep Israel away as with a flood. Even more rich for the historian is the information carefully deduced from the innocent starting point that "all the people of Judah took Azariah, who was sixteen years old, and made him king in place of his father Amaziah" (2 Kings 14:21). It is shown that this came about, not as a sequel to the assassination of the old king, but instead only five years after Amaziah's accession when as a young man he had let his impetuosity lead him into a disastrous campaign against the kingdom of Israel (vv. 8–14). Similarly, it is shown that we must take account of Manasseh's elevation at the age of twelve to a coregency with his father, Hezekiah, because of the latter's ill health. Somewhat different in kind is the discovery of the date of the termination of the reign of Tibni, who disputed with Omri for the throne of Israel.

Still, most readers will feel that the major by-product of Professor Thiele's careful study is more striking. He has taken passages commonly regarded as patent disclosures of carelessness, if not of ignorance, on the part of the Hebrew historians and shown them to be astonishingly reliable. It is an achievement of far-reaching significance. We have, it is true, come some distance from the radical criticism of half a century ago. In treatment of the text and in appraisal of the historic reliability of the records, we are now in a much more cautious mood. As we have seen one uncertain point after another clarified, our skepticism has dissipated under the new facts. But many uncertainties remain. And it is a matter of first-rate importance to learn now that the Books of Kings are reliable in precisely the features that formerly excited only derision.

Similar are the implications in regard to the long process through which the biblical writings have come down to us. Here too we have learned caution through our mistakes. It has been a sobering experience to discover that in some cases the text of the Old Testament passages has been preserved and accurately transmitted by the scribes, apparently for ages, after they had lost the meaning of the words that they copied. And Professor Thiele's findings enforce this result. He has shown that suspicion of the accuracy of the received text actually arose in pre-Christian times and is fully evidenced in manuscripts of the Septuagint and then later in the work of Josephus; and further in his account of recent theories in regard to Hebrew chronology, he has pointed out how the latest of these proceeds on the basis that "it is incredible that all these numbers can have been handed down through so many editors and copyists without often becoming corrupt." But Professor Thiele demonstrates conclusively that in reality they were so handed down "without often becoming corrupt." The vast bulk of them are precise to the point of astonishment. The few errors that crept in are such as actually to enhance the reliability of the copyists, for with one exception they form a consistent pattern. And the amusing fact is that this one passage where error in transmission seems to have occurred—a real "corruption"—is exactly the one on which this latest theory just now mentioned bases its entire reconstruction!

In summary, then, Professor Thiele's work contributes very significantly both to our respect for the accuracy of the Hebrew historians and to a growing confidence in the soundness of the long process through which generation after generation of scribes handed on the sacred text to succeeding ages. No one who has wrestled seriously with the problems of biblical history or of textual criticism will be in danger of carrying either result to a foolish extreme; but it is a healthy corrective for Old Testament scholarship as a whole to have the demonstration here provided.

The larger implications of this situation will be variously interpreted. Some will seize it as one more evidence of this foolishness and frustration of "the critics"—little knowing who the critics are or what they seek. The great bulk of biblical scholarship will welcome it and without revolution find a place for it in their systems of biblical thinking. For, whatever limitations in the biblical record they have admitted, they have sought only the truth and have long since been inured to readjusting their thinking to discoveries that have shaken various of their views. True scholarship abjures dogmatism. It recognizes the relativity of all things human, aware that all our conclusions, even the most basic, are conditioned by very limited knowledge. The so-called laws of nature rest on nothing better than our observation, through a relatively minute moment of time, of processes that constitute only a part of the total of the reality of the universe—how great or small that part is, relative to the whole, again we do not know. As time goes on and these processes are seen to be consistent and dependable, the probability increases in similar proportion that our interpretation of them is reliable. But we shall never attain finality until we reach the total of truth—which obviously lies beyond human capacities. For a variety of reasons this ultimate uncertainty is greater in humanistic studies, where clearly the study of the Bible takes its place. The biblical scholar, insofar as he has felt the greatness and complexity of his task, is most of all ready to confess the things he does not know. His views and conclusions are held tentatively; against every one of them he writes the qualification "insofar as I can see at present." It is then no shock or hardship for him to abandon long-held positions. He is eager to do so—as soon as convincing reasons are presented to him. His concern is for truth.

But this does not mean that the immense activity of biblical scholars is futile—that they are always and totally failing to arrive at worthy results. Only those ignorant of Bible study methods and results would ever entertain such a view. Out of the confusion of theory and countertheory, and the conflict of debate, little by little biblical scholarship through the years has been building its structure of meaning. Such theories, readily abandoned as truth advances, and commonly exciting scorn on the part of the ill-informed, are the scaffolding of construction. They are a mark of health and vigor. And the building is steadily going up. Even were it otherwise, what alternative have we? To rest secure in ancient opinion is not a solution of the problem, but only its repudiation. Ancient opinion may be held, after it has been subjected to searching, unrelenting examination, and found dependable—as commonly it is. Otherwise, it is a snare and deception. Truth is absolute and can be found only by the fallible methods of human research and confirmation.

Professor Thiele has made an important contribution to our common quest of truth.

WILLIAM A. IRWIN

Chicago, Illinois
2 January 1950

CHAPTER ONE

The Problems of Old Testament Chronology

HRONOLOGY IS THE BACKBONE of history. Absolute chronology is the fixed central core around which the events of the nation must be correctly grouped before they may assume their exact positions in history and before their mutual relationships may be properly understood. Without exact chronology there can be no exact history. Until a correct chronology of a nation has been established, the events of that nation cannot be correctly integrated into the events of neighboring states. If history is to be a true and exact science, then it is of fundamental importance to construct a sound chronological framework about which may be fitted the events of states and the international world.

Of particular interest and importance is the history of the Hebrew nation. If the establishment of a correct chronology is important for any nation, then it is important for the Hebrews. Never will the manifold details of the Old Testament writings be correctly integrated into each other, never will the events of the Old Testament record be properly fitted into the events of the Near Eastern world, and never will the vital messages of the Old Testament be thoroughly or correctly understood until there has been established a sound chronology for Old Testament times. If Old Testament scholarship is to achieve the degree of confidence that is its due, then it must move forward on the basis of a sound chronology. Not until there has been established for the Old Testament a chronological pattern that is consistent with both itself and the world of that time will there exist a foundation that will make possible that degree of sound and scientific study so necessary in this important field.

Anyone who is acquainted with the difficulties of the chronological problem in general, and with the special intricacies of biblical chronological data, will understand something of the task confronting those who would venture into this trying field. Every Old Testament scholar knows of the many chronological details in the biblical record that seem to be in hopeless disagreement with each other and with the chronological pattern of neighboring states. In spite of almost endless research and discussion, biblical chronology remained in a state of almost hopeless confusion.

Because of the many difficulties encountered in the endeavor to integrate Hebrew chronological materials into those of neighboring states, there has arisen a general impression that biblical chronology is something separate and apart from secular chronology and that these two are at hopeless variance with each other—that if the one is sound the other is fallacious. There is, of course, only one chronology that is correct chronology. Between the absolute chronology of the Hebrews and that of their neighbors there can be no conflict. If biblical chronology seems to be at variance with Assyrian chronology, it may be because of errors in the Hebrew records, but it may also be because the data preserved in those records are not correctly understood.

If the chronological materials recorded in the Hebrew Scriptures are basically sound, they will agree with whatever is sound in the annals of neighboring states. And if a pattern of Hebrew chronology can be established from biblical sources that will agree with the chronological pattern of neighboring states as built on the historical materials of those nations, and that will be in agreement with the required astronomical data, then we may be certain that we are on the track of that correct and absolute chronology that has long been the goal of students of ancient history. The agreement of sources also assures us that we are dealing with sources that are basically sound.

The present discussion will confine itself to a study of the chronology of the kings of Israel and Judah. This period is of greatest importance in Hebrew history, and it is here that the most trying problems of biblical chronology occur. This period also should offer the best opportunities for success, for it is here that the largest amount of chronological material, both biblical and secular, is found.

The amount and variety of chronological material found in the biblical record for the period of the kings is surprisingly extensive. First of all, there is a complete list of the kings of Israel and Judah for the period of the divided kingdoms, together with their lengths of reign. Thus Jeroboam I reigned twenty-two years (1 Kings 14:20), Asa forty-one years (1 Kings 15:10; 2 Chronicles 16:13), Zechariah six months (2 Kings 15:8), Zimri seven days (1 Kings 16:15), and Manasseh fifty-five years (2 Kings 21:1; 2 Chronicles 33:1). Furthermore, while the kingdoms of Israel and Judah were coexistent, synchronisms are given for the accessions of the kings of each nation in terms of the corresponding year of the ruler of the other nation. Thus Abijah came to the throne of Judah in the eighteenth year of Jeroboam I of Israel (1 Kings 15:1; 2 Chronicles 13:1), Jehoshaphat began to rule in Judah in the fourth year of Ahab of Israel (1 Kings 22:41), Nadab in Israel ascended the throne in the second year of Asa of Judah (1 Kings 15:25), Azariah took the throne of Judah in the twenty-seventh year of Jeroboam II of Israel (2 Kings 15:1), and Menahem of Israel in the thirty-ninth year of Azariah (Uzziah) of Judah (2 Kings 15:17). It will be noticed that many of the chronological details regarding the Hebrew rulers are recorded not only in the Books of Kings, but in Chronicles as well.[1]

In the case of the kings of Judah, the age at the time of accession is frequently given. Jehoshaphat was thirty-five years old when he came to the

---

[1]For a list of the data regarding synchronisms and lengths of reign as found in the Books of Kings and Chronicles, see Appendix A.

throne (1 Kings 22:42; 2 Chron. 20:31), Jehoram was thirty-two (2 Kings 8:17; 2 Chron. 21:5, 20), Joash was seven (2 Kings 11:21; 2 Chron. 24:1), and Manasseh twelve (2 Kings 21:1; 2 Chron. 33:1).

At times the year of reign is given when certain events took place. We are told, for instance, that in the twenty-third year of Joash the temple had not yet been repaired (2 Kings 12:6); in the seventh year of Hoshea, Shalmaneser began his siege of Samaria (2 Kings 18:9); in the fourteenth year of Hezekiah, Sennacherib captured the fortified cities of Judah (2 Kings 18:13; Isa. 36:1); and in the eighteenth year of Josiah the purifying of the land and the temple was completed and an important Passover was observed (2 Chron. 34:8; 35:19). Sometimes the day and month as well as the year of an event are given. Thus Nebuchadnezzar began his siege of Jerusalem in the ninth year of Zedekiah, on the tenth day of the tenth month (2 Kings 25:1; Jer. 52:4); in the eleventh year, the fourth month, and the ninth day, the city wall was broken through (2 Kings 25:3–4); in the seventh day of the fifth month of the nineteenth year of Nebuchadnezzar, Nebuchadnezzar came to Jerusalem and destroyed its temple, palace, and walls (2 Kings 25:8–10); and on the fifth day of the tenth month of that year, which was the twelfth year of Jehoiachin's captivity, word of the fall of Jerusalem reached the exiles in Babylon (Ezek. 33:21).

There are occasions when the number of years involved in the interval from one event to another is given. Thus the death of Amaziah of Judah took place fifteen years after the death of Jehoash of Israel (2 Kings 14:17); from the time that Jeremiah received his call as a prophet in the thirteenth year of Josiah (Jer. 1:2) to the fourth year of Jehoiakim was a period of twenty-three years (Jer. 25:1, 3); and Ezekiel's vision of the city and temple is declared to have taken place "in the fourteenth year after the fall of the city" (Ezek. 40:1).

Events recorded in both Hebrew and secular history are always of interest. In the fifth year of Rehoboam, Shishak of Egypt attacked Jerusalem (1 Kings 14:25; 2 Chron. 12:2). During the reign of Ahaz, Tiglath-Pileser III captured Damascus and received tribute from the king of Judah (2 Kings 16:7–9), and Menahem of Israel likewise paid tribute to Pul, i.e., Tiglath-Pileser III (2 Kings 15:19). Sennacherib attacked Jerusalem and the fortified cities of Judah in the fourteenth year of Hezekiah (2 Kings 18:13; Isa. 36:1). All these events are referred to in the records of the ancient East.

Of particular importance are synchronisms between the years of the Hebrew kings and the reigns of kings of the Near East. Thus the fourth year of Jehoiakim of Judah is synchronized with the first year of Nebuchadnezzar of Babylon (Jer. 25:1), and the tenth year of Zedekiah with the eighteenth of Nebuchadnezzar (Jer. 32:1).

A historian would normally look with delight on such a large amount of chronological material as is found in the Old Testament, for it would seem to facilitate the establishment of a sound chronological system. But for the biblical scholar this has not been the case. The more details that are found in the record, the greater have been the perplexities, for once the scholar has begun the development of a chronological pattern based on one set of data, a seemingly different pattern is found based on other data. And no amount of effort has made it possible to make all the biblical details harmonize with each other or with the historical pattern established by the chronological materials of contemporary powers.

One of the greatest perplexities concerning "biblical" chronology is that many of its details seem to be self-contradictory. A number of these difficulties occur in connection with the data regarding the accession of the kings. Thus in one place we are told that Ahaziah of Judah came to the throne in the eleventh year of Joram of Israel (2 Kings 9:29), while another reference states that it was the twelfth year (2 Kings 8:25). And Joram, the son of Ahab, began to reign in the eighteenth year of Jehoshaphat of Judah according to 2 Kings 3:1, while according to 2 Kings 1:17 it was the second year of Jehoram, son of Jehoshaphat. If 2 Kings 1:17 is correct, then Jehoram of Judah began his reign before Joram of Israel. But according to 2 Kings 8:16, Jehoram of Judah came to the throne in the fifth year of Joram of Israel. At first sight these statements sound hopelessly contradictory, and the reader may raise an eyebrow when told that, regardless of how they sound, they are all correct and fit perfectly into the chronological pattern of the times. How this may be will be shown later in this volume.

Yet again, the accession of Omri of Israel is said to have taken place in the thirty-first year of Asa of Judah and his reign lasted twelve years (1 Kings 16:23). In that case the termination of Omri's reign would not have occurred till after the death of Asa, who ruled forty-one years (1 Kings 15:10). But the record states that Omri died and was buried in Samaria and was succeeded by his son Ahab in the thirty-eighth year of Asa (1 Kings 16:28–29). But this was seven, not twelve years, after Omri's accession in Asa's thirty-first year.

Another group of difficulties is that experienced in the totals of the years of reign. Totals from one fixed point in the history of Israel and Judah to another fixed point in their common history are not the same. For instance, the accession of Jeroboam of Israel and of Rehoboam of Judah at the time of the schism coincide. And Joram of Israel and Ahaziah of Judah met their deaths simultaneously at the hands of Jehu. The totals of the reigns of the kings of Israel and Judah for these two periods should be the same but in consulting the Masoretic Text one finds that the figures in the Book of Kings yield the following:

ISRAEL			JUDAH	
Jeroboam I	22 years		Rehoboam	17 years
Nadab	2 years		Abijah	3 years
Baasha	24 years		Asa	41 years
Elah	2 years		Jehoshaphat	25 years
Zimri		7 days	Jehoram	8 years
Omri	12 years		Ahaziah	1 year
Ahab	22 years			
Ahaziah	2 years			
Joram	12 years			
Total	98 years, 7 days		Total	95 years

The deaths of Joram and Ahaziah were followed by the accession during the same year of Jehu in Israel and Athaliah in Judah. According to 2 Kings

18:10, the fall of Samaria took place in the ninth year of Hoshea, which was the sixth year of Hezekiah. Thus the totals of reigns for these two periods should again agree, but actually they are as follows:

ISRAEL			JUDAH	
Jehu	28 years		Athaliah	7 years
Jehoahaz	17 years		Joash	40 years
Jehoash	16 years		Amaziah	29 years
Jeroboam II	41 years		Azariah (Uzziah)	52 years
Zechariah		6 months	Jotham	16 years
Shallum		1 month	Ahaz	16 years
Menahem	10 years		Hezekiah	6 years
Pekahiah	2 years			
Pekah	20 years			
Hoshea	9 years			
Total	143 years, 7 months		Total	166 years

Thus in the first of these two periods that should be identical, we have a total of 98 years and 7 days for Israel as against 95 years for Judah, while in the second there are 143 years and 7 months for Israel as against 166 years for Judah. Compared with Assyrian figures, both of these last figures seem too high. There are only 120 years from 841 B.C., the eighteenth year of Shalmaneser III, when the latter reported having received tribute from Jehu— usually conceded to be very early in Jehu's reign—to the accession of Sargon in 722/21, when the latter claimed to have captured Samaria. Compared with Assyrian figures, then, the total of the reigns of kings of Israel for this period seems to be about 23 years too high, while for Judah there seems to be an excess of about 46 years.

Perhaps the hardest kind of problem in Old Testament chronology is the seeming disagreement between the synchronisms and the lengths of reign. Every scholar who has endeavored to work out a chronological pattern based on both the synchronisms and the lengths of reign knows something of the extreme difficulties involved. If a chronology is worked out according to the lengths of reign, then the synchronisms will not fit; and if the synchronisms are used, then it appears that the lengths of reign must be discarded. The two sets of data just do not seem to be in harmony. Only a few examples need be given. Amaziah of Judah came to the throne in the second year of Jehoash of Israel (2 Kings 14:1) and reigned twenty-nine years (2 Kings 14:2). Since the length of the reign of Jehoash was sixteen years (2 Kings 13:10), the first fourteen of Amaziah's twenty-nine years would fall within the reign of Jehoash, and the remaining fifteen years would fall within the reign of Jeroboam II, successor of Jehoash. It would be expected, then, that Azariah (Uzziah), son and successor of Amaziah, would have come to the throne in the fifteenth year of Jeroboam II. But we are told that Azariah came to the throne in the twenty-seventh year of Jeroboam (2 Kings 15:1). If Amaziah terminated his reign in the fifteenth year of Jeroboam II and his successor did not begin his reign till the twenty-seventh year of that king, who ruled over Judah during the intervening twelve years?

Yet again, Jeroboam II ruled forty-one years (2 Kings 14:23). Since Azariah came to the throne in the twenty-seventh year of Jeroboam (2 Kings 15:1), the death of Jeroboam II would come fourteen years after Azariah had begun his reign, and we would look for Zechariah, son and successor of Jeroboam, to come to the throne in the fourteenth year of Azariah. But the record states that Zechariah began to reign in the thirty-eighth year of Azariah (2 Kings 15:8). What should be done with the intervening twenty-four years? And yet again, Pekah of Israel began his reign in the fifty-second year of Azariah (2 Kings 15:27). Since Azariah reigned fifty-two years (2 Kings 15:2), Pekah began his reign in the year in which Azariah died and in which he was succeeded by his son Jotham. Jotham reigned sixteen years (2 Kings 15:33) and was followed by his son Ahaz. The length of Pekah's reign was twenty years (2 Kings 15:27), sixteen of which would then coincide with the reign of Jotham and the last four with the first four of the reign of Ahaz. Pekah was slain and succeeded by Hoshea in the twentieth year of Jotham (2 Kings 15:30). But 2 Kings 17:1 states that Hoshea began his reign in the twelfth year of Ahaz. If 2 Kings 17:1 is correct, then who ruled over Israel in the interval between the fourth and the twelfth years of Ahaz? How can this latter synchronism be made to harmonize with the previous synchronism of Hoshea's accession in the twentieth year of Jotham when the latter reigned only sixteen years?

Almost every one who has dealt with these and similar problems has eventually become baffled and finally concluded that no harmony is possible. Certain scholars have decided that in the construction of a sound chronological system only the lengths of reigns are to be considered. They have thought that the synchronisms were added at a late period and are irreconcilable with the years of reign. Yet others have come to the conclusion that the synchronisms provide the correct picture of Hebrew chronology and that the lengths of reign are artificial and erroneous.

Another type of difficulty is the seeming lack of harmony between the details of Old Testament chronology and the chronologies of neighboring states. The dates of Assyrian kings for the period in which the most frequent contacts between Assyrian and Hebrew history occur are quite definitely established. But frequently there seems to be a wide divergence between biblical and established Assyrian datings for the same events. The divergencies appear to vary at different periods but increase in extent the further we go back in time. There is, for example, the discrepancy of some thirteen years between the fourteenth year of Hezekiah, when Sennacherib invaded Judea (2 Kings 18:13), and the Assyrian date for this event. The biblical date for the beginning of Hezekiah's reign is secured from the synchronism of his accession with the third year of Hoshea of Israel (2 Kings 18:1). Since Hoshea ruled nine years (2 Kings 17:1), and since his reign terminated with the fall of Samaria, 723/22 B.C., Hoshea must have begun his reign in 732/31 B.C., which brings his third year and Hezekiah's accession to about 729/28 B.C. And if 729/28 B.C. was the accession year of Hezekiah, his fourteenth year would be 715/14 B.C. But this is nine years before Sennacherib began his reign and thirteen years before his famous third campaign against the land of the Hatti in which he went up against the cities of Judah. This period of Hezekiah, Ahaz, and Jotham is particularly difficult to synchronize with the events of Assyrian history. It presents the single greatest problem in the chronology of the kings and will be dealt with in detail later in this study.[2]

Only a few of the problems in the chronological field have here been mentioned, but they are sufficient to give some idea of the task confronting the Old Testament scholar. The reaction to these difficulties has been interesting and varied. As far back as the third century B.C., there are indications that these chronological problems were recognized and that attempts were made to deal with them. The Septuagint was at that time translated from the Hebrew. It contains a number of striking variations from the chronological data in the Masoretic Text, variations that were introduced to make possible a more harmonious pattern of the lengths of the Hebrew kings' reigns and the synchronisms.

In the early Christian centuries biblical scholars continued to struggle with the chronological difficulties. Jerome wrote:

> Relege omnes et veteris et novi Testamenti libros, et tantam annorum reperies dissonantiam, et numerorum inter Judam et Israel, id est, inter regnum utrunque confusum, ut hujuscemodi haerere quaestionibus, non tam studiosi, quam otiosi hominis esse videatur.[3]

> (Read all the books of the Old and New Testament, and you will find such a discord as to the number of the years, such a confusion as to the duration of the reigns of the kings of Judah and Israel, that to attempt to clear up this question will appear rather the occupation of a man of leisure than of a scholar.)

The opinion of some of the most careful modern students of Old Testament history is that some accidental errors of transmission and certain other mistakes may have occurred in working out the synchronisms. However, these same scholars believe that both the lengths of the reigns and the synchronisms are, in general, accurate and that the original data available to later scribes must have been sufficiently full and reliable to make possible the construction of a chronology that is neither fantastic nor artificial but basically sound.[4]

Another group of scholars, led by Ewald, Wellhausen, and Stade, holds the view that the chronology of the kings is essentially schematic and artificial and that the recorded data are worthless for the construction of any sound chronological scheme.[5]

---

[2]A discussion of the main facts concerning the nature and reliability of Assyrian chronology will be given in chapter 4.

[3]Hieronymus, *Traditio catholica*, ed. J. P. Migne (Paris, 1864), vol. 1, Ep. 72, *Ad Vitalem* (*Patrologia Latina*, vol. 22; col. 676).

[4]See Robert H. Pfeiffer, *Introduction to the Old Testament* (New York, 1941), pp. 393–95; Adolf Kamphausen, *Die Chronologie der hebräischen Könige* (Bonn, 1883), pp. 5ff.; Franz Rühl, "Chronologie der Könige von Israel und Juda," *Deutsche Zeitschrift für Geschichtswissenschaft* 12 (1894–95): 44ff.

[5]Heinrich Ewald, *The History of Israel* (London, 1876), 1:206ff.; 2:20ff., 297ff.; Julius Wellhausen, "Die Zeitrechnung des Buchs der Könige seit der Theilung des Reichs," *Jahrbücher für*

Some take the view that there has been "intentional mutilation of the text" and that certain "passages have been ruthlessly altered" in order to cover up various facts of history and to pass on to posterity, not a true record of what actually took place, but the type of picture that it was desired future generations should have in mind.[6]

There are today two main systems of chronology regarding the Hebrew kings. One is the long system employed by a group of men who place the main emphasis on their interpretation of the requirements of the Masoretic Text, regardless of the demands of contemporary chronology. To secure any degree of harmony between the lengths of reign and the synchronisms, the systems of chronology developed by this group have postulated the existence of interregna, or periods of political chaos during which no rulers occupied the throne. As a result these systems give us a chronology that for the early period of the Hebrew kings is about fifty years longer than the chronology of the nations round about.[7] Advocates of such systems usually think of their systems as constituting true biblical chronology.

The other main type of chronological system is that used by scholars whose primary purpose is to secure a system of Old Testament chronology that is in harmony with the chronology of contemporaneous nations. In order to secure such a chronology, it has been felt necessary in many instances to disregard the data recorded in the Masoretic Text and to secure dates for the Hebrew kings from such synchronisms as were available with contemporaneous history. This type of system in the early period of the kings is about fifty years shorter than the other[8] and is usually looked on with suspicion by conservative biblical scholarship.

Certainly, in our age of enlightenment we should have something better than this. If the scholar who makes use of the shorter chronology knows from a knowledge of the history of the Near East that this contemporaneous chronology is sound, it should be possible, if true biblical chronology is also sound, to appreciate this fact. The biblicist should not be forced to believe that in order to deal with historical facts it is necessary to sacrifice the basic details of biblical chronology. Or if the conservative Old Testament scholar knows that "biblical" chronology is indeed the true chronology of the Hebrew Scriptures, and that this longer chronology is indeed the absolute chronology of the period in question, it should be possible with the vast amount of historical data now at hand to put a finger on the specific chronological mistakes in secular history. Such a scholar should be able to harmonize secular chronology with "biblical" reckoning.

---

deutsche Theologie 20 (1875): 607–40; Bernhard Stade, *Geschichte des Volkes Israel* (Berlin, 1887–88), 1:88ff., 558ff.; *Encyclopaedia Britannica*, 9th ed. s.v. "Kings"; W. Robertson Smith, "The Chronology of the Books of Kings," *Journal of Philology* 10 (1882): 209–13; Friedrich Bleek, *Einleitung in das Alte Testament*, 4th ed. (Berlin, 1878), pp. 263–64.

[6]*Jewish Encyclopedia* (1903), s.v. "Chronology."

[7]Among those using early dates for the disruption of the kingdom are the following: Hales, 990; Anstey, 982; Oppert, 978; Graetz, 977; Bähr, Mangenot, Ussher, 975; Mahler, 953.

[8]Among those using late dates for the disruption of the kingdom are the following: Kamphausen, Kittel, Krey, Olmstead, 937; Robinson, 936; Kleber, 932; Couche, Rühl, Thilo, 931; Mowinckel, 930; Kugler, 929; Begrich, 926; Albright, Lewy, 922.

If it is true that the chronological data concerning the kings of Judah and Israel recorded in the Old Testament are fundamentally unsound, it would then indeed be a hopeless task to endeavor to establish any exact chronology on such a foundation. But are we altogether certain that such is the case? The fact that up to the present no scheme has as yet been devised that will bring harmony out of the many seeming contradictions does not of itself prove that harmony is impossible. The difficulties in the system that have induced the opinion that the figures are not dependable really establish no more than that the key that might provide the solution has not yet been produced. And an unsolved problem in any field is always a challenge to further effort and research till a final solution is reached.

Among the many appraisals of the chronological problem of the Old Testament, perhaps that of Professor Kittel is worthy of more attention than it has received:

> The Israelitish numbers and the parallel numbers referring to Judah do not agree at the points at which we are able to compare them. Besides, the well-established Assyrian dates differ considerably from those deduced from the Old Testament. Both facts show either that the numbers, originally given accurately, of the Books of Kings, were in course of time altered by disturbing influences (errors of scribes, misapprehensions of the meaning, etc.), or else that we are no longer in a position to discover the original method of reckoning according to which the sums of the several items were bound to agree; or finally, that both causes have contributed to bring about the present state of things. The latter is most likely the case.[9]

Certainly, at the current stage of Old Testament scholarship no one will be in a position to give categorical proof that any of the possibilities suggested by Professor Kittel may not have some part in accounting for the present situation as regards the chronology of the kings.

If errors on the part of the scribes may prove to be one possible source of our difficulties with Hebrew chronology, yet another source must be recognized in ourselves, for we today may simply no longer be in a position to determine the underlying factors whereby the available data will be found to agree. And does not this possibility constitute a challenge to further investigation on the assumption that the real difficulty may lie in our own present lack of information rather than in the insolubility of the problem itself? In other words does not the most promising method of attacking this problem lie in going forward on the basis that the Hebrew annalists and scribes who recorded and passed on these figures to us were at least normally honest and competent men who were in possession of certain sound historical data that they endeavored to preserve to the best of their ability and that, in so doing, they were performing a service of real value to the historian of the future? If an interpretation of the

---

[9]R. Kittel, *A History of the Hebrews* (London, 1896), 2:235–36.

given facts of the Hebrew chronological system and of its difficulties can be found—an interpretation at once sufficiently simple and in harmony with our knowledge of the customs of the times as to carry some intrinsic reasonableness—should it not deserve our serious consideration and, in the nature of the case, carry a high probability of its truth? Is it not the course of wisdom to proceed on the assumption that there may be in these figures something of value that is not now fully realized? Should we not endeavor to ascertain, if we can, just what lies back of these seemingly discordant figures and perhaps open up avenues of knowledge now closed to us? We will proceed on such a basis.

CHAPTER TWO

The Fundamental Principles of Hebrew Chronology

IN WORKING OUT the chronology of a nation, a primary requisite is that the chronological procedure of that nation be understood. The following items must be definitely established: (1) the year from which a king began to count the years of his reign—whether from the time of his actual accession, from the following year, or from some other time; (2) the time of the calendar year when a king began to count his reign; (3) the method according to which a scribe of one nation reckoned the years of a king of a neighboring state, whether according to the system used in his nation or according to that of the neighbor; (4) whether or not the nation made use of coregencies, whether or not several rival rulers might have been reigning at the same time, and whether interregna occurred; (5) whether during the period under review a uniform system was followed, or whether variations took place; and, finally, (6) some absolute date during the period in question from which the years can be figured backward and forward so that the full chronological pattern might be secured.

An understanding of each of the above items is necessary to a correct reconstruction of the chronologies of Israel and Judah, for unless one is acquainted with the type of chronological procedure in use, a wrong interpretation is likely to be placed on the available data and cause an erroneous pattern to ensue.

Just when did a king begin counting the years of his reign? When he ascended the throne did his first year begin immediately? Or, did he wait till the beginning of the next new year and designate that his first year? Customs were not the same. In Assyria, Babylon, and Persia when a king first came to the throne, the year was usually called the king's *accession* year, but not till the first day of the first month of the next new year did the king begin reckoning events in his own first year. This system of reckoning is called the *accession-year system*, or *postdating*. In other places a king began to reckon his first year from the day he first came to the throne. This method of reckoning is known as the *nonaccession-year system*, or *antedating*. It will be noticed that any particular year of a king's reign according to the nonaccession-year system is always one year higher than according to the accession-year method. Thus the first year according to the accession-year system would be called the second year according to the nonaccession-year system, and so on. Therefore, in order to know exactly what is meant by the data provided, it first becomes necessary to understand the system of reckoning involved.

Diagram 1

Accession- Versus Nonaccession-Year Reckoning

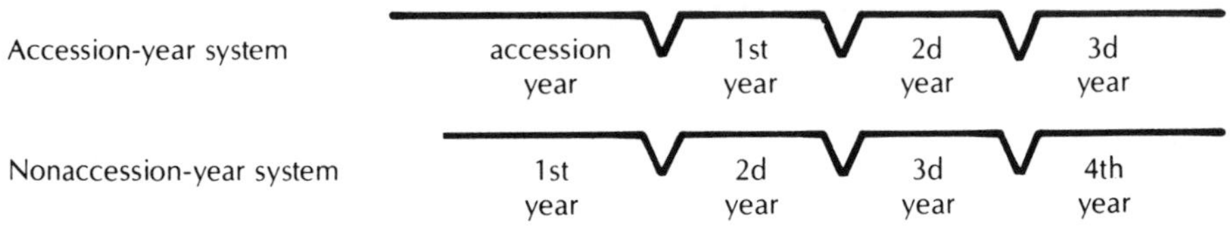

Accession-year system	accession year	1st year	2d year	3d year
Nonaccession-year system	1st year	2d year	3d year	4th year

The exact time of the year from which a king began to count his regnal year is also an important factor. Did a king begin counting his regnal years from the day he ascended the throne, or did his regnal years coincide with calendar years? Among the Hebrews there were two calendar years, one beginning with Nisan in the spring and the other with Tishri in the fall. With which of these months did the Hebrews begin reckoning their regnal years? And did both Israel and Judah follow the same practice? In regard to the latter, four possibilities exist: (1) both Israel and Judah began the regnal year with Nisan; (2) both Israel and Judah began the regnal year with Tishri; (3) Israel began the regnal year with Nisan and Judah began it with Tishri; (4) Israel began the regnal year with Tishri and Judah began it with Nisan.

It will be readily apparent that the month involved for the beginning of a king's regnal year might involve important differences in the chronological data regarding that king. This would be true where cross-synchronisms were involved regarding kings of two nations that followed different methods of chronological procedure. Let us take the case of two hypothetical kings, Jonathan of Judah and Ishmael of Israel, both of whom came to the throne on the same day, at the beginning of the month of Nisan. For the sake of simplicity let us imagine a case where both Israel and Judah were following the same method of reckoning their regnal years—the nonaccession-year system. If both nations also followed the same practice of commencing their regnal years with either Nisan or Tishri, then the reckoning of their years would correspond throughout their reigns.

But suppose Judah began its regnal year with Nisan and Israel began it with Tishri. For the first six months after coming to the throne, the first year of Jonathan would synchronize with the first year of Ishmael. But from 1 Tishri to the next 1 Nisan, the first year of Jonathan would synchronize with the second year of Ishmael. During the next six months both kings would be in their second year. But from the next 1 Tishri for another six months, the third year of Ishmael would synchronize with the second year of Jonathan; and so onward.

It will thus be seen that even though both of these hypothetical kings came to the throne at the same time, every alternate six months the years of Ishmael's reign would be numbered one year higher than those of Jonathan. During the other six months the numbers of their years would be the same. If Israel began reckoning its regnal year with 1 Nisan and Judah with 1 Tishri, it would be Jonathan whose second year would begin after he had been on the throne only six months, at 1 Tishri, while Ishmael's first year would continue another six months, till 1 Nisan, when he would begin reckoning his second year. It will thus be seen that with Jonathan and Ishmael beginning their reigns at the same time, the simple matter of the month from which they began to reckon their regnal years might give us the following variations as to their respective years of reign: (1) the first year of Jonathan would synchronize with the first year of Ishmael, (2) the first year of Jonathan would synchronize with the second year of Ishmael, (3) the second year of Jonathan would synchronize with the first year of Ishmael.

Diagram 2
Tishri Years Versus Nisan Years

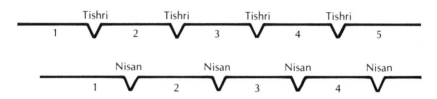

It might appear that such an item as this is too hypothetical to be worth discussing. Before we have proceeded far with our presentation of the chronological pattern of the kings of Israel and Judah, however, it will be seen that the points given here have a vital bearing on the data. An understanding of these principles is a prerequisite to a correct reconstruction of Hebrew chronology. So simple a matter as the determination of the months with which Israel and Judah began their regnal years can help clear up the problems of the chronology.

The above hypothetical case of Jonathan and Ishmael was worked out on the basis of Judah and Israel both reckoning their regnal years according to the nonaccession-year system. The matter would become even more involved, however, if in addition to using different months for the beginning of their regnal years, the two nations also used different systems for reckoning those years—one by the accession-year system and the other by the nonaccession-year system. These additional variations in the system would add greatly to the total possible permutations in the chronological pattern. As complicated as this might make the problem, these factors cannot be neglected in any scientific endeavor to work out the chronologies of the Hebrew kingdoms.

Still another factor to be taken into consideration is the method that might be used by each nation in referring to the chronological data of the other. If Judah were using the accession-year system and Israel the nonaccession-year system, how would Judah refer to the years of a king of Israel—according to the system used in Judah, or according to the system used in Israel? If Judah used Judah's system in referring to the years of a king of Israel, would Israel use Israel's system in referring to the years of a king of Judah?

Let us notice specific possibilities under a number of conditions. We will take a king of Judah who follows the accession-year system and whose years start with Tishri. His accession will be synchronized with a king of Israel who uses nonaccession-year reckoning, whose years start with Nisan, and who is in his own third year. If the Judean ruler began his reign between Tishri and Nisan and if he used Israel's nonaccession-year system for synchronizing his accession, (a) he came to the throne in the third year of the Israelite ruler. But if he used his own accession-year system for that synchronism, (b) he came to the throne in the second year. If, however, he started his reign between Nisan and Tishri and used Israel's nonaccession-year system for the synchronism, (c) he came to the throne in the fourth year of Israel's king. Finally, if he used Judah's accession-year system in expressing the synchronization, (d) he commenced his reign in the third year of Israel's king.

Diagram 3
Regnal Data According to Tishri and Nisan Years

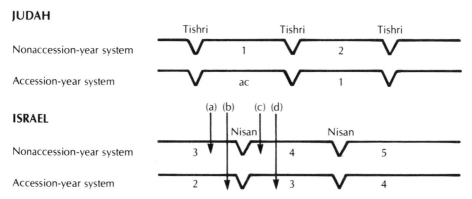

An understanding of the meaning of the regnal data in such involvements as above will go far to clear up many seeming discrepancies. It is such factors as these, long neglected, that provide the clues for unraveling the tangled chronological skein of the Hebrew kings.

Even so simple a statement as that a certain king ruled for a certain number of years may have a number of different meanings. It may be that this king had for a number of years ruled cojointly with his father. In some nations it was at certain periods quite the regular procedure for a king still ruling in the prime of his power to appoint his son as coregent. Such was the case in Egypt during the twelfth dynasty. In other nations a coregent was appointed to serve with the father at times of emergency. Just how frequent the appointment of a coregent was in any one country is a matter that usually has to be determined by careful study. In working out a correct chronology for a nation, the coregencies are of vital importance. Unless the coregencies are known, years that were overlapping might be made consecutive, causing the history of the nation to be stretched out beyond the actual years.

If there was a coregency, did the official length of reign include the years of coregency, or only of the sole reign? It will be seen that among the Hebrews in the same nation, the custom in such matters was not always the same. And yet again, did a coregency begin with an official first year or an accession year?

The matter of interregna is also important. In the history of nations there are few records of states passing through periods when they were without rulers. Even in time of trouble and crisis nations had their rulers, and at such periods those who would exercise control were usually present in increased numbers. History has shown that periods of political weakness and chaos have usually resulted in a multiplication of rulers rather than in a cessation of ruler-ship. The use of invented interregna to clear up seeming chronological dis-crepancies is something that must be done with extreme caution. When inter-regna are invented and inserted where they ought not to be, the resultant chronological pattern will be extended beyond the years of contemporary na-tions and beyond the terms of the true chronology.

Finally, in the endeavor to establish a chronology for a state, attention should be given to the question of whether or not the same method of chrono-logical procedure continued without change throughout the period in question, or whether modifications were introduced. A careful study of history often surprises us with the unexpected.

An understanding of each of the above items is necessary to a correct reconstruction of the chronology of the Hebrew kingdoms, but to obtain such an understanding is by no means easy. It is certain that no ancient authorities exist who can pass this information on to us. Some facts may be gleaned from the available data, but others can be worked out only by a laborious process of trial and error.

The chronologist must keep in mind that it is not his task to manufacture history but to recover history. In dealing with chronology he is dealing with something fundamental and absolute, something altogether fixed that allows no deviation in any way, even by a single year, if it is to be entirely correct. Adjustments cannot be made, a little here and a little there, in order to secure some desired result. Events happened as they did and when they did, and the task of the chronologist is to fit those events into their exact niches in history. Carefully and correctly performed, the chronologist's work will when finished comprise a complete and harmonious pattern, consistent with itself and in perfect harmony with the correct chronological pattern of all nations round about. If the chronologist's work cannot meet this test of absolute harmony with all else that is sound, then at some point the work is in error. The work has not been completed and must be started again in order to discover error, correct the mistakes, and keep on till harmony is achieved.

Our first task will be to discover the systems used by Israel and Judah in the reckoning of their regnal years. We have noticed that the systems usually used in the Near East were the accession- and the nonaccession-year systems. According to the accession-year method, that portion of the last calendar year during which a king reigned was assigned to him as his last year, and the balance of that year—the period during which the succeeding king reigned—was termed the accession year of the new king. Not until the termination of the calendar year during which the previous king died and the beginning of the new year did the new king begin reckoning his first year of reign. According to this system there was no duplication in the reckoning of years. If a ruler was said to have ruled ten years, then ten years was the length of his reign, and if there were ten rulers each of whom according to this system ruled ten years, the period covered by their reigns was one hundred years. When, however, the nonaccession-year system was used, that portion of the final calendar year during which a king reigned was assigned to him as his last year, and the remaining portion of the year during which his successor reigned was termed that king's first year. Consequently, that calendar year was assigned to two kings, being counted both as the last year of the old king and the first year of the new king. Thus in this method of reckoning, there was always a duplication of one year for each reign. According to this system if a king was said to have reigned ten years, the actual length of his reign was only nine years. If there were ten kings, each of whom according to this system were said to have ruled ten years, the total period covered by their reigns was only ninety years. If, then, one nation used the accession-year system and another nation used the nonaccession-year system, the years of the latter nation increased by one year for each reign as compared with the nation using the accession-year system. An understanding of these principles will help us to understand how to interpret the chronological data of the Hebrew kings.

Following are the data of the early kings of Judah and Israel:

JUDAH

Rehoboam	17 years	1 Kings 14:21
Abijah	18th of Jeroboam	1 Kings 15:1
Abijah	3 years	1 Kings 15:2
Asa	20th of Jeroboam	1 Kings 15:9
Asa	41 years	1 Kings 15:10
Jehoshaphat	4th of Ahab	1 Kings 22:41

ISRAEL

Jeroboam	22 years	1 Kings 14:20
Nadab	2d of Asa	1 Kings 15:25
Nadab	2 years	1 Kings 15:25
Baasha	3d of Asa	1 Kings 15:28, 33
Baasha	24 years	1 Kings 15:33
Elah	26th of Asa	1 Kings 16:8
Elah	2 years	1 Kings 16:8
Zimri	27th of Asa	1 Kings 16:10, 15
Zimri	7 days	1 Kings 16:15
Omri	27th of Asa	1 Kings 16:15, 16
Omri	12 years	1 Kings 16:23
Ahab	38th of Asa	1 Kings 16:29
Ahab	22 years	1 Kings 16:29
Ahaziah	17th of Jehoshaphat	1 Kings 22:51
Ahaziah	2 years	1 Kings 22:51
Joram	18th of Jehoshaphat	2 Kings 3:1

Let us observe the results secured from a comparison of the data of Judah and Israel for the period immediately following the disruption:

Diagram 4
Increase in the Totals of Israel Over the Totals of Judah

```
JUDAH
Totals:              20    22     23     46     47     58   61            78       79

Rehoboam 17| Abijah 3| Asa 2d    3d   26th   27th  38th  41| Jehoshaphat 17th   18th

         Jeroboam 22| Nadab | Baasha | Elah 2| Zimri   Ahab 4th        22| Ahaziah | Joram
ISRAEL                   2      24           Omri 12                         2

Totals:              22    24     48     50     62     66            84       86
Excess years for Israel:  0     1      2      3      4      5             6        7
```

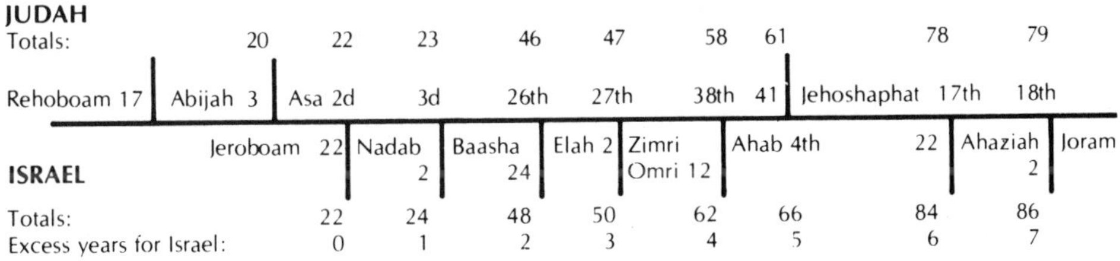

Diagram 4 shows that at the eighteenth year of Jehoshaphat in Judah, when the decease of Ahaziah in Israel took place, there are seventy-nine regnal years for Judah as against eighty-six regnal years for Israel. During this period Israel's totals increased by one year for every reign over the totals of Judah. This is positive evidence of the use of the accession-year system in Judah and the nonaccession-year system in Israel. When the lengths of reign of the Israelite rulers are expressed in actual rather than official years, the totals of the two kingdoms are the same:

JUDAH			ISRAEL		
	Official years	Actual years		Official years	Actual years
Rehoboam	17	17	Jeroboam	22	21
Abijah	3	3	Nadab	2	1
Asa	41	41	Baasha	24	23
Jehoshaphat	18	18	Elah	2	1
Total	79	79	Omri	12	11
			Ahab	22	21
			Ahaziah	2	1
			Total	86	79

In expressing synchronistic years, both Judah and Israel used their own systems for the years of the neighboring kings. Thus in Judah the lengths of reign of Judean kings were at this time expressed in terms of the accession-year system, and the synchronisms with the Israelite kings were also expressed by that system, although in Israel itself the nonaccession-year system was used. In Israel both the synchronisms with Judah and the lengths of reign of Israelite kings were expressed in terms of the nonaccession-year system. The rule was to use this procedure throughout the history of the two nations, both for the lengths of reign of local kings and also for the synchronisms with a neighbor, regardless of the system the neighbor used. This rule helps explain the patterns of reign to be developed for the rulers of both Israel and Judah. Thus when Baasha's accession is synchronized with the third year of Asa (1 Kings 15:28), it will be the third year of Asa according to the nonaccession-year system used in Israel, which according to Judah's accession-year system and absolute time would be Asa's second year. Since Baasha was succeeded by Elah in the twenty-sixth year of Asa (1 Kings 16:8), this would be the twenty-sixth year according to the nonaccession-year system, or the twenty-fifth year of Asa according to the accession-year system and actual years. Similarly when Zimri's and Omri's accession and Elah's death took place in the twenty-seventh year of Asa (1 Kings 16:10, 15–16), nonaccession-year reckoning, this would actually be Asa's twenty-sixth year, and Omri's death and Ahab's accession in the thirty-eighth year of Asa (1 Kings 16:29), nonaccession-year reckoning, would be the thirty-seventh year of Asa according to Judah's accession-year system and absolute time.

When the above adjustments are made, so that the figures for both nations stand in terms of the same method of reckoning and in accord with actual rather than official years, it will be noticed that there is perfect harmony for the totals of Israel and Judah.

As this pattern of lengths of reigns and synchronisms is carefully studied, we see that the individuals who first recorded these data were dealing with contemporary chronological materials of the greatest accuracy and the highest historical value. Back of the seeming discrepancies lies an underlying harmony not previously appreciated because of failure to understand the principles of the chronological systems then in use.

The records of the Assyrian king Shalmaneser III throw light on the method of reckoning used in the northern kingdom during the ninth century B.C. During the sixth year of Shalmaneser the famous battle of Qarqar was fought. Ahab joined forces at Qarqar with the western allies in resisting the Assyrian king.[1] Thus Ahab was still alive during the sixth year of Shalmaneser III. Ahab was succeeded by Ahaziah, who ruled two years (1 Kings 22:51), and Ahaziah was followed by Joram, who ruled twelve years (2 Kings 3:1), making a total of fourteen official years for these two kings. After Joram came the usurper Jehu (2 Kings 9:24; 10:36), who paid tribute to Shalmaneser III in the eighteenth year of the latter's reign.[2] So Jehu was already ruling over Israel in the eighteenth year of Shalmaneser, twelve years after Ahab fought at Qarqar. The reigns of Ahaziah and Joram must thus have taken place in the twelve-year interval between Shalmaneser's sixth and eighteenth years. But how can fourteen years be fitted into twelve? It is evident that the total years of Ahaziah and Joram could not have exceeded twelve. This would be exactly the case if Ahaziah's official two years were reckoned on the nonaccession-year basis, which would give him only one actual year, and if Joram's twelve years were reckoned on the same basis, or eleven actual years, giving a total of twelve years for these two kings. Thus the ancient records of Assyria provide this interesting

---

[1] Daniel David Luckenbill, *Ancient Records of Assyria and Babylonia* (Chicago, 1926), vol. 1, secs. 563, 610–11, 646–47.

[2] Ibid., sec. 672.

additional and conclusive evidence that Israel at this time was reckoning the reigns of its kings on the nonaccession-year basis.

Our next task is to ascertain the time of the year from which the kings of Israel and Judah began to reckon their regnal years. Most biblical chronologists have followed a Nisan-to-Nisan year in dealing with the Hebrew kings.[3] The statement in the Mishnah tract Rosh Hashana that 1 Nisan is the new year for kings[4] is no doubt largely responsible for this point of view. Such outstanding authorities as Begrich and Morgenstern point out, however, that in view of the late date of the Mishnah notice, we might expect to find recorded there merely a late tradition.[5] It is quite possible that, by the time the Mishnah statement was prepared, all memory of the exact chronological arrangements of the Hebrew kings had disappeared and that any statements from the authorities of that age are as arbitrary as those of more recent investigators.

Kleber uses a Nisan-to-Nisan year for Judah but a Tishri-to-Tishri year for Israel.[6] Many of the best modern students of chronology follow a Tishri-to-Tishri reckoning for both Judah and Israel.[7] Begrich believes that a shift was made from a Tishri-to-Tishri reckoning in the early period to a Nisan-to-Nisan year in later times.[8] Mahler holds that the regnal and the calendar years were not identical but that the former was counted from the day on which the king first came to the throne.[9]

The difficulty with the above systems, however, is that they do not succeed in clearing up the discrepancies in the synchronisms. If the position is taken that these discrepancies are irreconcilable, there might be no way of proving with absolute finality whether the above systems are right or wrong, for complete evidence on this point is not at present available, as has been expressed by some who have made a most careful study of the subject.[10]

There is evidence, however, that gives some indications as to the type of regnal year used in Judah. That a Tishri-to-Tishri year was used in the reckoning of Solomon's reign is indicated by the data available concerning the building of the temple. Work on the temple was begun in the second month of the fourth year of Solomon (1 Kings 6:1, 37), and it was completed in the eighth month of

---

[3]Isaac Newton, *The Chronology of Ancient Kingdoms Amended* (London, 1728), p. 296; Karl Friedrich Keil, *Commentary on the Books of Kings* (Edinburgh, 1857), 1: 206; Franz Xaver Kugler, *Von Moses bis Paulus* (Münster, 1922), p. 26; Julius Lewy, "Forschungen zur alten Geschichte Vorderasiens," *Mitteilungen der vorderasiatischen Gesellschaft* 29 (1924): 25; Willis Judson Beecher, *The Dated Events of the Old Testament* (Philadelphia, 1907), p. 11.

[4]Babylonian Talmud, Tract Rosh Hashana ("New Year") 1.1.

[5]Joachim Begrich, *Die Chronologie der Könige von Israel und Juda und die Quellen des Rahmens der Königsbücher* (Tübingen, 1929), p. 70; Julian Morgenstern, "The New Year for Kings," *Occident and Orient: Gaster Anniversary Volume* (London, 1936), pp. 439, 454–55.

[6]Albert M. Kleber, "The Chronology of 3 and 4 Kings and 2 Paralipomenon," *Biblica* 2 (1921): 15.

[7]Sigmund Mowinckel, "Die Chronologie der israelitischen und jüdischen Könige," *Acta orientalia*, 10 (1932): 175ff.; Morgenstern, "New Year," pp. 439–56; "Supplementary Studies in the Calendars of Ancient Israel," *Hebrew Union College Annual* 10 (1935): 1ff.; and *Amos Studies* (Cincinnati, 1941), 1:127–79.

[8]Begrich, *Die Chronologie*, pp. 70–90.

[9]Edward Mahler, *Handbuch der jüdischen Chronologie* (Leipzig, 1916), pp. 236–42.

[10]F. K. Ginzel, *Handbuch der mathematischen und technischen Chronologie* (Leipzig, 1911), 2:27; Martin P. Nilsson, *Primitive Time Reckoning* (Lund, 1920), pp. 232ff., 272ff.

Solomon's eleventh year, having been seven years in building (1 Kings 6:38). In the Hebrew Scriptures the months are numbered from Nisan, regardless of whether the reckoning of the year was from the spring or fall.[11] And reckoning was according to the inclusive system, whereby the first and last units or fractions of units of a group were included as full units in the total of the group.[12] If Solomon's regnal year began in Nisan, then according to the above method of counting, the construction of the temple would have occupied eight years instead of seven. Diagram 5 below makes it clear that the figure of seven years for the building of the temple can be secured only when regnal years are computed from Tishri-to-Tishri but with a Nisan-to-Nisan year used for the reckoning of ordinary events and the ecclesiastical year.

Diagram 5

Years That the Temple Was in Building

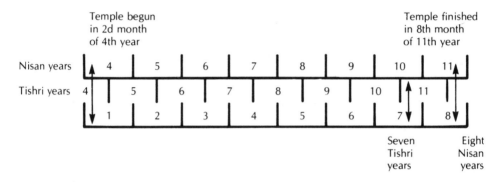

If the regnal years of Solomon were figured from Tishri-to-Tishri, this would almost certainly be the method used by the successors of Solomon in the southern kingdom. That Judah almost at the close of its history was still counting its regnal years from Tishri-to-Tishri is indicated by 2 Kings 22:3 and 23:23, for it was in the eighteenth year of Josiah that the work of repair was begun on the temple; and it was still in the same eighteenth year, after 1 Nisan had passed, that the Passover was celebrated on 14 Nisan. The proof turns on the fact that there are too many events to be performed in a short two-week period

---

[11]See Exod. 12:2; Lev. 23:5, 24, 27; Num. 9:1, 5, 11; 28:16; 29:1, 7; 1 Kings 8:2; 2 Kings 25:25; 2 Chron. 5:3; 7:10; 29:3, 17; 30:1–3, 13, 15; Jer. 36:9; 41:1, 8; Ezra 6:19; Neh. 1:1; 7:73–9:1; Esther 3:7, 12–13; 8:9; Zech. 7:1.

[12]See 2 Kings 18:9–10 where the period from the seventh to the ninth years of Hoshea is given as three years; Lev. 12:3 and Gen. 17:12, where a child was eight days old on its eighth day; Gen. 42:17–18, where Joseph's brothers were placed in ward for three days that terminated on the third day; and Lev. 23:15–16, where the fifty days of Pentecost began to be counted with the day after a certain Sabbath and terminated with the day after a Sabbath seven weeks later. Cf. also Matt. 12:40 and Mark 8:31, where the period from Christ's crucifixion on Friday afternoon to His resurrection on Sunday morning is counted as three days; and Acts 10:3–30, where the period from a certain day on which Cornelius had a vision, the next day when he sent messengers to Peter at Joppa, the following day when they arrived at the home of Peter, and the day after that, when Peter arrived at the home of Cornelius, is reckoned as four days.

narrated between 2 Kings 22:3 and 23:23. These events include the delivering of funds for the repair of the temple to the carpenters, builders, and masons who were to perform this work, the accomplishment of the work of repair, the finding of the book of the law, the reading of the book by Shaphan the secretary and before the king, the consultation with Huldah the prophetess, the gathering of the elders of Judah to Jerusalem to hear the reading of the law, the destruction of the vessels of Baal, the doing away with the idolatrous priests, the tearing down of the houses of the male shrine prostitutes, the defilement of the high places from Geba to Beersheba, the destruction of the emblems dedicated to the sun, the desecration of the altar and high place at Bethel, the doing away with all the houses of the high places in the cities of Samaria, and the slaying of the idolatrous priests. If all this could have been performed in the short period of two weeks between 1 and 14 Nisan, then there would be no evidence here for beginning the regnal year with 1 Tishri. But since it is quite clear that all the above events could not have taken place in a two-week period, it is evident that Josiah's eighteenth year of reign must have commenced before 1 Nisan and been carried over beyond 1 Nisan, and that 1 Tishri must thus have been the beginning of the regnal year. Furthermore, it is clear from Nehemiah 1:1 and 2:1 that Nehemiah reckoned the years of the Persian king Artaxerxes from Tishri-to-Tishri, for the month Kislev (Nov./Dec.) fell within the twentieth year of the king and the following Nisan was still in the same twentieth year. But why would Nehemiah do this, when the custom in Persia was to reckon the year from Nisan-to-Nisan? Is it not reasonable to suppose that Nehemiah was acquainted with the custom formerly followed by the kings of Judah to begin their regnal years with Tishri and, in a spirit of intense nationalism, applied the customary Jewish practice even to a Persian king? In the double-dated Aramaic papyri from Elephantine of the fifth century B.C., the reigns of Persian kings were also dated according to Judean Tishri years rather than Persian Nisan years.[13]

Perhaps the strongest argument for the use of a Tishri-to-Tishri regnal year in Judah is that this method works, giving us a harmonious pattern of the regnal years and synchronisms, while with a Nisan-to-Nisan regnal year the old discrepancies remain.

For Israel there seems to be no direct scriptural evidence as to the time of the beginning of the regnal year. However, when a Nisan-to-Nisan regnal year is used for Israel together with a Tishri-to-Tishri year for Judah, the perplexing discrepancies disappear and a harmonious chronological pattern results. Diagram 6, below, shows this arrangement. It will be recalled, moreover, that Jeroboam I spent some time as a political refugee in Egypt during the reign of Solomon (1 Kings 11:40) and before returning to Israel to become the northern kingdom's first king (1 Kings 12:2–3, 20). While in Egypt he had, of course, become acquainted with the Egyptian "wandering" year, which at that time happened to begin in the middle of April. On his assumption of the royal power in Israel, he would be more inclined to adopt the practice of a spring new year,

---

[13]S. H. Horn and L. H. Wood, "The Fifth-Century Jewish Calendar at Elephantine," *Journal of Near Eastern Studies* 13 (1954): 1–20.

as it was observed both in Egypt and Mesopotamia, than to follow the custom observed in the rival kingdom of Judah.[14]

Diagram 6

Regnal Years in Judah and Israel

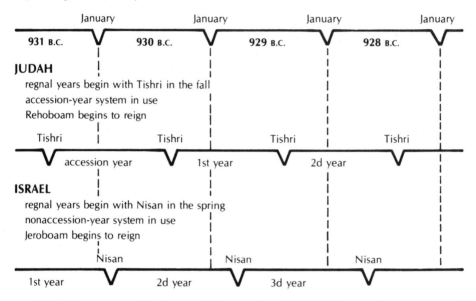

The diagrams and charts of the years of the Hebrew kings scattered throughout this volume portray the completeness of chronological harmony made possible by an application of the principles set forth. Diagram 7 shows how these principles work. In the Israelite record at left, where the nonaccession-year system is used, the years of the various kings are always one year higher than in Judah's record at right, where the accession-year system is used. Perfect harmony between all the chronological data, here and with the rulers to follow, is thus made possible.

In the construction of a sound chronology the question of coregencies must be considered. Kings were prone at times to associate their sons with them on their thrones, but they did not always leave direct evidence of having done so. Often the evidence for a coregency is indirect. But if a coregency existed it is important to know this, for otherwise years that overlapped might be treated as consecutive.

Whether or not coregencies were used is not a question that can be settled a priori. The evidence must be carefully examined, and if it points to the existence of a coregency the historian should accept that fact. Double datings at

---

[14]For a study of the question of intercalation among the Hebrews see J. B. Segal, "Intercalation and the Hebrew Calendar," *Vetus Testamentum* 7 (1957): 250–307.

Diagram 7

	ISRAELITE RECORD Nonaccession-year system in use			JUDEAN RECORD Accession-year system in use		
	ISRAEL Nisan years	JUDAH Tishri years	JUDAH Tishri years	ISRAEL Nisan years		
	Jeroboam 20			Jeroboam 19		ASA—41 years 20th of Jeroboam 1 Kings 15:9–10
		Abijah 3	Abijah 2			
	21					
		4 ASA	3 ASA →	→ 20		
NADAB—2 years 2d of Asa 1 Kings 15:25	22 NADAB	1	ac	21 NADAB		
	1 → → 2		1	ac		
	2			1		
BAASHA—24 years 3d of Asa 1 Kings 15:28, 33	BAASHA 1 → → 3		2	BAASHA ac		
	2			1		
		4	3			

times provide the necessary clue. Thus in Egypt it is known that the year 30 of Amenemhet I corresponds to the year 10 of Sesostris I, that the year 44 of Sesostris I corresponds to the year 2 of Amenemhet II, and that the year 35 of Amenemhet II corresponds to year 3 of Sesostris II.

In the case of Israel two dates are given for the accession of Joram, the second year of Jehoram of Judah (2 Kings 1:17) and the eighteenth year of Jehoshaphat (2 Kings 3:1). This undoubtedly points to a coregency between Jehoshaphat and his successor Jehoram, a coregency that is again referred to in 2 Kings 8:16. In 2 Kings 15:5 mention is made of Jotham's judging the land during the illness of his father, Azariah. Valuable evidence regarding the existence of a number of other coregencies is found in the synchronistical data or the data concerning the years of reign. When the evidence points to the existence of a coregency, the alert historian will recognize and accept it; and the result will be a correct historical pattern, harmonious with itself and with the years of contemporary history. When that evidence is neglected or rejected, the result will be a distorted pattern in which harmony is not possible.

Concerning the regnal data for coregencies and rival reigns, it is vital to know that in five of the nine such reigns the datum for the length of reign is the number of years from the beginning of the period of overlap to the end of the sole reign, but the synchronism of accession marks the end of the overlap and the commencement of the sole reign. This I term *dual dating*. Failure to understand this practice more than anything else has been responsible for the confusion and bewilderment that has arisen concerning the data in Kings.

The question of interregna has already been briefly mentioned. There is no evidence anywhere in the Old Testament of the existence of a single interregnum in either Israel or Judah during the period of the divided monarchies. When there was no king there was no nation. During periods of political unrest several kings might have been ruling simultaneously in various parts of the land, but once kingship ceased, the existence of the monarchy was at its end. Nothing in the Bible, nothing in contemporary history, calls for any interregna anywhere during the period of the Hebrew kings. When Bible students fail to understand the basic principles of chronological procedure and invent inter-regna to clear up supposed chronological discrepancies, the result is not greater harmony but less. We are then left with a distorted historical pattern out of harmony with contemporary history and with the correct chronology of the times. It is largely the unwarranted insertion of nonexistent interregna into the chronology of the kings that accounts for the so-called long systems of Hebrew chronology. The latter is often regarded as biblical but actually presents perplexing variations from the established chronology of the ancient East.

Having set forth certain of the fundamental principles of Hebrew chronol-ogy in the early period of the divided monarchies, we may well ask whether these principles were retained without modification to the end of Hebrew history, or whether variations were introduced. The course of history brings frequent and sometimes violent modifications of political procedure. In such a technical matter as the type of chronological method in use, the possibility of occasional modifications must not be overlooked. Such modifications took place in other nations, and they could well have taken place among the Hebrews.

Diagram 8
Use of Nonaccession-Year Reckoning in Judah

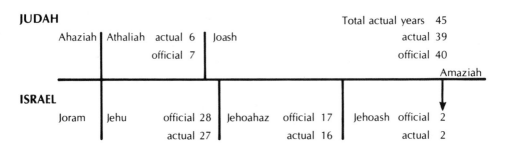

We have already examined the data concerning the kings immediately after the schism and have seen how certain phenomena point definitely to the use at that time of the accession-year system in Judah and of the nonaccession-year system in Israel. Let us now notice the data from a later period. It will be remembered that Ahaziah of Judah and Joram of Israel were slain simultane-ously by Jehu (2 Kings 9:24, 27). Their successors, Athaliah in Judah and Jehu in Israel, thus began their reigns at the same time. Athaliah ruled seven years (2 Kings 11:4, 16, 20), and Joash, her successor, forty (2 Kings 12:1), for a total of forty-seven years. During the same period in Israel, Jehu ruled twenty-eight years (2 Kings 10:36), which if reckoned on the accession-year basis would be an actual twenty-seven years. Jehoahaz, the successor of Jehu, reigned seventeen official years (2 Kings 13:1), or sixteen actual years. Jehoahaz was succeeded by Jehoash, in whose second year Amaziah, son and successor of Joash of Judah, came to the throne (2 Kings 14:1). Amaziah ascended to the throne at the death of Joash. If these years are reckoned according to the accession-year system in harmony with the custom for cross-synchronisms previously mentioned, this would be an actual two years that Jehoash of Israel, son and successor of Jehoahaz, had ruled when the termination of the reign of Joash of Judah took place. Adding together these years for Israel—twenty-seven for Jehu, sixteen for Jehoahaz, and two for Jehoash—we have a total of forty-five years from the time Jehu came to the throne, to the second of Jehoash, accession-year reckoning, as shown in Diagram 8, above. For Judah we should have this same total of forty-five years for the corresponding period from the accession of Athaliah to the death of Joash and the accession of Amaziah. But the figures for Judah for this period are forty-seven years, not forty-five. What is wrong? If the official years of Judah for this period were reckoned not according to the accession- but the nonaccession-year system and were reduced accordingly to bring them in line with actual years—six years instead of seven for Athaliah and thirty-nine instead of forty for Joash—we would have a total of forty-five years for Judah. This would be in harmony with the total of forty-five years for Israel for the same interval. But this would presuppose that during the period in question both Judah and Israel were reckoning their reigns according to the nonaccession-year system. This assumes that Judah at some time previous to this must have made a shift from the accession- to the nonaccession-year system. It would also presuppose that at the close of the period Judah shifted back to the accession-year method, for the synchronism of Amaziah's accession in the second year of Jehoash of Israel (2 Kings 14:1) was reckoned above on the basis of accession- and not nonaccession-year reckoning.

A shift in Judah from one type of reckoning to another is a matter of considerable interest. That such a shift did occur is indicated not only by the above totals of reign but also by the synchronism for the accession of Jehoram of Judah in the fifth year of Joram of Israel (2 Kings 8:16), for this synchronism is possible only on the basis of a reckoning of the years of Judah according to the nonaccession-year method. In fact, it was the impossibility of working out this synchronism on the basis of accession-year reckoning up to that time used in Judah that first called my attention to the possibility that such a shift had taken place. Up to the time of Jehoram's reign in Judah, the procedure previously outlined had provided a harmonious pattern based on the chronological data of the Masoretic Text of Kings. But the reign of Jehoram produced a difficulty. Harmony was possible only if the reigns of Judah as well as Israel were reckoned according to the nonaccession-year system. The question was whether at that time Judah made a shift in the method used in reckoning the regnal years, abandoning her own accession-year system and adopting the nonaccession-year system of Israel. Further investigation provided a number of indications that such a shift had indeed taken place. One clue was the totals of years discussed in the previous paragraph. Another was the continued impossibility to secure harmony in the synchronisms for the rulers of Judah from Jehoram to Joash inclusive unless these reigns were computed on the basis of nonaccession-year reckoning.

Still another indication was the double synchronism for the accession of Ahaziah, given in one place as the eleventh year of Joram of Israel (2 Kings 9:29) and in another place as his twelfth year (2 Kings 8:25). Here we have the interesting possibility of one scribe continuing to give the year of Ahaziah's accession according to the old accession-year system, the eleventh year of Joram, and another giving it according to the newly adopted nonaccession-year method, Joram's twelfth year. The valuable clue to this change found in the Masoretic Text of 2 Kings 8:25 has been lost in the Lucian (Greek) text, whose editor changed the "12" to an "11" to correspond to 2 Kings 9:29.

What might have been the reason for Judah's abandonment of the old accession-year method and the adoption of the nonaccession-year system in use in Israel? We have noticed the indications that this shift in system was introduced during the reign of Jehoram. It will be remembered that the wife of Jehoram was Athaliah, the daughter of Ahab and Jezebel of Israel (2 Kings 8:18, 26). A period of *rapprochement* between Judah and Israel had been introduced by Jehoshaphat, with the royal families intermarrying (2 Kings 8:18, 26; 2 Chron. 21:5–6), adopting the same names for their children (2 Kings 3:1; 8:16),[15] and exchanging visits (2 Kings 8:29; 2 Chron. 18:1–2). The two nations, moreover, united in joint ventures for foreign trade (2 Chron. 20:35–36; 1 Kings 22:48–49), and made a common disposition of their forces in battle (1 Kings 22:2–4; 2 Chron. 18:3–31; 22:5–6). Israel, rather than Judah, seemed to be the leading force in these matters of affiliation, with the southern kingdom following the lead of her northern neighbor (1 Kings 22:2; 2 Kings 8:27; 2 Chron. 18:2–3; 22:2–5) and being rebuked by her prophets (2 Chron. 19:2; 20:37). With such a strong-willed daughter of Jezebel as his wife (2 Chron. 22:2–3, 10–12; 2 Kings 11:1–3), it is only to be expected that Jehoram would be induced to adopt certain customs of the northern kingdom. Indeed, the record expressly declares, "He walked in the ways of the kings of Israel, as the house of Ahab had done" (2 Kings 8:18; 2 Chron. 21:6). Israel so influenced the southern kingdom at this time that Judah changed her method of reckoning the years of her kings to correspond to that of Israel. Once introduced, the nonaccession-year system was to continue in Judah for fifty-two years and through four reigns.

Although we have mentioned that the change from the accession- to the nonaccession-year system was introduced into Judah at the time of Jehoram, Athaliah may have made the shift when she took the throne of her slain son, with the reckoning in the latter instance thrown back by the scribes to include the reign of Jehoram.[16]

---

[15]For the sake of clarity, we are using in this volume the name *Jehoram* for the ruler of Judah and the name *Joram* for the king of Israel.

[16]I am indebted for this latter suggestion to Prof. W. A. Irwin. Inasmuch as both the accession- and the nonaccession-year systems were still in use at the end of Jehoram's reign, Professor Irwin has called my attention to the fact that the actual shift in reckoning may well have been introduced by Athaliah and then thrown back by the scribes or annalists to include the reign of Jehoram, but with the conservative element continuing for a time to cling to the old system.

Mention has been made of the fact that the nonaccession-year system was used for reckoning the reigns of Judah from Jehoram to Joash inclusive, and that beginning with Amaziah a shift back to the accession-year system took place. The indications are that Israel at this same time also shifted from the nonaccession- to the accession-year system, beginning this method of reckoning with Jehoash, who was the successor of Jehoahaz and the contemporary of Amaziah of Judah. The evidence for this shift is found in the pattern of synchronisms and lengths of reigns that from this time forward can be worked out harmoniously only on the basis of accession-year reckoning in both Israel and Judah.[17]

It can hardly be a mere coincidence that Israel and Judah adopted the accession-year system at practically the same time. A number of indications of friendship exist, possibly even of an alliance between the two nations at this time. One finds parallels in the days of Ahab and Jehoshaphat when they sent their common forces into battle against Aram, when an intermarriage between the two houses took place, and when the children of both houses bore the same names and were no doubt named after each other. At this latter period we find much the same situation, with Aram a common enemy of both nations (2 Kings 10:32–33; 12:17–18; 13:3–4, 17–19, 22; 2 Chron. 24:23–24) and perhaps a powerful force in driving the two nations together. The fact that Jehoahaz of Israel, who ruled from the twenty-third to the thirty-seventh years of Joash of Judah (2 Kings 13:1, 10), gave the name of that king to his son and successor is a clear indication of friendship. And the fact that Amaziah, the son of Joash, hired an army from Jehoash of Israel to assist him in his campaign against Edom (2 Chron. 25:6–10) gives definite proof that Judah and Israel were now on very friendly terms. We notice too the disdainful reply of Jehoash to Amaziah's later challenge to war, where the thistle (Amaziah), evidently visiting the cedar (Jehoash) in Lebanon, made the proposal that the cedar give his daughter in marriage to the son of the thistle—Azariah, then somewhat less than sixteen years of age (2 Kings 14:9, 21; 2 Chron. 25:18; 26:1, 3). Here we undoubtedly have a reflection of an earlier proposal of Amaziah to Jehoash for a marriage

---

[17]The author is happy to call attention to the existence of a number of striking parallels between the details of his chronological scheme and that of Prof. V. Coucke of the Grand Seminaire de Bruges (see his "Chronologie biblique," in *Supplément au Dictionnaire de la Bible* edited by Louis Pirot, vol. 1 [1928]). Not until the author had worked out the details of his chronological scheme and the resultant dates for the kings of Israel and Judah, did he become aware of the earlier work of Professor Coucke. It is a matter of gratification to know that these two independent studies have produced essentially the same results on a number of important points, such as Tishri-to-Tishri regnal years in Judah and Nisan-to-Nisan years in Israel (though Professor Coucke suggests that in the latter instance this might have been 1 Thoth instead of Nisan), and accession-year reckoning in Judah except for a period when a shift was made to the nonaccession-year system, and nonaccession-year reckoning in Israel with a later shift to the accession-year system. Professor Coucke, however, commences Judah's shift to the nonaccession-year system with Athaliah instead of Jehoram and continues it through to the reign of Jotham or Ahaz instead of to the accession of Amaziah; Israel's shift to the accession-year system he commences with Menahem instead of Jehoash, with a shift back to the nonaccession-year system under Pekah, and then again to the accession-year system under Hoshea. Other vital points, however, were not ascertained by Professor Coucke, and in consequence he retains a number of discrepancies and uncertainties in his completed scheme.

alliance. As Israel and Judah were closely bound together in 848 B.C. when Judah adopted Israel's accession-year method of reckoning, so no doubt the two nations moved together in a joint decision to adopt the accession-year system formerly used in Judah. Assyria may have had some influence on this decision, for she used the accession-year system. Assyria was also at the time of these kings manifesting a great interest in the west; so this shift to the accession-year system in both Israel and Judah is no doubt in some way connected with the growth of Assyrian influence in the countries of western Asia and may point to a rather wide adoption of this system of reckoning in these areas at this time.

The methods used by Israel and Judah in the reckoning of the reigns of their kings would thus be as follows: Israel at the time of the schism followed the nonaccession-year system and continued its use till the close of the ninth century B.C. when under Jehoash a shift was made to the accession-year system, which continued to be used to the close of Israel's history. Judah at the time of the schism used the accession-year system and continued its use to the middle of the ninth century; from Jehoram to Joash reigns are reckoned according to the nonaccession-year system; and from Amaziah, at about the beginning of the eighth century, to the close of Judah's history the accession-year system was again in use. At the time of the schism, Israel and Judah were thus using different systems of chronological reckoning, Israel the nonaccession-year system and Judah the accession-year method; and from the middle of the ninth century to the close of their respective histories both nations used the same method—the nonaccession-year system to the beginning of the eighth century, and the accession-year system from then to the end.[18]

The best argument for the correctness of the above outline of chronological procedure among the Hebrews is that it works, giving us a chronological scheme of the kings of Israel and Judah that has internal consistency and that harmonizes with the chronological pattern of neighboring states. When these principles are applied to the Hebrew kings, the alleged discrepancies of Old Testament history disappear. We will apply these principles to the data of the Masoretic Text available for the kings of Israel and Judah and seek to establish the chronology for the royal period.

---

[18]A list of the chronological data of the kings of Israel and Judah arranged according to the systems here set forth will be found in Appendix A.

CHAPTER THREE

Coregencies and Rival Reigns

O SECURE AN ACCURATE reconstruction of ancient Hebrew history and chronology, it is necessary to recognize the existence of a number of coregencies and overlapping reigns. Some of these are specifically mentioned in Kings, but others are brought to light only by the regnal data. These data precisely reflect the true nature of the reigns to which they apply; and if they clearly point to a rival, the only proper course is to acknowledge it. Only in this way can a correct historical pattern of Hebrew history be secured and seemingly conflicting numbers be made to harmonize. Data set forth by the early Hebrew recorders to denote the details of overlapping reigns must not be expected to fit nonoverlapping reigns that some scholars have invented.

Coregencies and Rival Reigns in Israel and Judah

Israel	Cause
Omri and Tibni	Israel divided into two parts (1 Kings 16:21–22)
Jehoash and Jeroboam II	Imminent war (2 Kings 14:8–13; 2 Chron. 25:18–23)
Menahem and Pekah	Two nations in the north (Hos. 5:5)[1]

Judah	
Asa and Jehoshaphat	Asa gravely ill (1 Kings 15:23; 2 Chron. 16:12)
Jehoshaphat and Jehoram	Imminent war (1 Kings 22:4, 32–33; noted in 2 Kings 8:16)
Amaziah and Azariah (Uzziah)	Amaziah captive in Israel (2 Kings 14:8–13, 21; 2 Chron. 25:21–24)
Azariah and Jotham	Leprosy of Azariah (2 Kings 15:5; 2 Chron. 26:21)
Jotham and Ahaz	Ahaz involved in a pro-Assyrian coup (2 Kings 16:7)
Hezekiah and Manasseh	Illness of Hezekiah (2 Kings 20:1–6; 2 Chron. 32:24)

---

[1]Hosea 5:5 indicated that Ephraim and Israel are separate nations. Some translations fail to clearly indicate this, but the plural pronoun at the end of the verse—"Judah also stumbles with *them*"—shows that the prophet had two nations in mind. The argument here is based on the Masoretic Text and not any single English translation. The entire Book of Hosea reflects the existence of two nations in the north at this time.

The tabulation on the previous page gives the overlapping reigns of the Hebrew kingdoms, three of them in Israel and six in Judah. Sufficient information is given in the biblical record to point to the probable reason for each overlap.

Here there will be an explanation of some of the outstanding details of each of these overlapping reigns. Fuller presentations will be given later in discussions of the specific reigns.

The first overlap took place when Israel was divided into two parts, with Tibni ruling half of the nation and Omri the other (1 Kings 16:21–22). The regnal data for Omri in this period are of great importance because they are in accord with dual dating—an unusual type of dating that is used for all three of the overlapping reigns in Israel and for two in Judah.[2] In Israel dual dating was used for the regnal data of Omri, Jeroboam II, and Pekah. In Judah dual dating was used for Jehoshaphat and Azariah. An awareness of this procedure solves chronological problems over two thousand years old.

Omri was raised to the throne in the twenty-seventh year of Asa when he brought about the death of Zimri, who reigned only seven days (1 Kings 16:15–18). The synchronism given for Omri's accession is the thirty-first year of Asa, and the length of his reign was twelve years (1 Kings 16:23). Omri died in the thirty-eighth year of Asa and was succeeded by Ahab (1 Kings 16:29). The synchronism for Omri's accession, the thirty-first year of Asa, marks the end of the rival rule of Tibni and the beginning of Omri's sole reign. But the datum for the length of Omri's reign includes both the years of his overlap with Tibni and those of his sole reign. It is thus in accord with dual dating.

Wide divergencies from the Masoretic Text in the regnal data of the Septuagint and the Lucianic recension show that misunderstandings concerning dual-dating procedure already prevailed in the pre-Christian centuries. Since evidence shows that many Greek variants go back to still earlier Hebrew *Vorlagen* (manuscripts that are the basis of later material), the variant numbers found in the Greek in all likelihood go back to very early Hebrew manuscripts from which the Greek translations were made. A detailed illustration of this will be given in connection with the discussion of Omri's reign in chapter 5.

The second overlapping reign in Israel was a coregency of Jeroboam II with Jehoash. Jeroboam II came to the throne in the fifteenth year of Amaziah (2 Kings 14:23). Since Amaziah lived fifteen years after the death of Jehoash (2 Kings 14:17), and since he was succeeded by Azariah in the twenty-seventh year of Jeroboam (2 Kings 15:1), Jeroboam II must have reigned twelve years with Jehoash. Jeroboam reigned forty-one years (2 Kings 14:23). This consisted of twelve years of overlap with Jehoash, fifteen years between the death of Jehoash and the death of Amaziah, and fourteen years between the accession of Azariah in Jeroboam's twenty-seventh year and Jeroboam's death in his forty-first year. Thus the forty-one years of Jeroboam's reign included twelve years of overlap with Jehoash and twenty-nine years of sole reign, but the synchronism of his accession marked the end of his overlap with Jehoash and the commencement of his sole reign. This is another example of dual dating. In connec-

---

[2]The reader should carefully review the definition for dual dating that appears on page 55.

tion with the discussion of the reigns of Jehoash and Jeroboam, it has been suggested that the reason for this coregency was the fact that Jehoash was about to embark on a war with Amaziah of Judah (2 Kings 14:8–13; 2 Chron. 25:18–23). Jehoash evidently placed Jeroboam on the throne as coregent as a matter of prudence.

The third overlapping reign in Israel was that of Pekah in Gilead during the reigns of Menahem and Pekahiah in Samaria. That there were two kingdoms in the north at this time in addition to Judah in the south is testified to in Hosea 5:5 where the prophet declared, "Therefore shall Israel and Ephraim fall in their iniquity; Judah also shall fall with them" (KJV). Pekah began as a rival of Menahem in 752 B.C., the same year that Menahem began in Samaria. He had twelve years of overlap that paralleled the ten years of Menahem (2 Kings 15:17) and the two years of Pekahiah (2 Kings 15:23), and he also had eight years of sole reign from 740, the second and last year of Pekahiah, to 732. His twenty years terminated in 732 when he was slain by Hoshea.

The synchronism of Pekah's accession in the fifty-second year of Azariah (2 Kings 15:27), when he eliminated Pekahiah, marks the commencement of his sole reign. His twenty years of reign included twelve years of overlap with Menahem and Pekahiah and also eight years of sole reign. These facts show that the data of his reign are in accord with dual dating. It will be shown in chapter 6 that dual dating for Pekah was not understood at the time the final editorial work on Kings was being concluded. It was thought that Pekah's twenty years commenced in 740, the fifty-second year of Azariah, which is the synchronism of his accession in 2 Kings 15:27.

In Judah the first overlapping reign was a coregency between Jehoshaphat and Asa. The regnal data of Kings call for his twenty-five years (1 Kings 22:42) to begin with the thirty-ninth year of Asa. The record of 2 Chronicles 16:12 is "In the thirty-ninth year of his reign Asa was afflicted with a disease in his feet" that was "severe." Although the twenty-five years of Jehoshaphat begin with the thirty-ninth year of Asa, the synchronism of his accession is the fourth year of Ahab (1 Kings 22:41), which corresponds with Asa's forty-first and last year. The regnal data of Jehoshaphat are thus also in accord with dual dating, since the datum of his twenty-five years (1 Kings 22:42) includes both his years of overlap with Asa and his sole reign, whereas the synchronism of his accession denotes the commencement of his sole reign.

The second overlapping reign in Judah was a coregency of Jehoram with Jehoshaphat. It is indicated by the two synchronisms given for the accession of Joram in Israel, "in the second year of Jehoram son of Jehoshaphat" (2 Kings 1:17) and "in the eighteenth year of Jehoshaphat" (2 Kings 3:1). The eighteenth year of Jehoshaphat was the second year of Jehoram's coregency. This coregency was prompted by Jehoshaphat's agreeing to join Ahab in battle for recovering Ramoth Gilead from Aram. In this battle Ahab received a fatal wound and Jehoshaphat also found himself in mortal danger (1 Kings 22:2–37).

The third overlapping reign in Judah was a period of twenty-four years of overlap during the twenty-nine years of Amaziah (2 Kings 14:2) and the fifty-two years of Azariah (Uzziah) (2 Kings 15:2). The synchronism for Azariah's accession, the year when Amaziah died, is the twenty-seventh year of Jeroboam

(2 Kings 15:1). Since Jeroboam had a reign of forty-one years (2 Kings 14:23), his death took place fourteen years after Amaziah's death in Jeroboam's twenty-seventh year. But at that time, when Zechariah succeeded Jeroboam, Azariah was already in his thirty-eighth year (2 Kings 15:8); so he must have reigned twenty-four years before the death of Amaziah. The synchronism of Azariah's accession marks the end of his overlap with Amaziah and the commencement of his sole reign. The datum for his length of reign—fifty-two years—includes both his years of overlap with Amaziah and his sole reign. Therefore, these data are in accord with dual-dating procedure.

The overlap between Azariah and Amaziah was occasioned by Amaziah's being taken prisoner by Jehoash on his invasion of Judah. When the people of Judah found themselves without a king, they placed young Azariah on the vacant throne (2 Kings 14:13, 21).

The fourth overlapping reign in Judah was the coregency of Jotham with Azariah. This is specifically mentioned in 2 Kings 15:5, where we are told that because of the leprosy of Azariah, Jotham "had charge of the palace and governed the people of the land."

The fifth reign in Judah was between Ahaz and Jotham—from 735/34 to 732 B.C. It was brought about by Ahaz being raised to the throne in a pro-Assyrian coup. Jotham, however, was not slain, for although he terminated his sixteen official years of reign (2 Kings 15:33) in the seventeenth year of Pekah when Ahaz came to the throne (2 Kings 16:1), he lived to his twentieth year (2 Kings 15:30). It was during this period of overlap that the Pekah-Rezin incursions against Judah took place, resulting in Ahaz's desperate appeals to Tiglath-Pileser for aid. That there was an overlap between Jotham and Ahaz at this time is testified to by the fact that the Pekah-Rezin attack on Judah is mentioned in the accounts of both Jotham and Ahaz. In the account of Jotham it is noted in the postscript (2 Kings 15:37), indicating that his reign was officially over at the time when the attack was made. The main account comes in the record of Ahaz at 2 Kings 16:5-9, showing that it was he, not Jotham, who was then in control.

Judah's sixth and last overlapping reign was a coregency between Manasseh and Hezekiah. After the account of Sennacherib's attack on Hezekiah in 701 B.C., we are told in 2 Kings 20:1 that "Hezekiah became ill and was at the point of death" and that the Lord through Isaiah gave him the following message: "Put your house in order, because you will die." In answer to Hezekiah's earnest prayer, the Lord granted him an additional fifteen years (2 Kings 20:6). Under such circumstances Hezekiah would no doubt wish to place Manasseh on the throne at the earliest possible moment to give him a training in kingship. The indications are that Manasseh was placed on the throne as coregent when he had reached the age of twelve. Thus a part of his long reign of fifty-five years (2 Kings 21:1) was spent in a coregency with Hezekiah.

This completes our brief survey of the nine Hebrew overlapping reigns.

In a previous discussion of overlapping reigns,[3] I concluded my remarks as

---

[3]Edwin R. Thiele, "Coregencies and Overlapping Reigns Among the Hebrew Kings," *Journal of Biblical Literature* 93 (1974): 174–200.

follows: "There is no good reason to doubt the accuracy of the chronological data in the Hebrew text that call for the overlappings here set forth, nor of the authenticity of the overlapping reigns thus called for in ancient Hebrew history." The more carefully this subject is studied, the more clear it becomes that the nine overlappings here mentioned constituted integral components of ancient Hebrew history. When these overlappings are recognized, it becomes possible to construct an accurate pattern of Hebrew history, a pattern in harmony with the regnal data in Kings and in agreement with the established chronology of Israel's neighbors at every point where a precise contact can be secured.

CHAPTER FOUR

The Establishment of an Absolute Date in Hebrew Chronology

MAJOR OBJECTIVE in the reconstruction of the history of a nation is the establishment of its chronology. Not until a central core of exact and dependable chronological reckoning has been secured may the historian move forward with confidence toward the correct grouping and interpretation of the events of that state and of its neighbors.

In the Old Testament no absolute dates are given, and it becomes our task to establish, if we can, some absolute date in the history of Israel that can be used as a starting place to establish other dates in the desired chronological scheme. Our only hope of doing this is to find some cardinal point of contact where Hebrew history ties with certainty into the history of some other nation whose chronology is known.

In the early period of the Hebrew monarchies the most frequent and definite contacts were with Assyria, and in the later period most contacts were with Neo-Babylonia. Fortunately, the chronologies of these two nations, at least for the period with which we are most concerned, have been definitely established. There were also frequent Hebrew contacts with Egypt, Aram, and other lesser states, but the contacts were in most instances very indefinite in point of time, and the chronologies of those nations are likewise far from being positively established.

Assyrian chronology back to the beginning of the ninth century B.C. rests on a highly dependable basis. The various items essential to a sound chronology were present, and so scholars have been able to produce a sound chronological system for that nation.

First to be noted is the nature of the Assyrian year, for if years as they were reckoned then did not mean solar years as we know them, anything in the way of absolute chronology would be extremely difficult or impossible to achieve. The Assyrians during the period here under discussion measured time by lunar months and solar years. A new month was begun with each new moon. Since the moon makes a complete revolution of the earth once each 29 days, 12 hours, 44 minutes, and 2.8 seconds, or approximately once every 29½ days, the Assyrian months as a rule were alternately 29 or 30 days in length. Twelve of these months made up the year. But since this procedure gave a year that was approximately eleven days short of the solar year, it was necessary, if the year was to be kept in line with the sun and the annual seasons, for frequent adjustments to be made. Such adjustments were made whenever necessary by the addition of an intercalary month to the yearly calendar. Thus once in every two or three years—seven intercalations within a nineteen-year period—the calendar contained thirteen months instead of the usual twelve, and by this means the Assyrian year was kept in line with the solar year. This was also the procedure followed in Babylon and among the Hebrews. When in Assyrian chronology we are dealing with the passage of a certain number of years, we can have confidence that the years involved are solar years that may be precisely determined by reckoning from the data of recorded astronomical phenomena.

Of the greatest importance to the historian in the reconstruction of a sound chronological outline is the use of some device whereby events may be dated into the exact years when they took place and whereby the passage of the years may be reckoned correctly over extended intervals of time. The Seleucid and the Christian eras, the Olympic periods in Greece, and the custom of dating events in terms of the founding of Rome all have been of incalculable assistance to the chronologist in the correct reconstruction of history. The Assyrians did not make use of an era as such, but they did possess a system of eponymous years that serves a similar purpose. From some period very early in their history—possibly from the very beginning of the kingdom—to the end, the Assyrians followed the practice of each year appointing to the office of eponym, or limmu, some high official of the court, the governor of a province, or the king himself. The limmu held office for a calendar year, and to that year was given the name of the individual then occupying the position of limmu. Historical events in Assyria were usually dated in terms of these limmus, although at times they might be dated in terms of the year of the reign of the king, and on occasions both the year of reign and the eponymous year were given.

Thus if we have a list of eponyms, we have a list of Assyrian years. For any period for which there is available a complete and accurate list of eponyms, there is available a device making possible an accurate reconstruction of the chronological outline of the period covered. Fortunately, the Assyrians followed the custom of preserving lists of eponyms, many of which are available today. Some of these contain only a few names, while others contain several hundred names. Among the cuneiform tablets found at Nineveh by Austen Layard, Sir Henry Rawlinson identified four that were copies of the Assyrian eponym canon; and to these he assigned the numbers I, II, III, and IV. Canon I covered the period from 911 to 659 B.C., II extended from 893 to 692 B.C., III from 792 to 649 B.C., and IV from 753 to 701 B.C. None of these lists is perfect for the entire period, each being broken in places. Canon IV originally contained some sixty additional names; so it probably ended later than the other three. But where one tablet may be broken, the missing name or names may in many instances be supplied from other tablets, for in addition to the above a number of other lists are at present available. Among these are the following listed by

Ebeling and Meissner:[1] C^{a}5, 743–682 B.C.; C^{b}1, 816–727; C^{b}2[7], 810–745; C^{b}4, 840–706; C^{b}6, 818–703; C^c, 872–660; and C^d, 719–661.

Of particular interest among the limmu lists are a number of tablets that give not only the names of the eponyms but their titles or positions and the principal events during the various eponymies. Of this type are tablets listed in the C^b group by Ebeling and Meissner and canons V, VI, and VII of George Smith.[2] One item of unusual importance is a notice of an eclipse of the sun that took place in the month Simanu in the eponymy of Bur-Sagale. Astronomical computation has fixed this as 15 June 763.[3] With the year of the eponymy of Bur-Sagale fixed at 763 B.C., the year of every other name of the complete canon can likewise be fixed. The Assyrian lists extant today provide a reliable record of the annual limmu officials from 891 to 648 B.C.;[4] and for this period they provide reliable dates in Assyrian history.

In addition to the various limmu lists two other Assyrian documents are of great historical and chronological importance. These are the Khorsabad King List[5] found at Khorsabad, the ancient site of Dur-Sarrukin, capital of Sargon, in excavations conducted there during the season of 1932/33 by the Oriental Institute of the University of Chicago, and the SDAS King List, brought to America in 1953.[6] The Khorsabad List has a subscription stating that it was copied from a king-list tablet in the city of Ashur during the second eponymy of Adad-bel-ukin, which is the eighth year of Tiglath-Pileser III (738 B.C.). On the tablet was recorded a complete list of the kings of Assyria from the beginning to Ashur-nirari V (755–745), immediate predecessor of Tiglath-Pileser III. For the earliest kings only the names are given, then comes a section giving the name of

---

[1]"Eponymen," *Reallexikon der Assyriologie*, ed. Erich Ebeling and Bruno Meissner, vol. 2 (1938). A number of additional lists are given in this volume, but they are so short that they need not be mentioned in detail here.

[2]George Smith, *The Assyrian Eponym Canon* (London, 1875), pp. 28, 42–55.

[3]Various efforts have been put forth to identify this eclipse with that of 24 June 791, or with that of 13 June 809. These efforts have usually been prompted by the attempt to create some system of Assyrian chronology that will be more in keeping with certain preconceived ideas of "biblical" chronology. Such attempts introduce not harmony but confusion into both Hebrew and Assyrian history. In the endeavor to discredit the reliability of the testimony of the eponym canon, efforts are made to postulate a break in the canon, usually early in the eighth century B.C. The suggestion has been made that a whole block of fifty-one consecutive names, from 834 to 783 B.C., has been dropped from the canon and that all dates based on the canon beyond 783 B.C. are fifty-one years too low. According to this hypothesis, the Assyrian date of 911 B.C., the first year of Adad-nirari II, which synchronizes with the accession of Asa, should be 962 B.C., based on the evidence of "biblical" chronology (see Martin Anstey, *The Romance of Bible Chronology* [London, 1913], p. 220). George Smith describes a number of earlier attempts in this regard (*Assyrian Eponym Canon*, pp. 4ff.). There exists no evidence of any kind of a break in the eponym canon, particularly at the period in question, and certainly not in true biblical chronology. All the available evidence from Assyrian, Babylonian, and Egyptian records and from the Hebrew Scriptures points to the complete reliability of the canon in the matter of chronological reckoning. Any modern attempts to postulate a break in the canon at the very period when the evidence in regard to its reliability is so overwhelming will be disdained by the careful historian.

[4]For a list of these eponyms see Appendix F.

[5]For a description of the tablet and a discussion of its contents see A. Poebel, "The Assyrian King List from Khorsabad," *Journal of Near Eastern Studies* 1 (1942): 247ff, 460ff.; 2 (1943): 56–90.

[6]For a description, transliteration, and translation of these two lists see I. J. Gelb, "Two Assyrian King Lists," *Journal of Near Eastern Studies* 13 (1954): 209–30.

a king and his father, and finally there is a third section giving also the number of years of the king's reign. The SDAS King List is practically identical to the Khorsabad List, with the exception that it gives the names of two kings at the end of the list not found on the Khorsabad List, namely, Tiglath-Pileser III, with eighteen years (745–727 B.C.), and Shalmaneser V, with five years (727–722). The two lists provide a number of checks on each other.

The importance of these documents in providing vital chronological information concerning Assyrian history for the periods covered will be immediately apparent. Of vital concern to us is having here a pattern of Assyrian chronology exactly paralleling that of the divided Hebrew monarchies. And we likewise have a check on the accuracy of the Assyrian eponym canon where these sources parallel each other. There is a remarkable agreement. The fact that the king lists close with the reigns of Ashur-nirari V (755–745) and Shalmaneser V (727–722 B.C.) would point to the immediately preceding period as the area of greatest accuracy, for it would be from that period that the most reliable information would be available. This is a matter most gratifying to the biblical chronologist, for it is precisely in this period that he finds many of his most difficult problems; and it is in that area where gaps in the Assyrian records have been invented in order to bolster support for certain proposed schemes of Old Testament chronology.

In addition to these important documents that provide a check on the accuracy of the eponym canon prior to the middle of the eighth century B.C., there is another document that provides a check on its accuracy for the period following the middle of the eighth century B.C., namely, Ptolemy's canon. Ptolemy (70–161 A.D.) was a scholar of outstanding ability. He was an astronomer, geographer, historian, and chronologist. His famous canon begins in 747 B.C. with the start of the reign of Nabonassar in Babylon. First appears a list of the rulers of Babylon and their lengths of reign, from Nabonassar to Nabonidus, the ruler when the Neo-Babylonian empire came to its end. Then follow the rulers of Persia, from Cyrus, the conqueror of Babylon, to Darius III, the last ruler of Persia when it was overthrown by Alexander the Great. Following Alexander and Philip, Ptolemy lists the Ptolemaic rulers of Egypt to Cleopatra and then goes on with the rulers of Rome, from Augustus to Antoninus Pius (138–161 A.D.).[7] In addition to the number of years for each king, the sum of the years for the period of each ruler from the beginning of the canon is also given, this figure being secured by merely adding the sums of the previous reigns. We thus have what is called the Nabonassar era that began on 27 February 747 B.C. (astronomically noon, 26 February). Following the years of the Babylonian and Persian rulers up to the time of Alexander the Great, the years are again numbered beginning with Philip, and the totals are thus expressed to Antoninus Pius and the end of the canon.

What makes the canon of such great importance to modern historians is the large amount of astronomical material recorded by Ptolemy in his *Almagest*, making possible checks as to its accuracy at almost every step from beginning to

---

[7]For a good discussion of Ptolemy's canon, see F. K. Ginzel, *Handbuch der mathematischen und technischen Chronologie*, vol. 1 (Leipzig, 1906–14), pp. 138ff.

end. Over eighty solar, lunar, and planetary positions, with their dates, are recorded in the *Almagest* and these have been verified by modern astronomers. The details concerning eclipses are given with such minuteness as to leave no question concerning the exact identification of the particular phenomenon referred to and make positive verification possible. Early in the canon, for instance, its correctness can be checked by an eclipse of the moon that took place in the first year of Mardokempados on the night of 29/30 Thoth; it began in Babylon one hour after the rise of the moon and was a total eclipse. This was the twenty-seventh year of the Nabonassar era. The eclipse has been fully verified as having taken place on 19 March 721. Ptolemy also mentions an eclipse in the seventh year of Cambyses, which would be the year 225 of the Nabonassar era (523 B.C.). This eclipse has been computed to have taken place on 16 July 523. And once more, Ptolemy states in the *Almagest* that an eclipse of the moon took place in the thirty-first year of Darius on 3/4 Tybi. Since the death of Cambyses occurred in 522 B.C. (year 226 of the Nabonassar era), the thirty-first year of Darius would bring us to 491 B.C. (year 257 of Nabonassar's era). The eclipse took place 25 April 491 B.C. The dates of the Nabonassar era have thus been fully established, and once the method of procedure involved in the reckoning of the years of the kings is understood,[8] the canon of Ptolemy may be used as a historical guide with the fullest confidence.

Since Ptolemy's canon gives precise and absolutely dependable data concerning the chronology of a period beginning with 747 B.C., and since the Assyrian eponym canon carries us down to 648 B.C., it will be seen that there is a century where these two important chronological guides overlap and where they may be used as a check on each other. The canon of Ptolemy provides the date 709 B.C. (year 39 of the Nabonassar era) when Sargon, king of Assyria, became king of Babylon. From Assyria come two tablets, K 5280 and K 2688, that provide the information that the eponymy of Mannu-ki-Ashur-li', the thirteenth year of Sargon as king of Assyria, was his first year as king of Babylon.[9] We thus secure 709 B.C. as the year of the eponymy of Mannu-ki-Ashur-li' and the thirteenth year of Sargon as king of Assyria. Now on the basis of Ptolemy's canon we are able to provide dates to all the other eponymies on the Assyrian

---

[8]The years reckoned in Ptolemy's canon are Egyptian years of 365 days each, with no leap years. For this reason the 907 years of the canon are 226¾ days shorter than 907 Julian years, and the year of the canon was thus a wandering year, beginning with 26 February 747 B.C. and commencing one day earlier every four years. By A.D. 160 the Egyptian New Year's Day had moved back to 14 July. In the Babylonian and Persian sections the canon reckons each reign from 1 Thoth, the Egyptian New Year's Day, after the king came to the throne. For the Greek and Roman rulers the canon reckons each reign from 1 Thoth preceding the ruler's accession. It will be noticed that this method employed by Ptolemy is equivalent to the use of the accession-year system for Babylon and Persia and the nonaccession-year system for Greece, Egypt, and Rome—the very systems used by the rulers of those lands at those times. A king whose reign was less than a year (which did not embrace the New Year's Day) would not be mentioned in the list. No fractions of years are counted, these being taken care of by throwing the beginning of a ruler's reign forward to the New Year's Day following or back to the New Year's Day preceding his actual accession. For a good discussion of this and other related phases of this problem see Josef Hontheim, "Die Chronologie des 3. und 4. Buches der Könige," *Zeitschrift für katholische Theologie* 42 (1918): 463–82, 687–718.

[9]Smith, *Assyrian Eponym Canon*, p. 86.

lists, and we thus secure 763 for the eponymy of Bur-Sagale—the same date as was secured for that eponymy by the evidence of the solar eclipse that took place that year in the month Simanu. So the date 763 for the eponymy of Bur-Sagale has been established not only by the astronomical evidence of Assyria but also by that of Ptolemy's canon. We thus have complete assurance that 763 is the correct date for Bur-Sagale and that the other dates of the eponym lists, whether reckoned backward or forward from that date, are likewise correct.

Many other cross references between the Assyrian eponym list and the canon of Ptolemy are possible, such as the fourteenth year of Sargon as king of Assyria and second year as king of Babylon, in the eponymy of Shamash-upahhir,[10] the fifteenth year of Sargon as king of Assyria and third year as king of Babylon, in the eponymy of Sha-Ashur-dubbi,[11] the sixteenth year of Sargon as king of Assyria and fourth year as king of Babylon, in the eponymy of Mutakkil-Ashur,[12] and others.[13]

When the student has at his disposal chronological materials so dependable as the Assyrian eponym list and the Ptolemaic canon, he may have complete assurance that he has a solid foundation on which to build. And if, in turn, he finds a chronological pattern for some other nation that is in full accord with that of Babylon and Assyria as established by the evidence of Ptolemy and the limmu lists, he may have confidence that his pattern is entirely accurate.[14]

The earliest point where a positive synchronism between Israel and Assyria may be secured is from the reigns of Ahab, Jehu, and Shalmaneser III. We have already noticed that the latter in giving the events of his sixth year in the eponymy of Daian-Ashur lists Ahab as one of the western allies who fought against him at the battle of Qarqar.[15] Since in this inquiry we propose to deal

---

[10]Ibid., p. 87.

[11]Ibid.

[12]Ibid.

[13]Ibid., pp. 102ff.

[14]*The Scientific American* (Oct. 1977) pp. 79–81, published a vicious attack on Ptolemy entitled, "Claudius Ptolemy Fraud." There it presented the views of Robert R. Newton in his book *The Crime of Claudius Ptolemy* (Johns Hopkins University Press) that Ptolemy had "deliberately fabricated observations" and had invented "the length of reigns of Babylonian kings." Such allegations are totally groundless and have been shown to be false. In March 1979, pp. 91–92, *The Scientific American* published a repudiation of its previous article under the title "The Acquittal of Ptolemy." There it stated that noted astronomers after reviewing Newton's charges had "concluded that the charges of fraud were groundless." Such outstanding authorities as Noel M. Swerdlow of the University of Chicago, Owen J. Gingerich of Harvard University, and Victor E. Thoren of Indiana University had shown that "Newton's case against Ptolemy collapses because it is based on faulty statistical analysis and a disregard of the methods of early astronomy." Prof. Gingerich in a paper delivered before the American Astronomical Meeting at Honolulu on 18 January 1977 gave a detailed refutation of Newton's charges and concluded with his own resounding vindication of Ptolemy: "I prefer to think of him as the greatest astronomer of antiquity." Ptolemy was not a fraud. Rather, he was an extremely competent scholar in such fields as astronomy, history, mathematics, and geography. He left to posterity information of amazing accuracy and of priceless value, and there is every reason to trust and honor him.

[15]Daniel David Luckenbill, *Ancient Records of Assyria and Babylonia*, vol. 1 (Chicago, 1926), secs. 610–11.

with absolute chronology and since Ahab's contact with Shalmaneser at Qarqar is a cardinal point of departure, the establishment of the exact date of Qarqar is a matter of vital importance. The question is whether this date is 854 as given by one group of scholars,[16] or 853 as given by others.[17] The reason for these two datings lies in the fact that on one eponym list, C^{a}3, the symbol of Ebeling in *Reallexikon der Assyriologie,* 2, 423, one more eponym is found, Balatu, than occurs on parallel lists for the period, C^{a}6, C^{b}2, and C^c. Either list C^{a}3 is correct and the other lists have mistakenly omitted the name of Balatu, or the latter three lists are correct and some explanation must be found for the insertion of the name Balatu on list C^{a}3. If list C^{a}3 is correct and the insertion of the name Balatu stands for an extra eponymy and an extra year, then all dates beyond Balatu will be one year higher than if the other three lists omitting the eponymy of Balatu are historically correct. This is the reason for the divergent dates of 854 and 853 for the battle of Qarqar and for all years beyond 786 B.C.

Not only does list C^{a}3 contain the extra name Balatu, but on this list the eponym Nabu-shar-usur occupies a different position than it does on the other lists. On C^{a}3 the sequence is as follows:

788	Sil-Ishtar	785	Marduk-shar-usur
787	Balatu	784	Nabu-shar-usur
786	Adad-uballit	783	Ninurta-nasir

But on the other lists the following sequence occurs:

787	Sil-Ishtar	784	Marduk-shar-usur
786	Nabu-shar-usur	783	Ninurta-nasir
785	Adad-uballit		

It will thus be seen that on the latter three lists the name of Nabu-shar-usur occupies the place which on C^{a}3 is held by Balatu, following Sil-Ishtar and preceding Adad-uballit. If all four lists are correct in placing these two names in this particular place—C^{a}3 in placing Balatu in this position, and the other three in placing Nabu-shar-usur in that place—then Balatu and Nabu-shar-usur would both have been eponyms during the same year. In that case, however, the latter three lists for some reason gave only Nabu-shar-usur as limmu for the year 786, omitting the name of Balatu, while C^{a}3 gave the names of both Balatu and Nabu-shar-usur, with the latter name for some strange reason following that of Marduk-shar-usur. If C^{a}3 alone is correct in listing both the names of Balatu and Nabu-shar-usur and placing them in the positions they hold on that list, then the other three lists are guilty of two errors, the omission of the name

---

[16]See Smith, *Assyrian Eponym Canon,* p. 81; A. T. Olmstead, *History of Assyria* (New York, 1923), pp. 134ff.; Robert William Rogers, *Cuneiform Parallels to the Old Testament,* 2nd ed. (New York, 1926), pp. 220, 289; Robert H. Pfeiffer, *Introduction to the Old Testament* (New York, 1941), p. 395; and Luckenbill, *Ancient Records,* vol. 2 (Chicago, 1927), p. 431.

[17]See H. R. Hall, *The Ancient History of the Near East,* 9th ed. rev. (London, 1936), p. 449; Theodore H. Robinson, *A History of Israel* (Oxford, 1934), 1:296; Ebeling and Meissner, "Eponymen," pp. 420, 434; and Emil Forrer, "Zur Chronologie der neuassyrischen Zeit," *Mitteilungen der vorderasiatischen Gesellschaft* 20 (1915): 5ff.

Balatu and the eponym year for which it would stand, and the misplacement of the name Nabu-shar-usur.

Professor Olmstead strongly championed the view that C[a]3 was the correct list and that the peculiarities of the other three lists were due to scribal errors.[18]

Professor Forrer, on the other hand, accepted the witness of the lists containing the eponym Nabu-shar-usur for the year 786 as correct. He explained the inclusion of the name Balatu on C[a]3 by the suggestion that the name of the eponym for an ensuing year was in all likelihood announced before 1 Nisan of the year in which he was to hold office. Forrer said that the death of Balatu, who had been selected as the eponym for 786, took place after the announcement of his name but before his assumption of office. In consequence, Forrer continued, a new eponym, Nabu-shar-usur, was appointed; however, in the most distant provinces datings during the first few months of the year, before word could reach them of the newly appointed eponym, were in the name of the eponym already deceased, with the scribe responsible for C[a]3 inserting the name Nabu-shar-usur in the wrong place, and with the scribes responsible for the other lists simply omitting the name of the deceased Balatu.[19]

A determination of the question of whether there were one or two eponyms during the year 786 and whether the longer or the shorter chronology is correct, even though the difference is only one of a single year, is vital to our inquiry. One way in which the answer to this question might be obtained is to endeavor to find some fixed point on one side of 786 and another fixed point on the other side of 786 and then to try to find some means by which the number of years for that interval might be obtained. Beyond 786 we can take as one fixed point the year when Shalmaneser III came to the throne, which according to the Assyrian Chronicle was in the eponymy of Tab-Bel. On this side of 786 another fixed point is the year when Tiglath-Pileser III came to the throne, which according to the Assyrian Chronicle was in the eponymy of Nabu-bel-usur. The date of the eponymy of Nabu-bel-usur is on this side of the eclipse in Bur-Sagale's eponymy of 763 and is thus firmly established by the eponym canon as 745 B.C. If it is true that Balatu and Nabu-shar-usur were both eponyms during the year 786, then the eponym canon gives us the date 859 for the eponymy of Tab-Bel and the accession of Shalmaneser III. But if Balatu and Nabu-shar-usur occupied two separate eponymies, the eponym canon would provide the date 860 for the eponymy of Tab-Bel and the accession of Shalmaneser III. The exact number of years between the accession of Shalmaneser III and that of Tiglath-Pileser III may be easily discovered from the known lengths of reign of the kings in that interval. According to the Khorsabad List and other reliable sources, these are as follows:

---

[18]A. T. Olmstead, "The Assyrian Chronicle," *Journal of the American Oriental Society* 34 (1915): 344ff.; idem., "Shalmaneser III and the Establishment of the Assyrian Power," *Journal of the American Oriental Society*, 41 (1921): 374, n. 61; idem., "Bruno Meissner," *Archiv für Orientforschung* 5 (1928–29): 30.
[19]Forrer, "Zur Chronologie," pp. 5ff.

Shalmaneser III	35
Shamshi-Adad V	13
Adad-nirari III	28
Shalmaneser IV	10
Ashur-dan III	18
Ashur-nirari V	10
Total	114

Since it was in the year 745 that Ashur-nirari V died and that Tiglath-Pileser III came to the throne, and since it was 114 years before that that Shalmaneser III became king, 859 would be the correct date for the accession of Shalmaneser III and the eponymy of Tab-Bel.[20] We thus know that 786 is the eponym year of both Balatu and Nabu-shar-usur, that the chronology of eponym lists C^{a}6, C^{b}2, and C^e is indeed correct, that the recording of the name of Nabu-shar-usur between those of Marduk-shar-usur and Ninurta-nasir on C^{a}3 is wrong, and that all dates of the eponym canon beyond 786 will have to be reduced by one year on the part of those who have accepted the longer chronology.

The following lists show the relationship of eponyms and kings according to the long and short chronology. In the selection of their eponyms the Assyrians at this time were following a specific order of sequence under which the king occupied this position during the second year of his reign.

LONG CHRONOLOGY

Date	Name and Position of Eponym		Years between Eponymies	Years of Reign
883	Ashur-nasir-apli	the king	25	25
858	Shulman-asharid	king of Ashur	35	35
823	Shamshi-Adad	king of [Assyria]	13	13
810	Adad-nirari	[king] of Assyria	29	28
781	Shulman-asharid	king of Assyria	10	10
771	Ashur-dan	king of Assyria	18	18
753	Ashur-nirari	king of Assyria	10	10
743	Tukulti-apal-eschar-ra	king of Assyria		

SHORT CHRONOLOGY

Date	Name and Position of Eponym		Years between Eponymies	Years of Reign
882	Ashur-nasir-apli	the king	25	25
857	Shulman-asharid	king of Ashur	35	35
822	Shamshi-Adad	king of [Assyria]	13	13
809	Adad-nirari	[king] of Assyria	28	28
781	Shulman-asharid	king of Assyria	10	10
771	Ashur-dan	king of Assyria	18	18
753	Ashur-nirari	king of Assyria	10	10
743	Tukulti-apal-eschar-ra	king of Assyria		

[20]It will be noted that this accord between the chronological evidence provided by the lengths of reign of the Assyrian kings for this period and of the names on the limmu lists makes utterly untenable the postulation of a gap in the eponym canon, for it is in this period that the existence of such a gap has been proposed.

As long as this order was followed, the number of years between the eponymy of one king and that of his successor should be equal to the years of his reign. It will be noticed that, according to the short chronology in the period under review, the official length of a king's reign is in each instance identical with the number of years between the royal eponymies, whereas in the long chronology this is the case with each king except Adad-nirari, where under this arrangement an extra year has somehow crept in. It will be immediately noticed that this is the reign covering the eponymies of Balatu and Nabu-shar-usur. It is only when each of these men is assigned an eponymous year that this abnormality of an extra calendar year occurs. It must be evident, then, that Balatu and Nabu-shar-usur were both eponyms during the year 786 and that the longer chronology is in error.

It should also be noticed that if Balatu and Nabu-shar-usur occupy separate eponymies, then Adad-nirari must have held the eponymy during the first year of his reign or Shalmaneser held it during his third year, whereas the regular practice during this period and for a century thereafter was for a king to hold the eponymy during his second year of reign.

The evidence here presented points definitely to the correctness of the shorter system of Assyrian chronology and thus to 853 rather than to 854 as the date for the eponymy of Daian-Ashur and the battle of Qarqar, and it is in accord with this dating that we will proceed.

An exact synchronism between Hebrew and Assyrian history is made possible in the early period of the kings by an interesting correlation of events in Israel and Assyria that begins and ends the twelve-year period of 853 to 841 B.C. It has already been mentioned that Ahab is listed by Shalmaneser III as one of the kings of the Westland who fought against him in the battle of Qarqar, and we have seen that this battle was fought in the year 853. Therefore, Ahab was still alive and reigning in Israel sometime in the year 853. Shalmaneser also mentions that he received tribute from Jehu during his expedition to the west in his eighteenth year. This would be in the eponymy of Adad-rimani (841). Thus Jehu was already reigning over Israel sometime in 841. Two questions need to be answered: (1) How long after 853 did Ahab continue to reign, and (2) how long before 841 did Jehu begin to reign? The facts are that Ahab could not have reigned beyond 853 and Jehu could not have begun to reign before 841, because the interval between the death of Ahab and the accession of Jehu is exactly twelve years, being made up of the reigns of Ahaziah, the son and successor of Ahab, and Joram, who was slain and succeeded by Jehu. The official length of Ahaziah's reign is given as two years (1 Kings 22:51), which when reckoned according to Israel's nonaccession-year system would make one actual year. The official length of Joram's reign was twelve years (2 Kings 3:1), or eleven actual years, which would give a total of twelve years for the reigns of Ahaziah and Joram. Since the interval between the battle of Qarqar, at which Ahab fought in 853, and the time when Jehu paid tribute to Shalmaneser in 841 is also a period of just twelve years, it is in this period that the reigns of Ahaziah and Joram must have taken place, with 853 as the last year of Ahab and 841 for Jehu's accession.

It might be argued that the battle of Qarqar need not have taken place in the last year of Ahab's reign, and that he might have continued to live, say, two or three years after Qarqar was fought. That is true, and the death of Ahab, as far as Qarqar alone is concerned, might have taken place in 851 or 850. But if that were the case, then the accession of Jehu would have to be thrust ahead two or three years, to 839 or 838, which is not possible, for we know that he was on the throne in 841, Shalmaneser's eighteenth year. Likewise, it could be argued that Jehu did not necessarily pay tribute to Shalmaneser in the year that he ascended the throne and that 841 could conceivably have been the second or third year of his reign. That certainly would be possible as far as Jehu alone is concerned. But if Jehu's accession were pushed back two or three years, to 843 or 844, the death of Ahab would also need to be thrust back two or three years, to 855 or 856. But that would not be possible, for we know that Ahab was still alive in 853, Shalmaneser's sixth year, when Qarqar was fought. On the basis of these facts, the date of Ahab's death and Ahaziah's accession can be established as 853 and the date of Joram's death and Jehu's accession, as 841.

Having established these two dates as a starting point for an absolute chronology of the Hebrew kings, we should be able to go backward and forward, knowing that if our chronological pattern is correct, we will obtain exact synchronisms at all points of contact with any absolute chronology of neighboring states.

One point that should not be overlooked concerning the year 853 for the accession of Ahaziah and 841 for the death of Joram is that we have here from an Assyrian source a complete confirmation of the use in Israel of the nonaccession-year system of reckoning. If the official length of Ahaziah's reign was two years (1 Kings 22:51) and if the official length of Joram's reign was

Diagram 9

Years From the Schism to the End of Ahab

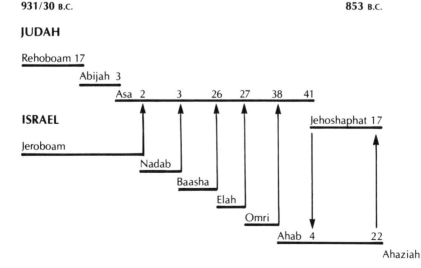

twelve years (2 Kings 3:1), and if these two reigns totaling fourteen official years were only twelve actual years, from 853 to 841, it is obvious that Israel was at this period using the nonaccession-year system.

With 853 fixed as the last year of Ahab, the data in the Masoretic Text should enable us to ascertain the date of the first year of Jeroboam I and the schism between Judah and Israel. The official and actual years of reign for this period, deducting from the reign of each king the one year overlap involved when the nonaccession-year system of reckoning is used, are as follows:

	Official Reign	Actual Reign
Jeroboam I	22 years	21 years
Nadab	2 years	1 year
Baasha	24 years	23 years
Elah	2 years	1 year
Zimri	7 days	7 days
Omri	12 years	11 years
Ahab	22 years	21 years
Total	84 years, 7 days	78 years, 7 days

With an interval of 78 years between the accession of Jeroboam I and the death of Ahab, and with the latter taking place in 853 B.C., we thus secure the date 931/930 B.C. as the year of Jeroboam's accession and of the schism between Judah and Israel. And, being in possession of this date, we are in a position—if the data with which we shall work are basically sound and if the principles of Hebrew chronology we have set forth are indeed correct—to ascertain the dates for the kings of Judah and Israel to the close of their histories. That is the task before us.

A solid synchronism between Judah and Assyria at which our pattern of Hebrew dates could begin is 701 B.C. That is a definitely fixed date in Assyrian history and is the year in which Sennacherib in his third campaign "went against the Hittite-land" (Aram), and shut up "Hezekiah the Jew . . . like a caged bird in Jerusalem, his royal city." That took place in the fourteenth year of Hezekiah (2 Kings 18:13), that is, in the year 701. The regnal data in Kings should enable us to work backward from 701 to 841 as the year when Athaliah began to reign in Judah and Jehu began to reign in Israel and to 853 as the year when Ahab was slain in battle and succeeded by Ahaziah.

However, instead of working backward from 701, we will work forward from 930. We will proceed reign by reign as the accounts are given in Kings and will give year-by-year charts from the disruption of the monarchy in 930 to the release of Jehoiachin from prison in Babylon in 561.

CHAPTER FIVE

The Chronology of Judah and Israel (930–841 B.C.)

AVING SET FORTH the basic chronological principles used by the ancient Hebrew recorders in the period of the kings and having fixed 931/30 as the year of the division of the monarchy and the beginning of the nations of Judah and Israel, I will proceed with the chronological pattern of the Hebrew rulers as based on the data of the Masoretic Text.

In the interests of simplicity the date 930 is being used for the division of the kingdom instead of the dual symbol 931/30. It should be noted, however, that the year 931 might have been equally appropriate or even more accurate than 930, depending on the season of the year when Jeroboam's rebellion took place. Nevertheless, whether 931 or 930 is used, none of the succeeding dates will be affected.

My procedure will be to deal with the reigns in the order in which they appear in Kings. From 930 for the beginning of Rehoboam, I will go on year by year and reign by reign, proceeding down an unbroken chronological chain in accord with the recorded data to the end of the nation of Israel and then to the end of Judah.

There will be a series of charts and diagrams that cover all the years from the beginning to end, set forth all the relevant regnal data, and denote the scribal procedures in use at the various times.

In dealing with the regnal data of Kings, it is of prime importance to understand the chronological principles in use at any given time and the procedures being followed by the recorders in dealing with their data. At the time of the schism Judah used accession-year reckoning for its own data and also for the years of Israel given in the synchronisms. Israel at this time used the nonaccession-year system for itself and for its synchronisms with Judah. The charts will be in accord with these details.

Rehoboam was the first ruler to follow Solomon; and so we begin with his reign.

1. Rehoboam—Judah—930–913

1 Kings 12:1–24; 14:21–31; 2 Chronicles 10:1–12:16
Synchronism: none since Israel was not yet in existence
Length of reign: 17 years, accession-year reckoning = 17 actual years
925—attack by Shishak of Egypt in the 5th year of Rehoboam (1 Kings 14:25; 2 Chron. 12:2)

The Shishak who came against Judah in the fifth year of Rehoboam was the vigorous and able Sheshonk I, founder of Egypt's twenty-second dynasty. He left his own record of this invasion of Palestine and gave a list of the cities he captured there. The fifth year of Rehoboam was between Tishri in the fall of 926 and Tishri in the fall of 925. Breasted gives the date of this invasion as "probably about 926 B.C."[1] This date is in almost complete accord with the date here given as based on biblical sources. If the invasion took place in the fall of the year after Tishri, then the date is 926. But that is not the usual season of the year when attacks on Palestine were made. If Shishak made his attack at the usual season in the spring, the date is 925.

Chart 1 below gives the chronological details of Judah and Israel from 930 to 921 B.C. in accord with the principles set forth above.

Chart 1

930–921 B.C.

930—Rehoboam—17 years—1 Kings 14:21
930—Jeroboam—22 years—1 Kings 14:20

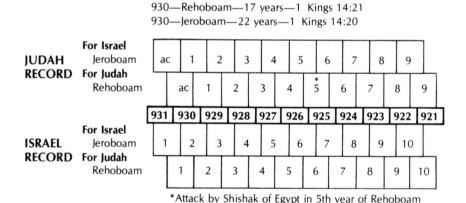

*Attack by Shishak of Egypt in 5th year of Rehoboam

The chart above gives details of how Judah and Israel kept their chronological records. Rehoboam of Judah succeeded Solomon between Tishri 931, and Tishri 930, which was Rehoboam's accession year. But according to the records kept in Israel that was his first year. Jeroboam ascended the throne of Israel between Nisan 931 and Nisan 930, and the records kept in Israel indicate this was the first year of his reign. But according to the records of Judah this was his accession year. Charts to follow will show the details of the chronological methods used in Judah and Israel at any given time.

---

[1]J. H. Breasted, *History of Egypt* (New York, 1921), p. 529.

After the opening part of Rehoboam's reign is presented in Kings, there comes the account of Jeroboam's rebellion and of his reign. Let us now notice the chronological details.

2. Jeroboam—Israel—930–909

1 Kings 12:25–14:20

Length of reign: 22 official years, nonaccession-year system = 21 actual years

Synchronism: not given; he began to reign shortly after Rehoboam in Judah

After the record of Jeroboam in Kings and the remaining details of Rehoboam, the next account is that of Abijah in Judah. The sequence of accounts below follows that of Kings. This is in accord with the sequence of the synchronisms.

Chart 2
921–911 B.C.

913—Abijah—18th of Jeroboam—3 years—
1 Kings 15:1–2

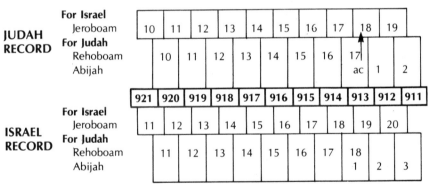

Judah's record is according to the accession-year system;
Israel's is nonaccession.

3. Abijah—Judah—913–910

1 Kings 15:1–8; 2 Chronicles 13:1–22

Length of reign: 3 official years, accession-year reckoning = 3 actual years

Synchronism: 18th of Jeroboam, accession-year reckoning = 19th official year of Jeroboam. This is the only synchronism with a ruler of Israel given in Chronicles.

Mother: Maacah daughter of Abishalom. 1 Kings 15:2. But see 2 Chronicles 13:2, "Maacah, a daughter of Uriel of Gibeah."

Chart 3

911–901 B.C.

910—Asa—20th of Jeroboam—41 years—1 Kings 15:9
909—Nadab—2d of Asa—2 years—1 Kings 15:25
908—Baasha—3d of Asa—24 years—1 Kings 15:33

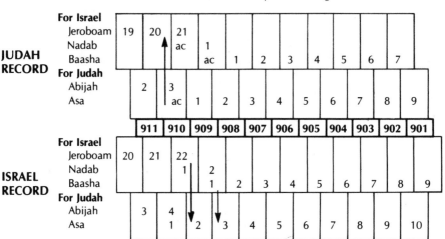

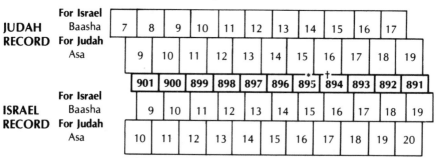

Judah's record is according to the accession-year system; Israel's is nonaccession.

Chart 4

901–891 B.C.

Judah's record is according to the accession-year system; Israel's is nonaccession.
*Asa routed Zerah and held a victory celebration.
†Baasha fortified Ramah.

Chart 5

891–880 B.C.

886—Elah—26th of Asa—2 years—1 Kings 16:8
885—Zimri—27th of Asa—7 days—1 Kings 16:15
885—Tibni—1 Kings 16:21
885—Omri—27th of Asa—1 Kings 16:15–16
　　—12 years—1 Kings 16:23
880—31st of Asa—1 Kings 16:23—Omri's sole reign

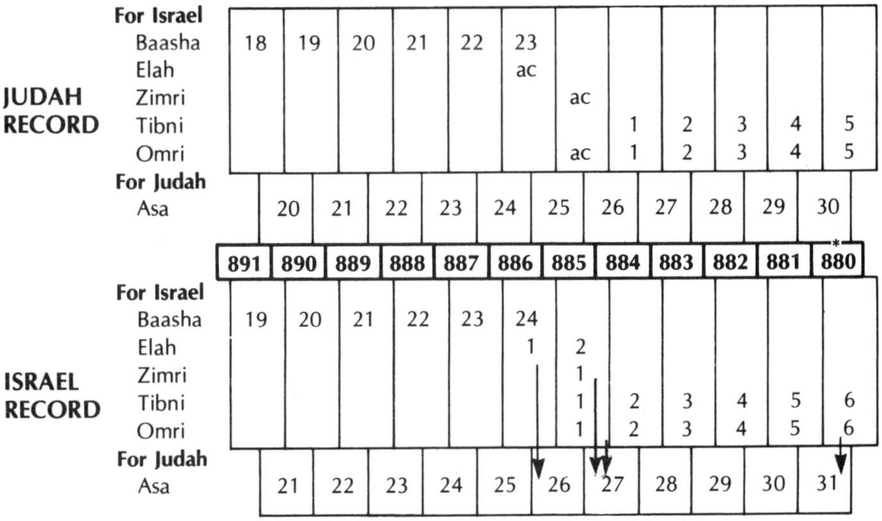

JUDAH RECORD

For Israel	891	890	889	888	887	886	885	884	883	882	881	880
Baasha	18	19	20	21	22	23						
Elah						ac						
Zimri							ac					
Tibni								1	2	3	4	5
Omri							ac	1	2	3	4	5
For Judah												
Asa		20	21	22	23	24	25	26	27	28	29	30

| **Year** | 891 | 890 | 889 | 888 | 887 | 886 | 885 | 884 | 883 | 882 | 881 | 880* |

ISRAEL RECORD

For Israel	891	890	889	888	887	886	885	884	883	882	881	880
Baasha	19	20	21	22	23	24						
Elah						1	2					
Zimri							1					
Tibni							1	2	3	4	5	6
Omri							1	2	3	4	5	6
For Judah												
Asa	21	22	23	24	25	26	27	28	29	30	31	

*Omri's sole reign.
Judah kept its record according to the accession-year system.
Israel kept its record according to the nonaccession-year system.
The data of Omri are in accord with dual-dating procedure.

4. Asa—Judah—910–869

1 Kings 15:9–24; 2 Chronicles 14:1–16:14

Synchronism: 20th of Jeroboam, accession-year reckoning = 21st official year of Jeroboam

Length of reign: 41 years, accession-year reckoning = 41 actual years
　　15th year (895 B.C.); victory celebration (2 Chron. 15:10–11)
　　35th year "of Asa" (KJV) "no more war" until this time (2 Chron. 15:19)
　　36th year "of Asa" (KJV) Baasha fortified Ramah (2 Chron. 16:1)
　　39th year (871 B.C.); Asa stricken with serious illness (2 Chron. 16:12)

From a chronological standpoint the long reign of Asa is of great importance. Six kings of Israel have their accessions synchronized with him; thus he provides vital information as to their dates. A reference in 2 Chronicles 16:12 to the grave illness of Asa in his thirty-ninth year (871 B.C.), throws light on the commencement of the reign of Jehoshaphat at that time in a coregency with Asa.

References to the thirty-fifth and the thirty-sixth years "of Asa" (KJV) in 2 Chronicles 15:19 and 16:1 have given rise to serious chronological misunderstandings. When correctly interpreted, however, these references provide important confirmatory evidence as to the exact number of years thus far involved since the beginning of the nations of Judah and Israel.

A vital factor was the threatened invasion of Judah by a large Ethiopian army under Zerah, who was met by a fierce counterattack from Asa. Zerah was completely routed and Asa took much plunder in the southern Philistine area of Gerar to which Asa had pursued the enemy (2 Chron. 14:9–15). The ensuing victory celebration in the fifteenth year of Asa (2 Chron. 15:10–11) provides the date of 895 B.C. for this battle.

With this serious engagement in Asa's fifteenth year, why does 2 Chronicles 15:19 say, "Up to the thirty-fifth year of Asa's reign there was no war" (JB)? This is the sense of the Hebrew of this verse, and it is reflected in NAB, KNOX, BERKELEY, and others. But to meet the difficulty of a definite war in Asa's fifteenth year, the KJV and other translations have added the word *more*, making the statement read, "There was no more war unto the five and thirtieth year of the reign of Asa."

The difficulty concerning the thirty-fifth year is solved by noticing that it is exactly thirty-five years from 930 B.C., when the nations of Judah and Israel came into being, to 895, the fifteenth year of Asa when his encounter with Zerah took place. It is my view that the original annalistic recording concerning the thirty-fifth year mentioned in 2 Chronicles 15:19 had only a reference to that year. The phrase "of Asa" was a late editorial addition introduced when the Book of Chronicles was brought into being.

That this must have been the meaning of the "thirty-fifth" year in 2 Chronicles 15:19 is made clear by a reference to a thirty-sixth year in 2 Chronicles 16:1. There we read, "In the thirty-sixth year of Asa's reign Baasha king of Israel went up against Judah, and fortified Ramah to prevent anyone from leaving or entering the territory of Asa king of Judah." But such an undertaking by Baasha in Asa's thirty-sixth year would not have been possible, because Baasha at that time had already been dead ten years. It was in the twenty-sixth year of Asa that Baasha was succeeded by his son Elah (1 Kings 16:6, 8). So the meaning of the thirty-sixth year when Baasha fortified Ramah is again a reference back to 930. Thirty-six years after 930 is 894, the year following Asa's defeat of Zerah in 895.

That year would have been the appropriate time for Baasha to undertake the fortification of Ramah in order "to prevent anyone from leaving or entering the territory of Asa king of Judah" (2 Chron. 16:1). The result of Asa's stunning victory over Zerah was that many of the citizens of Israel were coming over to Asa in Judah, "for large numbers had come over to him from Israel when they saw that the LORD his God was with him" (2 Chron. 15:9). Greatly perturbed by these developments, Baasha would lose no time before taking measures to put a stop to the influx to Judah out of Israel. So in 894, the year after the crushing defeat of Zerah, Baasha fortified Ramah as a barrier against Judah. This was thirty-six years after the beginning of the nation of Israel in 930.

Those who are acquainted with Professor Albright's studies of the disrup-

Chart 6

880–869 B.C.

874—Ahab—38th of Asa—22 years—2 Kings 16:29
872—Jehoshaphat as regent
869—Jehoshaphat's sole reign—4th of Ahab—25 years from start
of coregency—1 Kings 22:41–42

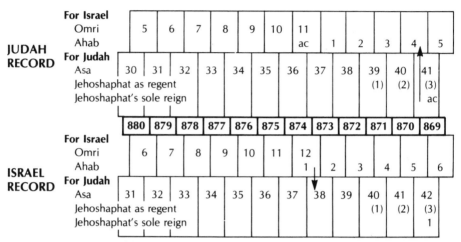

Judah kept its record according to the accession-year system.
Israel kept its record according to the nonaccession-year system.
The year that begins a coregency is the first official year of that
coregency.
Jehoshaphat's regnal data are in accord with dual-dating procedure.

tion of the monarchy will be interested to note that his acceptance of 2 Chronicles 16:1 as historically correct is responsible for his date of 922 rather than 930 for the schism. His argument is that "the 36th year of Asa would be the 54th year of a Rehoboam era, while according to the transmitted numbers for Israel Baasha died in the 46th year of a Rehoboam era, some eight years earlier! . . . It follows that, unless we increase the Israelite numbers drastically, we must reduce the reign of Rehoboam by at least 8, probably 9 years."[2]

But a reduction of the reign of Rehoboam from 17 to 8 or 9 years on such a flimsy basis involves extensive revisions in the data of synchronisms and lengths of reign for almost all the early Hebrew rulers recorded in Kings. With the exception of the late synchronisms of 2 Kings 17 and 18, the biblical data are in full harmony and there is no reason to reject them. The dates give evidence of having come down from early contemporary recorders and deserve our confidence and respect. We should not assume that a pattern of early Hebrew years based on Albright's modern invention is the original historical pattern of reigns for Israel or Judah or that it will be in more complete accord with the

---

[2]W. F. Albright, "The Chronology of the Divided Monarchy of Israel," *Bulletin of the American Schools of Oriental Research* 100 (1945): 20.

years of Israel's ancient neighbors. On the contrary, there is evidence indicating that Albright's date of 922 for the disruption of the monarchy is not historically sound.[3] Widely accepted though this date has been, it should be recognized as an aberration. Although coming from a scholar who was truly great, the date of 922 is not valid.

The concluding item concerning Asa reported in Kings is that "in his old age, however, his feet became diseased" (1 Kings 15:23). That statement occurs in the closing formula of his reign, seemingly when the reign had come to its end. In the closing formula of the parallel account we read, "In the thirty-ninth year of his reign Asa was afflicted with a disease in his feet" (2 Chron. 16:12). The text adds that the "disease was severe." Interestingly, the regnal data of Jehoshaphat call for the commencement of his twenty-five years in a coregency with his stricken father during the thirty-ninth year of Asa. But the synchronism of Jehoshaphat's accession is the fourth year of Ahab (1 Kings 22:41), which is the forty-first year of Asa. Both these data for Jehoshaphat are in accord with dual-dating procedure.

Diagram 10 below sets forth in simplified form the relationships between the kings of Judah and Israel from the disruption of the monarchy in 930 to the death of Asa in 869. Due to the fact that regnal years in Judah began in Tishri in the fall and in Israel they began in Nisan in the spring, absolute delineations

---

[3]There is an Assyrian text mentioning Ba'li-ma-AN-zêri of Tyre as having paid tribute to Shalmaneser III in the same year as did Jehu—in 841 B.C. See F. Safar, "A Further Text of Shalmaneser III from Assur" *Sumer* 7 (1950): 11–12, col. iv, 10–12; and J. Liver, "The Chronology of Tyre at the Beginning of the First Millennium B.C.," *Israel Exploration Journal* 3 (1953): 113–20. If this ruler is to be identified with Balezoros II of Josephus' list of Tyrian kings, and if Albright's date of 814 for the founding of Carthage is correct, the date 922 is historically disproved, for such a reconstruction would call for the dates 835 to 829 for Balezoros' reign, whereas it was in 841 that this ruler paid tribute to Shalmaneser III.

Albright endeavors to meet the situation by denying the identity of Ba'li-ma-AN-zêri with Balezoros on the ground of certain phonetic divergences, and proposes the name of another king, Ba'al-manzer, who he claims has dropped out of Josephus' list. See Albright, "Mélanges Isidore Lévy," *l'Annuaire de l'Institut de Philologie et d'Histoire Orientales et Slaves* 13 (1955): 1–9. If this is true, and if Josephus' list of the Tyrian kings is so imperfect that it has lost the entire reign of a certain king together with the number of years involved, then how can that list provide such a "tremendous advantage," as he has claimed for his date of 922 as against my date of 930? Certainly, Josephus' list cannot at one time be absolutely accurate and yet so admittedly wrong in such a vital essential.

A denial of the identity of Ba'li-ma-AN-zêri from an Assyrian cuneiform text of the ninth century B.C. with Balezoros of a Greek text of the first century A.D. on the ground of the slight phonetic divergences involved is open to serious question. What scholar cannot cite numerous such divergencies in texts of different languages a thousand years apart? If every such a divergence justifies the invention of a new king, river, country, city, or god, what would that do to the facts of ancient history? Whether the names represent the same individual or not, Albright's date of 922 derives no historical support from such testimony as this. If the names are not the same, and if an entire reign together with the years involved has been lost, then Josephus' list of Tyrian kings can hardly be used to establish any absolute date in ancient history. If the two names are the same, and if Albright's date of 814 for the founding of Carthage is sound, then his date of 922 is demonstrably wrong. See my study, "A Comparison of the Chronological Data of Israel and Judah," *Vetus Testamentum* 4 (1954): 188ff. Let me say in brief that I know nothing, biblical or historical, that would provide any support of any kind for the date 922 as against 930. The date 922 is not biblical, and there is not the slightest evidence that it is historical. The claim that the date 930 cannot be squared with Tyrian chronology is without foundation in fact.

cannot be set forth in such a condensation as this. For more precise details see charts 1 to 6 (pages 80–85).

Diagram 10

Rehoboam and Jeroboam to the Death of Asa (930–869 B.C.)

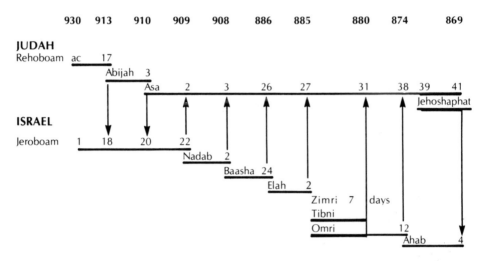

Following the record of Asa the Book of Kings has the accounts of seven rulers of Israel. All these came to the throne during the long reign of Asa, and six have their accessions synchronized with him, namely, Nadab, Baasha, Elah, Zimri, Omri, and Ahab. For Tibni there is no synchronism or length of reign. However, we note that his account follows that of the seven-day reign of Zimri, who ruled in the twenty-seventh year of Asa (when Omri was made king) and that Tibni ruled as a rival of Omri; hence Tibni also must have begun his reign in Asa's twenty-seventh year. The reigns of the above seven rulers will be considered next in the order in which they come in Kings.

5. Nadab—Israel—909–908

1 Kings 15:25–31
Synchronism: 2nd of Asa, nonaccession-year reckoning = 1st official year of Asa, accession-year reckoning
Length of reign: 2 official years, nonaccession-year reckoning = 1 actual year

6. Baasha—Israel—908–886[4]

1 Kings 15:32–16:7
Synchronism: 3rd year of Asa, nonaccession-year reckoning = 2nd year of Asa, accession-year reckoning

---

[4]The complexities of coordinating the New Years of the ancient calendars with the modern Julian calendar year make it a common practice to date ancient events with the two Julian years that contain the ancient date in question, for example 908/7 B.C. In this work a single date is generally used to simplify the discussion, but occasionally this approach is problematic. The same difficulties that are encountered between Tishri years and Nisan years (cf. chap. 2) are encountered when

Length of reign: 24 official years, nonaccession-year reckoning = 23 actual years

   36th year "of Asa" (KJV); fortified Ramah (2 Chron. 16:1). This was not the 36th year of Asa, for Baasha died in the 26th year of Asa when Elah succeeded him (1 Kings 16:6, 8); but it was the 36th year after the beginnings of Israel and Judah in 930, or 894 B.C.

7. Elah—Israel—886–885

1 Kings 16:8–14
Synchronism: 26th year of Asa, nonaccession-year reckoning = 25th year of Asa, accession-year reckoning
Length of reign: 2 official years, nonaccession-year reckoning = 1 actual year

8. Zimri—Israel—885

1 Kings 16:15–20
Synchronism: 27th of Asa, nonaccession-year reckoning = 26th year of Asa, accession-year reckoning
Length of reign: 7 days

9. Tibni—Israel—885–880

1 Kings 16:21–22
Synchronism: not given
Length of reign: not given

Although no data are recorded for the synchronism or length of reign of Tibni, these details may be deduced from the context. When Zimri killed Elah and ruled seven days in the twenty-seventh year of Asa, the people made Omri king (1 Kings 16:15–16). But Omri ruled only half the nation, for the other "half supported Tibni son of Ginath for king, and the other half supported Omri" (1 Kings 16:21). Since the account of Tibni's reign in 1 Kings 16:21–22 follows that of Zimri in 1 Kings 16:15–20, and since the records of the rulers in Kings are given in accord with the sequence of their accessions, it would appear that it was in the 27th year of Asa that Tibni as well as Omri followed Zimri. And the fact that Omri ruled six years in Tirzah after which his accession is synchronized with the thirty-first year of Asa (1 Kings 16:23), in accord with dual-dating procedure, would indicate that Tibni ruled six official years (five actual years) as a rival of Omri. At the close of this time Omri began his sole reign.

10. Omri—Israel—885–880 (kingdom divided with Tibni)
—885–874 (total rule)

1 Kings 15:23–28
Accession: 27th year of Asa when the people made him king at Zimri's subversion

attempting to date ancient events in modern Julian years. In some instances when single dates are used for ancient events, the time span of Julian years will differ by one year from the elapsed time given in the ancient record. When studied carefully it will be seen that this is because of the difference in calendars; it is not due to an incorrect chronology. Such is the case in the instance noted above.

Synchronism: 31st year of Asa when he began his sole rule at Tibni's death
Length of reign: 6 official (5 actual) years at Tirzah during Tibni's reign; 12
   official (11 actual) years from the beginning of his kingship
Dual-dating procedure was followed for his regnal data.

From before the commencement of the Christian era, there has been
uncertainty concerning the meaning of the regnal data of Omri. Did the time
when he began his reign of twelve years commence with the twenty-seventh
year of Asa when he was made king by the people? Or, did it begin with the
thirty-first year of Asa according to the official synchronisms of 1 Kings 16:23?[5]
There are a number of variant data for the rulers of this period in the early
Greek manuscripts. These data portray a pattern that commences the twelve
years of Omri with the thirty-first year of Asa and carry that pattern through to
the end of the Omride dynasty.

In order to understand the Greek departures from the Masoretic Text, it is
first necessary to see the true picture. Diagram 11 below depicts the vital
details of the reigns of Asa and Jehoshaphat in Judah, and in Israel of Tibni,
Omri, and Ahab, in accord with dual-dating procedure for Omri.

Diagram 11
Hebrew Pattern for the Accessions of Omri, Ahab, and Jehoshaphat

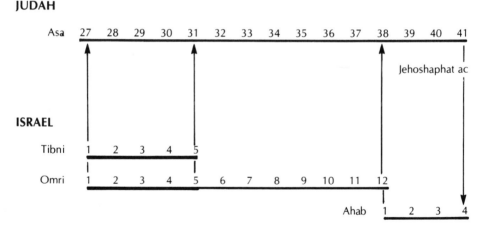

In such a simplified diagram as this not every detail of every reign can be
given. For a more complete picture see charts 5 and 6 (pages 83 and 85).

It should first be noted that Omri began his reign in the twenty-seventh
year of Asa when he was elevated to the throne by the people at the time of
Zimri's brief reign of seven days (1 Kings 16:15–17). Omri reigned twelve
official years (1 Kings 16:23), nonaccession-year reckoning, or eleven actual
years. This brought the end of his reign in the thirty-eighth year of Asa at the

---

[5]For a fuller discussion of this problem and details concerning overlapping reigns, see Edwin
R. Thiele, "Coregencies and Overlapping Reigns Among the Hebrew Kings," *Journal of Biblical
Literature* 93 (1974): 174–200.

accession of Ahab (1 Kings 16:29), according to the Hebrew record.

It must also be remembered that during the early part of Omri's reign Tibni ruled over part of the land (1 Kings 16:21–22). The regnal details of Omri are given in accord with dual-dating procedure, where in an overlapping reign the datum for the length of reign includes both the period of overlap and that of sole reign, but the synchronism of accession denotes the end of the period of overlap and the commencement of the sole reign. Thus the length of Omri's reign includes both his overlap with Tibni and his sole reign, but his synchronism of accession marks the end of his overlap with Tibni and the commencement of his sole reign.

Greek variants came into being because of a failure to understand the meaning of the Hebrew data and from an effort to correct supposed errors. Among these are variants as given by Burney as in the following list:[6]

		Masoretic Text	Septuagint	Lucian
1 Kings 16:29	I Ahab	38th of Asa	*2nd of Jehoshaphat*	*2nd of Jehoshaphat*
1 Kings 22:41	J Jehoshaphat	4th of Ahab	*11th of Omri*	*11th of Omri*
1 Kings 22:51	I Ahaziah	17th of Jehoshaphat	17th of Jehoshaphat	*24th of Jehoshaphat*
2 Kings 1:17	I Jehoram (also called Joram)	2nd of Jehoram J	*18th of Jehoshaphat*	2nd of Jehoram J
2 Kings 3:1	I Jehoram	18th of Jehoshaphat	18th of Jehoshaphat	....
2 Kings 8:25	J Ahaziah	12th of Jehoram I	12th of Jehoram I	11th of Jehoram I

It is evident that the Greek variants set forth a pattern of reign for Omri quite different from that in the Hebrew. The Hebrew synchronism at 1 Kings 22:41 for the accession of Jehoshaphat of Judah is the fourth year of Ahab of Israel. There the Greek synchronism for the accession of Jehoshaphat is also the fourth year of Ahab. But the Greek has another account of Jehoshaphat's reign, at 1 Kings 16:28, that places the accession of Jehoshaphat in the eleventh year of Omri.

Furthermore, at 1 Kings 16:29 the Hebrew synchronism for the accession of Ahab is the thirty-eighth year of Asa, but there in the Greek it is the second year of Jehoshaphat.

Accounts of reigns appear in Kings in the order of sequence in which the rulers began their reigns; this means that if Jehoshaphat began in the fourth year of Ahab, the account of Ahab should precede that of Jehoshaphat. Ahab does precede Jehoshaphat in both the Hebrew and the Greek where Ahab's account comes at 1 Kings 16:29–22:20 and the account of Jehoshaphat follows at 22:41–50.

The question is whether the Greek preceded the Hebrew text, or the Hebrew preceded the Greek. Conclusive proof that the Hebrew was in existence before the Greek is found in the Greek placing an additional account of Jehoshaphat at 1 Kings 16:28. That verse constitutes the concluding statement

[6]C. F. Burney, *Notes on the Hebrew Text of the Books of Kings* (Oxford: Clarendon, 1903, pp. xlii–xliv. For an examination of these and certain other variants see chapter 9, "The Variant Figures of the Greek Texts," of Edwin R. Thiele's book, *The Mysterious Numbers of the Hebrew Kings* (Chicago: University of Chicago Press, 1951).

concerning the reign of Omri, and the account of the next ruler should begin with verse 29. In both the Greek and the Hebrew, verse 29 is where the account of Ahab begins. But in order to permit the account of Ahab to begin there in the Greek and yet have the account of Jehoshaphat precede that of Ahab, the Greek attaches the entire account of Jehoshaphat as an appendage to the account of Omri and compresses it into a single verse together with the last verse of Omri's reign. The account of Jehoshaphat at 1 Kings 22:41–50 occupies ten verses. If the Greek had been in existence before the Hebrew, the account of Jehoshaphat would have been given at 1 Kings 16:29–38, and it would then have been followed by the account of Ahab. There would have been no second account of Jehoshaphat after the account of Ahab at 1 Kings 22:41. It is not difficult to reconstruct what took place here. The Hebrew arrangement of chapters and verses was in existence when the additional account of Jehoshaphat was added in the Greek. In adding that account the Greek editor was endeavoring to follow the arrangement of chapters and verses found in the Hebrew.

A comparison of the Hebrew and Greek arrangements of chapters and verses is revealing. The Hebrew arrangement is as follows:

1 Kings 16:23–28	Omri	31st of Asa
1 Kings 16:29–22:40	Ahab	38th of Asa
1 Kings 22:41–50	Jehoshaphat	4th of Ahab

In the Greek we have the following:

1 Kings 16:23–28	Omri	31st of Asa
1 Kings 16:28	Jehoshaphat	11th of Omri
1 Kings 16:29–22:40	Ahab	2nd of Jehoshaphat
1 Kings 22:41–51	Jehoshaphat	4th of Ahab

With the exception of the additional account of Jehoshaphat at 1 Kings 16:28, the sequences in the Greek and the Hebrew are the same. This is significant, for the additional account of Jehoshaphat in the Greek was placed at 1 Kings 16:28 in order that it might follow Omri and precede Ahab. The reason for this is seen in the Greek synchronism of Jehoshaphat's accession in the eleventh year of Omri. With that synchronism the account of Jehoshaphat had to follow that of Omri, whereas with the Hebrew synchronism of Jehoshaphat's accession in the fourth year of Ahab, the account of Jehoshaphat would follow that of Ahab. The Hebrew is perfectly consistent in the matter of sequence, with Ahab following Omri and with Jehoshaphat following Ahab. The Greek, however, is utterly inconsistent, with Jehoshaphat at 1 Kings 22:41–51 following Ahab but at 1 Kings 16:28 preceding him.

It is clear that in placing Jehoshaphat at 1 Kings 22:41–51 the Greek was following the Hebrew with its synchronism of Jehoshaphat's accession at the fourth year of Ahab. However, in placing another account of Jehoshaphat at 1 Kings 16:28, the Greek followed its own divergent synchronism of Jehoshaphat's accession in the eleventh year of Omri.

It is important that we see why the Greek places the synchronism of

Jehoshaphat's accession in the eleventh of Omri and the accession of Ahab in the second of Jehoshaphat (instead of the thirty-eighth of Asa as in the Hebrew). Let us notice the diverse Hebrew and Greek arrangements in accord with these synchronisms. The Hebrew pattern is as follows:

```
                                                          Jehoshaphat
Asa    (27)  28  29  30  (31)  32  33 34  35  36  37  (38) 39  40  (41)
Zimri  (1)
Tibni   1   2   3   4    5
Omri    1   2   3   4    5    6   7   8   9  10  11   12
                                              (1)   2   3   (4)
                                              Ahab
```

The following is the Greek arrangement:

```
                                                          Jehoshaphat
                                                          (ac)  1  (2)
Asa         27  28  29  30  (31)  32  33  34  35  36  37  38  39  40  41
                           (1)   2   3   4   5   6   7   8   9  10  (11) 12
                           Omri
                                                                    (1)
                                                                    Ahab
```

Looking at the Hebrew regnal data, we notice that the Greek editor could not understand how a reign of twelve years for Omri that began in the thirty-first year of Asa could terminate in the thirty-eighth year of Asa with Ahab at that time coming to the throne.[7] So the Greek editor began the twelve years of Omri, not in the twenty-seventh year of Asa when Omri was first elevated to the kingship at the elimination of Zimri (1 Kings 16:15–18), but in the thirty-first year of Asa. Since Asa reigned forty-one years, the first part of Omri's twelve years would in such a case parallel the last part of Asa, and the final years of Omri would parallel the first years of Jehoshaphat. Under such an arrangement Jehoshaphat would come to the throne in the eleventh year of Omri in accord with the Greek synchronism of 1 Kings 16:28, and Ahab would begin in the second year of Jehoshaphat in accord with the Greek synchronism of 1 Kings 16:29.

When this anomalous Greek arrangement was brought into being, the Hebrew enumeration of chapters and verses was already in existence, and this the Greeks endeavored to follow.[8] But they obviously faced a dilemma with the account of Omri ending at 1 Kings 16:28 and that of Ahab beginning at 1 Kings

---

[7]It also will be helpful here to review diagram 11 on page 89.

[8]James Donald Shenkel in his doctoral dissertation of 1964 made the claim that the Greek is the early and correct pattern for the Hebrew rulers and that the Hebrew regnal data arose as variants from an original Greek pattern. See J. D. Shenkel, *Chronology and Recensional Development in the Greek Text of Kings* (Cambridge: Harvard University Press, 1968). In a survey of the overlapping reigns in the Hebrew kingdoms, I have discussed the arguments presented by Shenkel. I have pointed out their numerous fallacies and inconsistencies and his failure to come to grips with the basic issues involved. See Edwin R. Thiele, "Coregencies and Overlapping Reigns Among the Hebrew Kings," *Journal of Biblical Literature* 93 (1974): 176–90. See also the extended review of Shenkel's book by D. W. Gooding, in *Journal of Theological Studies* 21 (1970): 118–31.

16:29. So the account of Jehoshaphat was added as an appendage to that of Omri at 1 Kings 16:28. Such an arrangement would never have been brought into being had the Greek been in existence before the Hebrew.

All this points unmistakably to the fact that the Hebrew was the original account, not the Greek, and that the Greek came into existence because of its failure to understand dual dating in connection with the regnal data of Omri. The Hebrew data were thought to be in error and in need of correction. It was thus that the Greek variants were produced concerning Omri, Ahab, and Jehoshaphat. Outwardly simple and seemingly correct though the Greek data may appear to be, they are far out of line with the original, correct Hebrew pattern of reigns. When carefully examined, the Greek arrangement reveals itself to be a late, artificial, and highly deceptive contrivance brought into being because of a failure to understand early, original Hebrew chronological procedures. This resulted in an attempt to correct something that was actually right but was looked on as wrong.

One indication of the artificiality of the Greek pattern is found in the dubious methods that they used for chronological procedure. In the Hebrew text there is a consistent use of the legitimate accession- and nonaccession-year methods of reckoning. When the use of these systems is understood, many of the most frequent difficulties disappear, and a pattern of reigns comes forth in accord with the regnal data and with the years of Israel's neighbors. In the Greek pattern, however, there is no consistency in methods of chronological procedure. There is only a haphazard jumping back and forth from one system to another, and often the resort is to an utterly fallacious system. At first glance the Greek pattern appears to be strangely akin to legitimate accession-year reckoning, but it is actually an erroneous and deceptive contrivance resorted to only because of involvements in which no legitimate method of chronological reckoning will work.

In my earlier discussions of the Greek variants, I termed this spurious system *inconsequent accession-year reckoning*. In this system the year when a ruler is set forth as having begun his reign is actually the year after his reign began. Thus in the Greek pattern previously given for the accessions of Omri and Ahab, the accession of Ahab is synchronized with the second year of Jehoshaphat, although according to that pattern it was in the previous year, the first year of Jehoshaphat, that Omri had his twelfth and last year, and there the pattern should have begun with the reign of Ahab. But that would not work in such an artificial pattern. Many such occurrences are found in the pattern of reigns based on the Greek variant data.

The list on the following page shows the haphazard use of chronological systems in the pattern called for by the Greek variant data and the frequent use of the delusive, artificial, inconsequent accession-year system of reckoning.

The use of the inconsequent accession-year method of reckoning in the Greek manuscripts provides prima facie evidence of the lateness and artificiality of their variant chronological data. Shenkel has called attention to the Greek Lucianic manuscript c_2 that uses this system throughout, from Rehoboam and Jeroboam to Hezekiah and Hoshea—changing the chronological data to be in accord with this admittedly late and arbitrary system of reckoning.[9] The vital fact that the Greek manuscript c_2 makes altogether clear is that the late Lucianic redactors were under the impression that the regnal data in the Hebrew text of the Books of Kings were in need of revision. They did not hesitate to make whatever adjustments they thought would improve the chronological data in Kings.

Chronological Systems Used in the Greek and Hebrew Texts

	Masoretic Text	Septuagint	Lucian
JUDAH			
Rehoboam	ac-year	inconsequent ac-year	inconsequent ac-year
Abijah	ac-year	inconsequent ac-year	inconsequent ac-year
Asa	ac-year	inconsequent ac-year	inconsequent ac-year
Jehoshaphat	ac-year	ac-year	ac-year
Jehoram	nonac-year	coregent, nonac-year	nonac-year
Ahaziah	nonac-year	ac-year	not clear
ISRAEL			
Jeroboam	nonac-year	inconsequent ac-year	inconsequent ac-year
Nadab	nonac-year	inconsequent ac-year	inconsequent ac-year
Baasha	nonac-year	ac-year	ac-year
Elah	nonac-year	not clear	not clear
Zimri	nonac-year	not clear	not clear
Omri	nonac-year	inconsequent ac-year	not clear
Ahab	nonac-year	inconsequent ac-year	inconsequent ac-year
Ahaziah	nonac-year	coregent, nonac-year	inconsequent ac-year
Joram	nonac-year	coregent, nonac-year	inconsequent ac-year

Additional shortcomings in the Greek pattern of Hebrew reigns will be set forth in my discussions of other rulers concerning whom variants occur.

At the death of Omri his son Ahab succeeded him, and it is his reign that will be presented next.

11. Ahab—Israel—874–853

1 Kings 16:29–22:40

Synchronism: 38th year of Asa, nonaccession-year reckoning = 37th official year of Asa's reign

Length of reign: 22 official years, nonaccession-year reckoning = 21 actual years

853—fought against Shalmaneser III at battle of Qarqar

During the reign of Ahab an accurately dated event in Assyrian history can for the first time be definitely tied in with Hebrew history. The Assyrian records list Ahab as among the allied powers of western Asia who fought against Shalmaneser III at the battle of Qarqar in Aram during the eponym year of

---

[9]Shenkel, *Chronology and Recensional Development*, pp. 28–31.

Daian-Ashur,[10] the sixth year of Shalmaneser III, verified as 853.[11] There is no mention of the battle of Qarqar in the Bible and thus no direct information as to the year of Ahab's reign when that battle was fought. But by a fortuitous combination of years in Hebrew and Assyrian history, it is possible to place this battle in Ahab's last year (see page 76–77). Ahab was followed by Ahaziah, who had an official reign of two years, nonaccession-year reckoning, or one actual year. Ahaziah was followed by Joram, with an official reign of twelve years, or eleven actual years. This makes a total of twelve years for Ahaziah and Joram. Joram was slain by Jehu; so there were twelve years between the death of Ahab and the accession of Jehu. In Assyrian history we also have a similar period of twelve years at this time. The Assyrian monarch Shalmaneser III fought at Qarqar in the sixth year of his reign; in his eighteenth year he reports having received tribute from Jehu.[12] That makes twelve years between the battle of Qarqar and the receipt of tribute from Jehu. And this combination provides 853 for the last year of Ahab and 841 for the commencement of Jehu.

But was Qarqar fought in the last year of Ahab and did Jehu pay tribute in his first year to Shalmaneser III? If the point is raised that Qarqar might have been fought at some time earlier than the last year of Ahab, thus bringing the death of Ahab to some time after 853, then the accession of Jehu would need to be thrust ahead an equal distance beyond 841. But that would not be possible because in 841 he paid tribute. Or if it should be argued that Jehu could have paid tribute at some time later than his first year, thus bringing his accession to some time before 841, then Ahab's participation at Qarqar would have to be pushed back an equal number of years before 853. But that could not be, for Qarqar was fought in 853. In this way the definite date of 853 is established for the death of Ahab[13] and 841 for the beginning of Jehu. Since the years of the Assyrian eponym canon are astronomically established, the dates 853 and 841 can be accepted with complete confidence as key points in a pattern of Hebrew history.

---

[10]Daniel David Luckenbill, *Ancient Records of Assyria and Babylonia*, vol. 1 (Chicago: University of Chicago Press, 1926), secs. 563, 610–11, 646.

[11]"Daian Assur," *Reallexikon der Assyriologie*, ed. Erich Ebeling and Bruno Meissner, 2 (1938); Arno Poebel, "The Assyrian King List from Khorsabad," *Journal of Near Eastern Studies* 2 (1943): 88.

[12]Luckenbill, *Ancient Records*, sec. 672.

[13]Inasmuch as Ahab was slain in battle by the Arameans at Ramoth Gilead (1 Kings 22:3, 34–35), this campaign must likewise have occurred in the year 853, following Qarqar. The month and day of the battle of Qarqar are not given, but Shalmaneser departed from Nineveh on this campaign on 14 Airu and crossed the Euphrates at its flood (Luckenbill, *Ancient Records*, sec. 610). This could not have been much later than the last of June, for in this month the flood is already on the decline and in late July the Euphrates reaches a low-water stage. For modern recordings of the Euphrates flow see M. G. Ionides, *The Regime of the Rivers Euphrates and Tigris* (London, 1937), pp. 39ff. The battle of Qarqar was thus probably fought during July or possibly early August. This would, however, leave Ahab ample time to return to Samaria and, with his forces already mustered, conduct the campaign at Ramoth Gilead well before the close of the season that year. For three years he had been at peace with Aram (1 Kings 22:1). The suggestion has been made that the alliance between Israel and Aram was prompted by a common fear of the growing power of Assyria (see Eberhard Schrader, *The Cuneiform Inscriptions and the Old Testament*, trans. Owen C. Whitehouse [London, 1885, 1888], vol. 1, 189–90; vol. 2, 323; Francis Brown, *Assyriology: Its Use and Abuse in Old Testament Study* [New York, 1885], pp. 53–62). Threatened by the same danger,

Chart 7

869–858 B.C.

		869	868	867	866	865	864	863	862	861	860	859	858
	For Israel												
	Ahab	5	6	7	8	9	10	11	12	13	14	15	
JUDAH RECORD	**For Judah**												
	Jehoshaphat												
	From regency	(4)	(5)	(6)	(7)	(8)	(9)	(10)	(11)	(12)	(13)	(14)	
	Sole reign	1	2	3	4	5	6	7	8	9	10	11	
	For Israel												
	Ahab	6	7	8	9	10	11	12	13	14	15	16	
ISRAEL RECORD	**For Judah**												
	Jehoshaphat												
	From regency	(4)	(5)	(6)	(7)	(8)	(9)	(10)	(11)	(12)	(13)	(14)	
	Sole reign	2	3	4	5	6	7	8	9	10	11	12	

The notations in Judah's record for both Judah and Israel are in accord with accession-year reckoning. The notations in Israel's record for both Israel and Judah are in accord with the nonaccession-year system. The initial year of a coregency is termed its first year, not an accession year. Dual-dating procedure was followed for the regnal data of Jehoshaphat.

12. Jehoshaphat—Judah—872-869—regent with Asa
      —872-848—total reign

1 Kings 22:41–50; 2 Chronicles 17:1–21:3
Synchronism: 4th of Ahab, commencement of sole reign, accession-year
    reckoning = 5th official year of Ahab
Length of reign: 25 official years, including 3 years of coregency with Asa, or
    24 actual years
Dual-dating procedure was used in his regnal data.

When all the regnal data of Jehoshaphat are put together, it is found that the commencement of his reign comes in 872, which is the thirty-ninth year of Asa, although the synchronism for his accession is given as the fourth year of Ahab, which is 869. The reason for this seeming discrepancy is that dual-dating procedure was followed in recording the regnal data of Jehoshaphat.

Ahab and Ben-Hadad were for a time able to bury their differences. The Aramean king was no doubt at the head of the western allies, for it is always he who is listed first in Shalmaneser's accounts of Qarqar. And it was he who furnished the largest number of infantry—twenty thousand out of the fifty-odd thousand involved are the figures given. It is altogether possible that Aram suffered a disproportionate share of the huge losses that Shalmaneser claims to have inflicted on the enemy and that Ahab with his chariots might have given a particularly good account of himself. At any rate, immediately after the battle was over, Ahab felt himself able to come to grips with his old foe and recent ally. On his return to Samaria he might have determined to square accounts with Aram before dispersing his troops. Jehoshaphat was probably invited to Samaria with a large retinue and showered with hospitality (2 Chron. 18:2) for the express purpose of securing his cooperation in the contemplated campaign for the recovery of Ramoth Gilead. The accession of Jehoram as coregent with Jehoshaphat in 853 was no doubt prompted by concern regarding the forthcoming campaign against Aram.

Chart 8
858–847 B.C.

853—Ahaziah—17th of Jehoshaphat—2 years—1 Kings 22:51
853—Jehoram—start of coregency
852—Joram—2d of Jehoram—2 Kings 1:17
    —18th of Jehoshaphat—2 Kings 3:1
    —12 years—2 Kings 3:1
848—Jehoram—5th of Joram—8 years—2 Kings 8:16-17

JUDAH RECORD

For Israel

	858	857	856	855	854	853	852	851	850	849	848	847
Ahab	16	17	18	19	20	21						
Ahaziah						ac	1					
Joram							1	2	3	4	5	6

For Judah

	858	857	856	855	854	853	852	851	850	849	848	847
Jehoshaphat		(15)	(16)	(17)	(18)	(19)	(20)	(21)	(22)	(23)	(24)	(25)
Sole reign		12	13	14	15	16	17	18	19	20	21	22
Jehoram as regent						1	2	3	4	5	6	
Jehoram's sole reign												1

858	**857**	**856**	**855**	**854**	**853**	**852**	**851**	**850**	**849**	**848**	**847**

ISRAEL RECORD

For Israel

	858	857	856	855	854	853	852	851	850	849	848	847
Ahab	17	18	19	20	21	22						
Ahaziah						1	2					
Joram							1	2	3	4	5	6
							(ac)	(1)	(2)	(3)	(4)	(5)

For Judah

	858	857	856	855	854	853	852	851	850	849	848	847
Jehoshaphat		(15)	(16)	(17)	(18)	(19)	(20)	(21)	(22)	(23)	(24)	(25)
Sole reign		13	14	15	16	17	18	19	20	21	22	23
Jehoram as regent						1	2	3	4	5	6	
Jehoram's sole reign												1

In accord with the practice up to this time, Jehoshaphat in Judah used accession-year reckoning for both Judah and Israel. But with his successor Jehoram, who married Athaliah, the daughter of Ahab and Jezebel of Israel, Judah shifted to the nonaccession-year system used in Israel. Judah followed this system for the reigns of Jehoram, Ahaziah, Athaliah, and Joash, and then shifted back to accession-year reckoning. The years of Jehoshaphat in parentheses are from the beginning of his coregency. Dual-dating procedure was followed for the regnal data of Jehoshaphat. The years of Joram in parentheses are in accord with accession-year reckoning.

It is of interest to note that in 2 Chronicles 16:12 we are told, "In the thirty-ninth year of his reign Asa was afflicted with a disease in his feet," which was "severe." Doubtless the cause for Jehoshaphat's having been raised to a coregency at that time was to carry on the affairs of state in behalf of his stricken father.[14]

A complete analysis of all the regnal data of Jehoshaphat requires that one examine the two accounts of his reign that are found in the Septuagint (LXX).

---

[14]A number of scholars have come to this same conclusion. Begrich calls attention to the fact that LXX Vaticanus a, b credits Asa with only thirty-nine years. See Joachim Begrich, *Die Chronologie der Könige von Israel und Juda und die Quellen des Rahmens der Königsbucher* (Tübingen, 1929), p. 130.

Since data were discussed in detail earlier in this chapter in connection with the reign of Omri, it will not be necessary to repeat that discussion here other than to make the following brief summary remarks. It cannot be argued successfully from the data that the Greek preceded the Hebrew; the evidence shows that the opposite is true. The explanation for the Greek variants is that the Greek editors did not understand dual-dating procedure.

13. Ahaziah—Israel—853–852

1 Kings 22:51–2 Kings 1:18
Synchronism: 17th of Jehoshaphat, nonaccession-year reckoning = 16th official year of Jehoshaphat
Length of reign: 2 official years, nonaccession-year reckoning = 1 actual year

Diagram 12 gives a simplified view of the coregencies in Judah of Jehoshaphat with Asa and of Jehoram with Jehoshaphat.

Diagram 12
874–841 B.C.

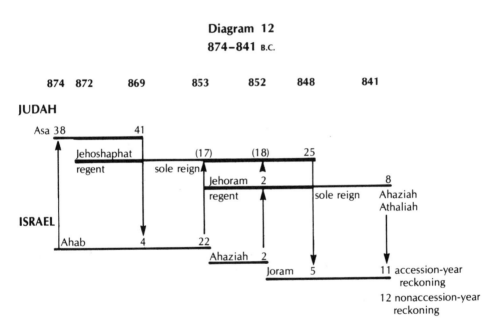

Judah

For Asa and Jehoshaphat accession-year reckoning was used for both the lengths of their reigns and their synchronisms with Israel. The twenty-five years of Jehoshaphat include the years of his regency with Asa, his sole reign that began in 869, and the regency of Jehoram. The synchronism of his accession in the fourth year of Ahab marks the beginning of his sole reign in 869.

Jehoram is the first king of Judah for whom nonaccession-year reckoning is used. Both the synchronism of his accession and the length of his reign are given in terms of nonaccession-year reckoning and start from the commencement of his sole reign in 848.

Ahaziah has two synchronisms for his accession, one in the eleventh year of Joram, which is in accordance with the accession-year method, and the other in the twelfth year of Joram, nonaccession-year reckoning.

Israel

For Ahab, Ahaziah, and Joram nonaccession-year reckoning is used for both the lengths of their reigns and the synchronisms of their accessions. The synchronisms of Ahaziah and Joram in the seventeenth and eighteenth years of Jehoshaphat, nonaccession-year reckoning, are in the actual sixteenth and seventeenth years from the time when Jehoshaphat began his sole reign in 869.

14. Joram—Israel—852–841

2 Kings 3:1–8:15

Synchronisms: 2nd of Jehoram (2 Kings 1:17)

      18th of Jehoshaphat (2 Kings 3:1), nonaccession-year reckoning, 17th official year of Jehoshaphat

Length of reign: 12 official years, nonaccession-year reckoning = 11 actual years

The official synchronism for Joram's accession given in 2 Kings 3:1 is the eighteenth of Jehoshaphat, but at the close of the account of Ahaziah it is stated that he was succeeded by Joram in the second year of Jehoram of Judah (2 Kings 1:17). The eighteenth year of Jehoshaphat's reign was the second year of Jehoram's coregency.

These two synchronisms for Joram's accession have often been regarded as contradictory and have been taken as evidence of the bungles involved in biblical chronology. That this was true in the early centuries before the Christian era is shown by the variant data in the Greek texts for these reigns. In the Septuagint the synchronism of 2 Kings 1:17 has been altered from the second of Jehoram to the eighteenth of Jehoshaphat to make it agree with 2 Kings 3:1. Lucian retains the second of Jehoram at 2 Kings 1:17 but at 2 Kings 3:1 omits the eighteenth of Jehoshaphat.

It should be noted that if Jehoram had been the sole ruler of Judah for two years before Joram came to the throne in Israel, then Jehoram began in Judah before Joram in Israel; in such a case Jehoram's record should have preceded that of Joram in the Book of Kings. That, however, is not the case. Also, although Lucian retained the synchronism of the second of Jehoram at 2 Kings 1:17, Lucian began the reign of Joram in Israel at 2 Kings 3:1 and that of Jehoram in Judah at 2 Kings 8:16, following the same sequence as in the Hebrew. Such an inconsistency in the Greek gives evidence of its dependence on an earlier Hebrew text. Again, this is positive proof that the Hebrew preceded the Greek.

15. Jehoram—Judah—853–848 regent
                —848–841 sole reign

2 Kings 8:16–24; 2 Chronicles 21:4–20

Synchronism: 5th of Joram, nonaccession-year reckoning; commencement of sole reign

Length of reign: 8 official years, sole reign, nonaccession-year reckoning = 7
actual years

The names "Jehoram" and "Joram" are variant spellings of the same Hebrew name. Thus the name Jehoram for this ruler of Judah is virtually identical
with that of his contemporary Joram of Israel. Both forms are given for these
kings at various places in the Hebrew text. One of these kings was certainly
named after the other at a period of close friendship between Israel and Judah.
To avoid confusion I am using Jehoram as the name of the king of Judah and
Joram as the name of the ruler of Israel.

Two synchronisms are given for Joram's accession in Israel, in the second
year of Jehoram at 2 Kings 1:17, and in the eighteenth year of Jehoshaphat at
2 Kings 3:1. These reveal the coregency between Jehoram and Jehoshaphat and
the year when it began.

If the eighteenth year of Jehoshaphat was the second year of Jehoram's
coregency, then the seventeenth year was its first year and the year when it
began. It was in the seventeenth year of Jehoshaphat that Ahaziah succeeded
his father Ahab on Israel's throne (1 Kings 22:51); the reason was that Ahab had
been slain in battle against Aram at Ramoth Gilead (1 Kings 22:34–37).
Jehoshaphat accompanied Ahab in that battle and found himself in mortal
danger (1 Kings 22:32–33). Since Jehoshaphat knew beforehand the risks he
would encounter in such an engagement, we can judge that prudence would
have caused him to place Jehoram on the throne as regent. That is no doubt the
reason for this coregency.

The translation that now appears in the King James Version of 2 Kings
8:16, "In the fifth year of Joram the son of Ahab king of Israel, Jehoshaphat
being then king of Judah, Jehoram the son of Jehoshaphat began to reign," is
not in full accord with the Hebrew and does not accurately present the facts. A
better rendering is "In the fifth year of Jehoram son of Ahab king of Israel,
Joram son of Jehoshaphat king of Judah became king" (NEB, cf. JB, NAB, GNB,
MOFFATT, AM. TRS., and others. The fifth year of Joram of Israel is not the year
when Jehoram of Judah became coregent, but is the year when Jehoshaphat
died and Jehoram became sole ruler.

Both the synchronism for Jehoram's accession in the fifth year of Joram and
the length of his reign, eight years, are given in accord with the date of 848 for
the death of Jehoshaphat and the beginning of Jehoram's sole reign. And, very
interestingly, both are given in terms of nonaccession-year reckoning, not in
accord with the accession-year system that had thus far been used in Judah.
This is a matter of vital importance in dealing with the regnal data of the period
immediately ahead, for it will be found that not only did Jehoram follow the
nonaccession-year system but also so did the three following Judean rulers,
namely, Ahaziah, Athaliah, and Joash. Unless one understands this point, one
will not be able to fit the regnal data for these rulers into a harmonious pattern.

The reason for this shift of reckoning in Judah to the nonaccession-year
system that was used in Israel has already been discussed in detail on page
58. Given the intermarriage of the ruling families between both kingdoms, it is
not strange that Judah, under the rulership of Jehoram and Athaliah, should

adopt Israel's nonaccession-year system of reckoning. A clear indication that this shift took place is found in the two synchronisms for the accession of Jehoram's son Ahaziah—in the twelfth year of Joram according to 2 Kings 8:25, in accord with the newly adopted nonaccession-year system, and in the eleventh year of Joram in 2 Kings 9:29, in accord with the former accession-year method. This clue that a change of reckoning had just taken place is lost in the Greek Lucianic text where the synchronism of 2 Kings 8:25 was altered to read the "eleventh" year of Joram so that it might be the same as 2 Kings 9:29.

Chart 9

847–835 B.C.

841—Ahaziah—11th year of Joram—2 Kings 9:29
—12th year of Joram—2 Kings 8:25
—1 year—2 Kings 8:26
841—Athaliah—regnal data not given
841—Jehu—28 years—2 Kings 10:36
835—Joash—7th of Jehu—40 years—2 Kings 12:1

	847	846	845	844	843	842	841	840	839	838	837	836	835
JUDAH													
Jehoram	1	2	3	4	5	6	7	8					
Ahaziah								1					
Athaliah								1	2	3	4	5	6
Joash													1
ISRAEL													
Joram	6 (5)	7 (6)	8 (7)	9 (8)	10 (9)	11 (10)	12 (11)						
Jehu							1	2	3	4	5	6	7

Tishri years for Judah; Nisan years for Israel.
Nonaccession-year reckoning used in both Israel and Judah.
The years of Joram in parentheses are according to accession-year reckoning.

16. Ahaziah—Judah—841

2 Kings 8:25–29; 2 Chronicles 22:1–9
Synchronisms: 11th year of Joram (2 Kings 9:29); accession-year system
              12th year of Joram (2 Kings 8:25); nonaccession-year system
Length of reign: 1 year, nonaccession-year system = part of a year

The two synchronisms for the accession of Ahaziah reflect the change in chronological reckoning that had recently taken place in Judah. This was from the former accession-year system to the nonaccession-year method used in Israel.

The fact that at this period we have kings with the same names—Jehoram and Ahaziah in Judah and Ahaziah and Jehoram (Joram) in Israel—speaks of the friendly relations between the two nations. Both royal houses were extending the courtesy of naming heirs to the throne after each other.

CHAPTER SIX

The Chronology of Judah and Israel (841–723 B.C.)

HE PERIOD BEFORE US is one of the most interesting in Hebrew history from a chronological standpoint. The problems here with the biblical data have long defied all efforts of scholars to find the solution. The answers can now be given.

There were many contacts during this period between the Hebrews and their neighbors, and these are often mentioned in contemporary documents. With Assyria the contacts were frequent and violent. Reliable dates can often be given.

This period began in 841 B.C. when Jehu brought an end to the Omride dynasty and when he also paid tribute to Shalmaneser III. Athaliah, daughter of Ahab and Jezebel, took the throne of Judah in 841 when Ahaziah fell at the hands of Jehu.

This period ends in 723 when Samaria fell and the northern kingdom of Israel came to its end after existing since 930. From then on no more synchronisms are possible between the rulers of Israel and Judah.

This chapter commences with the reign of Jehu, who left the marks of his violence on both Israel and Judah.

17. Jehu—Israel—841–814

2 Kings 9:1–10:36
Synchronism: not given
Length of reign: 28 official years, nonaccession-year reckoning = 27 actual years
841—paid tribute to Shalmaneser III of Assyria

Although no synchronism is given for the accession of Jehu, we can determine when he began by his contacts with the rulers of both Israel and Judah. Having received his commission to destroy the whole house of Ahab (2 Kings 9:5–10), Jehu on the same occasion in 841 killed Joram of Israel and Ahaziah of Judah (vv. 24, 27).

The date of 841 is established by Jehu's payment of tribute to Shalmaneser

III of Assyria in that year and, together with 853, becomes one of the basic dates in Hebrew history. Although the Bible makes no mention of Jehu's payment of tribute to Assyria, Shalmaneser III mentions that in the eighteenth year of his reign he went against "Hazael of Aram," shut him up in "Damascus, his royal city," and "received the tribute of the men of Tyre, Sidon and of Jehu, son of Omri."[1]

The meaning of "son of Omri" here as elsewhere in the Assyrian records is the nation of Israel. So important a personage was Omri in early contemporary history that his name was given by Assyria to the nation over which he ruled and for which he and his house had done so much. It is interesting to note that this Assyrian record applied to the nation of Jehu the name of the king whose dynasty he had destroyed.

The eighteenth year of Shalmaneser was twelve years after his sixth year, 853, the date of the battle of Qarqar in which Ahab was a participant. Since precisely twelve years elapsed from the death of Ahab to the accession of Jehu, we know 841 was the year when Jehu began to reign.

This fact of twelve years between the sixth and the eighteenth years of Shalmaneser provides Assyrian confirmation for the use of nonaccession-year reckoning at this time in Israel, where the two official years of Ahaziah plus the twelve official years of Joram equal twelve actual years.

18. Athaliah—Judah—841–835

2 Kings 11:1–20; 2 Chronicles 22:10–23:21
Synchronism: not given
Length of reign: not given

The Bible does not give the data concerning the year of Athaliah's accession or the length of her reign; however, these details can be learned from contextual items. We discover the date of the commencement of her reign from the fact that she took the throne immediately after Jehu had slain Ahaziah and Joram in 841. The close of her reign can be fixed from the fact that she was succeeded by Joash when he was seven years old in the seventh year of Jehu (2 Kings 11:21; 12:1). That was at some time between Nisan and Tishri of 835. Joash was a babe in arms when Athaliah tried to exterminate the royal family and took the throne. He was hidden for six years and then brought forth in the seventh year of Jehu at the age of seven (2 Kings 11:2–4, 21; 12:1). That gave Athaliah a reign of seven years, nonaccession-year reckoning, or six actual years.

19. Joash—Judah—835–796

2 Kings 11:21–12:21; 2 Chronicles 24:1–27
Synchronism: 7th year of Jehu, nonaccession-year reckoning = 6th actual year
Length of reign: 40 official years, nonaccession-year reckoning = 39 actual years

---

[1]Daniel David Luckenbill, *Ancient Records of Assyria and Babylonia*, vol. 1 (Chicago: University of Chicago Press, 1926), sec. 672.

20. Jehoahaz—Israel—814–798

2 Kings 13:1–9
Synchronism: 23d year of Joash, nonaccession-year reckoning
Length of reign: 17 official years, nonaccession-year reckoning = 16 actual
years

Diagram 13 below sets forth in simplified form the regnal details for
Athaliah and Joash in Judah, and for Jehu, Jehoahaz, and Jehoash in Israel.

Diagram 13
841–782 B.C.

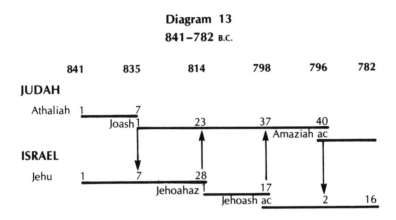

In Judah, Athaliah and Joash followed nonaccession-year reckoning. In
Israel nonaccession-year reckoning also was followed by Jehu and Jehoahaz.
With Amaziah as king of Judah, that nation shifted back to its original
accession-year system and continued to use it to the end of its history as a
kingdom in 586. With Jehoash in Israel, that nation adopted accession-year
reckoning and continued its use to its end in 723. Thus from these two rulers on
to the end both nations used the same method of reckoning—the accession-
year system.

Chart 10
835–823 B.C.

	835	834	833	832	831	830	829	828	827	826	825	824	823
JUDAH Joash		2	3	4	5	6	7	8	9	10	11	12	13
ISRAEL Jehu	7	8	9	10	11	12	13	14	15	16	17	18	19

Tishri years for Judah; Nisan years for Israel
Nonaccession-year dating for both Israel and Judah

Chart 11
823–811 B.C.

814—Jehoahaz—23d of Joash—17 years—2 Kings 13:1

	823	822	821	820	819	818	817	816	815	814	813	812	811
JUDAH Joash		14	15	16	17	18	19	20	21	22	23	24	25
ISRAEL Jehu	19	20	21	22	23	24	25	26	27	28			
Jehoahaz										1	2	3	4

Tishri years for Judah; Nisan years for Israel
Nonaccession-year dating for both Israel and Judah

Chart 12
811–799 B.C.

	811	810	809	808	807	806	805	804	803	802	801	800	799
JUDAH Joash	25	26	27	28	29	30	31	32	33	34	35	36	37
ISRAEL Jehoahaz		4	5	6	7	8	9	10	11	12	13	14	15	16

Tishri years for Judah; Nisan years for Israel
Nonaccession-year dating for both Israel and Judah

Diagram 14 on the following page shows the reigns in Israel and Judah from 798 to 732 and reveals the solution to some of the most perplexing problems concerning the regnal data of the kings. The main features for Israel are a coregency of Jeroboam II with Jehoash and a rival reign of Pekah that was concurrent with the reigns of Menahem and Pekahiah. Concerning Judah the diagram shows an overlap of Azariah with Amaziah and the well-known coregency of Jotham with Azariah. Dual dating was followed for Jeroboam II and Pekah in Israel and for Azariah in Judah. When once this is understood, the solution becomes clear and one of the most vexatious chronological problems in Kings can be handled with comparative ease. Only by these principles can the true historical pattern of this time be reconstructed and the seemingly insupportable regnal date in Kings be found to be correct. Therefore the arrangements of diagram 14 deserve careful study.

Both Israel and Judah used accession-year reckoning for the lengths of their reigns and synchronisms. A true coregency starts with an official first year, not an accession year. Dual dating was used in Israel for Jeroboam II in his coregency with Jehoash, for Pekah in his rival reign that was simultaneous with the reigns of Menahem and Pekahiah, and for Azariah in Judah in his overlap with Amaziah. Because of the failure to understand dual-dating procedure for these three reigns, the regnal data of this period have provided one of the most thorny problems for biblical chronologists. The difficulties go back to the centuries before the commencement of the Christian era. It has long been thought

Diagram 14
798–732 B.C.

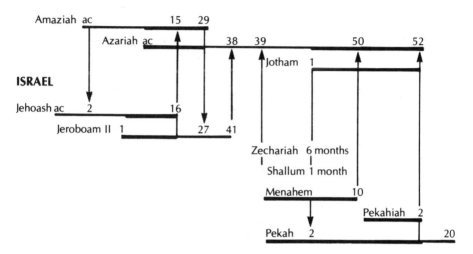

| 798 | 796 | 793 | 792 | 782 | 767 | 753 | 752 | 750 | 742 | 740 | 732 |

JUDAH

Amaziah ac   15   29

      Azariah ac   38   39   50   52

                        Jotham   1

ISRAEL

Jehoash ac   2   16

      Jeroboam II   1   27   41

                  Zechariah   6 months
                  Shallum   1 month
                  Menahem   10
                              Pekahiah   2
                  Pekah   2   20

that these data are impossible to harmonize. Many bitter remarks have been made concerning the supposed errors in these data and the carelessness of the scribes responsible, but entirely without justification. When the basic chronological methods used are understood and when the historical arrangements involved are perceived, the difficulties are brought to a solution. I will first present the problem and then the solution.

The problem is twofold. First, the biblical numbers appear to be in violent disarray, and in gross conflict with each other. Second, the pattern of reigns that the data seem to call for is far out of line with contemporary Assyria. In this period there are a number of contacts with Assyria where Hebrew and Assyrian years should coincide, but where they appear not to do so.

The Hebrew rulers involved and their lengths of reign are as follows:

JUDAH		ISRAEL		
Athaliah	7 years	Jehu	28 years	
Joash	40 years	Jehoahaz	17 years	
Amaziah	29 years	Jehoash	16 years	
Azariah	52 years	Jeroboam II	41 years	
		Zechariah		6 months
		Shallum		1 month
		Menahem	10 years	
		Pekahiah	2 years	
Total	128 years		114 years	7 months

The total years in Judah from the beginning of Athaliah to the fifty-second year of Azariah should be the same as the total years in Israel from the beginning of Jehu to the end of Pekahiah, for Athaliah and Jehu began at the same time, and the fifty-second and last year of Azariah was the year when Pekahiah was slain and succeeded by Pekah (2 Kings 15:27). But according to the above tabulation the totals are some 13 years apart, with 128 years for Judah against 114 years and 7 months for Israel.

But the difficulty is further aggravated when compared with contemporary Assyria. According to Assyrian history 841 was the year when Jehu paid tribute to Shalmaneser III. And it was from 743 to 738 that Tiglath-Pileser III conducted his great campaign in the Mediterranean area and mentioned contacts with Azariah, Menahem, and Pekah. From this scholars have long recognized that only about a hundred years were involved in this period. For Judah there appeared to be an excess of over a quarter of a century, while in Israel there was an excess of something like a dozen years. What does one do with this excess? The answer has long eluded biblical scholars and the opinion came to prevail that this was another evidence of grave errors in biblical chronology.[2]

The answer is found as far as Israel is concerned in a coregency of twelve years between Jeroboam II and Jehoash; in Judah there is found an overlapping of twenty-four years of the reign of Azariah with the years of his father, Amaziah. All these reigns are closely related, and once their nature is understood the seeming discordance vanishes and a historical pattern for Israel emerges that is in full harmony with that of Assyria.

The major difficulty in the past in solving this problem has been a failure to understand the involvement of dual-dating procedure in the regnal data of Jeroboam II and Azariah. When once it is seen that the regnal data of these two rulers are given in accord with dual-dating procedure, the seeming discrepancies vanish and a chronological pattern is established for the Hebrew monarchies that is in accord with the biblical numbers and the years of contemporary Assyria. I will here set forth the details of this pattern.

---

[2] A century ago the German scholar Schrader declared: " The chronological system of the Books of Kings, as compared with that of the monuments, is shown to be untenable. . . . Not a few discrepancies yawn within it, and unfortunately we cease to feel confidence in the scriptural computation just at the point where a comparison with another chronological system is rendered possible. . . . It is therefore in the most recent period of chronology that our verdict must be pronounced against the scriptural system, though we should have expected the most trustworthy and unassailable statements with respect to that period. The system must, however, be abandoned in presence of the corresponding statements of the monuments and the eponym canon" (Eberhard Schrader, *Cuneiform Inscriptions and the Old Testament,* trans. Owen C. Whitehouse (London: William and Norgate, 1888) 2:165.

Prof. Albright wrote: "It is incredible that all these numbers can have been handed down through so many editors and copyists without often becoming corrupt. . . . If we examine the chronological material for the century following Jehu's rebellion (which is fixed to within a year or two by Assyrian data), we note that the century between 842 and 742 B.C. is occupied in Kings by four Judahite reigns, totalling 128 years, from which 3–4 years must be deduced [sic] in accordance with antedating practice. The excess of some 24 years can be eliminated entirely by disregarding the total reigns attributed to the kings of Judah and basing our revised estimates of their reigns solely on the synchronisms with Israel (which throughout contradict the regnal totals of the kings of Judah)" (W. F. Albright, "The Chronology of the Divided Monarchy of Israel," *Bulletin of the American Schools of Oriental Research* 100 [1945]: 17, 19).

Jehoash in Israel and Amaziah in Judah began their reigns at a time of friendly relationships with each other. Jehoash (Joash) of Israel had the same name as Amaziah's father, Joash (Jehoash), in Judah. Amaziah on a visit to Jehoash had evidently proposed that a formal treaty be sealed by a marriage alliance involving his son and the daughter of Jehoash. This is indicated in the taunt expressed by Jehoash after their relationships had soured, namely, "A thistle in Lebanon sent a message to a cedar in Lebanon, 'Give your daughter to my son in marriage'" (2 Kings 14:9).

Amaziah was in a campaign against Edom and had hired a large contingent of Israelite troops to accompany him (2 Chron. 25:6–13). But in response to counsel from "a man of God" (v. 7), Amaziah dismissed the Israelite troops who were with him on his way to Edom. Taking this as an insult, the Israelites vented their rage by attacks on various towns of Judah as they proceeded on their way home. When Amaziah returned from his triumphal campaign in Edom, he sent a challenge of war to Jehoash. This Jehoash declined with a warning that Amaziah and Judah would be defeated. When Amaziah insisted on war, Jehoash invaded Judah. He took Amaziah prisoner, broke into Jerusalem, took hostages, and pillaged the palace and temple (2 Chron. 25:17–24).

The bizarre events of this episode explain the coregency of Jeroboam II with Jehoash and the overlap of Azariah with Amaziah. Before starting out against the exultant Amaziah, who was fresh from his triumph in Edom, Jehoash with thought for the future placed his son Jeroboam on the throne as regent. In Judah, with Amaziah having been taken to Israel as a prisoner of war, the people placed the young Azariah on the vacant throne. The fact that Azariah

Chart 13
799–788 B.C.

798—Jehoash—37th of Joash—16 years—2 Kings 13:10
796—Amaziah—2d of Jehoash—29 years—2 Kings 14:1–2
793—Jeroboam II—start of coregency
792—Azariah placed on throne by people

	799	798	797	796	795	794	793	792	791	790	789	788
JUDAH												
Joash		(38) 37	(39) 38	(40) 39								
Azariah									ac	1	2	3
Amaziah				ac	1	2	3	4	5	6	7	8
ISRAEL												
Jehoash		ac	1	2	3	4	5	6	7	8	9	10
Jehoahaz		(16)	(17)									
Jeroboam II							1	2	3	4	5	6

Tishri years for Judah; Nisan years for Israel
Accession-year dating for both Israel and Judah
Nonaccession-year dating in parentheses for Joash in Judah and Jehoahaz in Israel
Dual dating for Jeroboam II in Israel and Azariah in Judah

Chart 14
788–777 B.C.

782—Jeroboam II—15th of Amaziah—sole reign
—41 years—total reign—2 Kings 14:23

	788	787	786	785	784	783	782	781	780	779	778	777
JUDAH												
Azariah	4	5	6	7	8	9	10	11	12	13	14	
Amaziah	9	10	11	12	13	14	15	16	17	18	19	
Years of Amaziah after death of Jehoash							1	2	3	4	5	
ISRAEL												
Jehoash	10	11	12	13	14	15	16					
Jeroboam II	6	7	8	9	10	11	12	13	14	15	16	17
Jeroboam II's sole reign							(ac)	(1)	(2)	(3)	(4)	(5)

Tishri years for Judah; Nisan years for Israel
Accession-year dating for both Israel and Judah
Dual dating for regnal data of Jeroboam II and Azariah
Years of sole reign of Jeroboam II in parentheses

was raised to the throne at the age of sixteen is recorded as a postscript to the account of Amaziah. Chronologically this item does not belong at 2 Kings 14:21. Instead, it belongs after the events of verses 12–14, for it was twenty-four years before the death of Amaziah—only five years after Amaziah had begun to reign—that the people made Azariah king. In all probability Amaziah was given his freedom at the death of Jehoash to return to Judah to live out his remaining fifteen years (2 Kings 14:17; 2 Chron. 25:25), but not to sit on the throne as king.

The coregency of Jeroboam with Jehoash and the overlapping of Azariah with Amaziah are set forth in diagram 15 below.

Diagram 15
798–740 B.C.

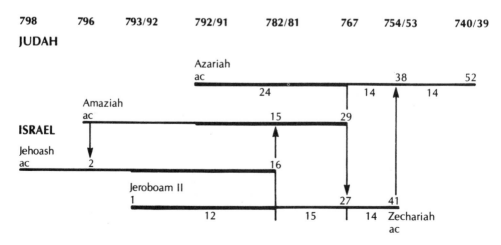

For a more precise setting forth of all the details in this period the yearly charts 13 to 18 (pages 109, 110, 116, 117, 119) should be consulted.

Jehoash began in 798. In his second year, 796, Amaziah began in Judah. The sixteen years of Jehoash terminated in 782/81.

This is the fifteenth year of Amaziah, the synchronism for the accession of Jeroboam II. The twenty-nine years of Amaziah terminate in 767, the twenty-seventh year of Jeroboam II, which is the synchronism of Azariah's accession. The death of Amaziah took place fifteen years after the death of Jehoash. So if 767 is the twenty-seventh year of Jeroboam II, and if Jehoash died only fifteen years before, Jeroboam II had ruled twelve years before his father's death.

Jeroboam II ruled forty-one years, to 754/53, and that is fourteen years after his twenty-seventh year, which is the synchronism for Azariah's accession. Jeroboam II was succeeded by Zechariah in the thirty-eighth year of Azariah (2 Kings 15:8). If in 754/53 Azariah had already been on the throne thirty-eight years, and if Amaziah had died only fourteen years before, then Azariah ruled twenty-four years before the death of Amaziah. That gives 792/91 for the commencement of Azariah's reign. And with a reign of fifty-two years, the termination of Azariah took place in 740/39.

It will be seen that the years given for both Jeroboam II and Azariah are the total years that they ruled, including twelve years of coregency for Jeroboam II with Jehoash, and twenty-four years of Azariah that overlapped the twenty-nine years of Amaziah. The synchronism given for Azariah's accession, however, is the year when Amaziah died, the twenty-seventh year of Jeroboam. And the synchronism for the accession of Jeroboam, the fifteenth year of Amaziah, is the year when Jehoash died and when Jeroboam began his sole reign. All this is in full accord with dual-dating procedure. And this serves to solve the vexatious chronological problems involved with the biblical regnal data of these rulers.

The year when Jeroboam began his forty-one years is reckoned as the first official year of his coregency, not his accession year, in accord with the practice followed in Kings for the regnal data of regents. However, since Azariah was not a regent, his reign began with an accession year.

The historical details of this interesting period of Hebrew history are not understood if the regnal data are not correctly interpreted. The numbers in the Books of Kings open up vistas of historical truth that would not otherwise be perceived. They are important for the study of historical as well as chronological facts. The alert investigator will study them carefully in order to secure the full and true picture of ancient Israel that otherwise would be missed.

21. Jehoash—Israel—798–782

2 Kings 13:10–25
Synchronism: 37th of Joash, accession-year reckoning
Length of reign: 16 official years, accession-year reckoning = 16 actual years
796—paid tribute to Adad-nirari III of Assyria

Beginning with Jehoash, regnal years in Israel were reckoned in accord with the accession-year system; and this was continued to the end of the nation.

At the same time in Judah, beginning with Amaziah, the southern kingdom returned to the accession-year system and continued its use to the end. Jehoash and Amaziah almost certainly collaborated with each other in their shift to accession-year reckoning.

The reason for this shift appears to have been due to the great influence of Assyria in western Asia at this time. In Assyria and Babylonia the accession-year system was in use. Under the Assyrian monarch Adad-nirari III (811–783), great efforts were being made to secure the mastery of the Mediterranean coastlands.

In 1967 a stele was found at Tell al Rimah that has twelve lines dealing with a campaign of Adad-nirari III in the Mediterranean area. Of particular interest to students of the Old Testament is the mention of the receipt of tribute from "Ja'asu of Samaria," or Jehoash. Also mentioned is the receipt of tribute from Mari', apparently Bir-Hadad III of Damascus, and from the rulers of Tyre and Sidon. The stele was published by Stephanie Page and has been widely discussed.[3]

The year when Jehoash paid tribute to Adad-nirari III is not specifically mentioned on the new stele, but the eponym canon provides the following possible dates: 804, "against Arpadda"; 803, "against Ba'ali"; 802, "against the seacoast"; and 796, "against Manṣuate." These frequent campaigns to the Mediterranean coastal area reveal the determination of Adad-nirari to bring the powers there under Assyrian control. Since Jehoash began his reign in 798, and since he paid tribute to Adad-nirari in 796—only two years after he took the throne—he must have been anxious to come to early terms with Assyria. The reason is not difficult to find. Damascus, a leader in the resistance against Assyria, was the archenemy of Israel.

We are told that under Jehoahaz, father of and predecessor of Jehoash, "Hazael king of Aram oppressed Israel throughout the reign of Jehoahaz," but that Jehoash "recaptured from Ben-Hadad the son of Hazael the towns he had taken in battle from his father Jehoahaz. Three times Jehoash defeated him, and so he recovered the Israelite towns" (2 Kings 13:22, 25). The heavy hand of Assyria on Damascus no doubt had so weakened its power that Jehoash was able to gain the upper hand over Israel's former oppressor. Jehoash was happy to voluntarily send a gift to Adad-nirari to be aligned with him against Aramean aggression.

We have the following delineation of the situation by Millar and Tadmor:

> It was probably either in Manṣuate or in Damascus that Israel,
> Edom and Philistia, formerly vassals or dependencies of Aram,
> sent tribute to Adad-nirari (imperial terminology for a free-will

[3]Stephanie Page, "A Stela of Adad-nirari III and Nergal-ereš from Tell āl Rimah," *Iraq* 30 (1968): 139–53; and plates XXXVIII–XLI; Aelred Cody, "A New Inscription from Tell āl-Rimah and King Jehoash of Israel," *The Catholic Biblical Quarterly* 32 (1970): 325–40; A. R. Millard and H. Tadmor, "Adad-nirari III in Syria," *Iraq* 35 (1973): 57–64; A. R. Millard, "Adad-nirari III, Aram, and Arpad," *Palestine Exploration Quarterly* 105 (1973): 161–64; Hayim Tadmor, "The Historical Inscriptions of Adad-nirari III," *Iraq* 35 (1973): 141–50; A. Jepsen, "Ein Neuer Fixpunkt für die Chronologie der Israelitischen Könige?", *Vetus Testamentum* 20 (1970): 359–61; William H. Shea, "Adad-nirari III and Jehoash of Israel," *Journal of Cuneiform Studies* 30 (1978): 101–13; E. Lipinski, "The Assyrian Campaign to Manṣuate in 796 B.C., and the Zakir Stele," *Annali dell' Instituto Orientale di Napoli* 30 (1970): 393–99; and others.

gift) now recognizing his overlordship. Among these the Rimah stele singles out tribute of Joash of Samaria. That king, who had ascended the throne a few years before, was especially grateful to Assyria for defeating Israel's oppressor and former suzerain. The embassy of Joash emphasized the renewed dependency of Jehu's dynasty upon the kings of Assyria in his bitter struggle with Aram. On the other hand, Assyria must have preferred a stronger but distant Israel, which would supplant the Aramaean hegemony in central and southern Syria, outside of Assyria's immediate political and economic interests.[4]

By putting together all the facts that can be learned about this period from such additional sources as the Saba'a stele, the Calah slab, and others, it may be possible to formulate a more detailed picture of the circumstances under which the energetic Hebrew king Jehoash (798–782) paid tribute to the conquering Assyrian monarch Adad-nirari III (811–783). But that is not vital to our present purpose. In the Old Testament there is no mention of Jehoash paying tribute to Adad-nirari III or of Adad-nirari's intervention against Damascus. And the details concerning Manṣuate are not definitely known—whether it was a city or the name of a region, or exactly where it was located. It is thought that it was in an area about fifty miles west of Damascus. But all these details are beyond our main chronological purpose. The reigns of Jehoash and Adad-nirari overlapped each other. Adad-nirari claimed that Jehoash paid tribute to him. The evidence presently available points to this as having been at Manṣuate in 796. Beyond that we need not go.

I have previously called attention to the friendly relations of Jehoash with Amaziah of Judah when Amaziah hired a large contingent of Israelite troops to accompany him on a campaign against Edom. But the situation changed drastically when on nearing Edom the Israelite soldiers were dismissed. The Israelites took this as a slight and vented their displeasure by pillaging the cities of Judah as they proceeded on their way home. When Jehoash reluctantly accepted the challenge of Amaziah to battle, he placed his son Jeroboam on the throne as regent. In the ensuing struggle Jehoash took Amaziah captive to Israel in 792. The people of Judah then placed the young Azariah on the vacant throne.

22. Amaziah—Judah—796–767

2 Kings 14:1–22; 2 Chronicles 25:1–28
Synchronism: 2nd of Jehoash
Length of reign: 29 official years, accession-year reckoning = 29 actual years
Lived 15 years after the death of Jehoash

A correct understanding of the regnal data of Amaziah and his son Azariah is of vital importance to the correct reconstruction of the pattern of Hebrew history for this period. When an overlap of twenty-four years of Azariah with Amaziah and a twelve-year coregency of Jeroboam II with Jehoash are recog-

---

[4]A. R. Millar and H. Tadmor, "Adad-nirari III in Syria," *Iraq* 35 (1973): 64.

nized, and when the principle underlying these data is understood, it becomes possible to recreate the original historical pattern for the reigns of these Hebrew rulers as based on the seemingly irreconcilable regnal data.

The problems of interpreting the biblical data here caused Sanders to declare, "The exact chronology of this century is beyond any historian's power to determine. . . . What to do with the extra twenty-five years is uncertain."[5]

To Albright it appeared that the original pattern of reigns could only be reconstructed by discarding the biblical numbers and supplying figures of his own. His comments on this difficulty have already been noted on page 108, n. It was Albright's proposal to reduce the reign of Athaliah by one year, from seven to six years; of Joash by two years, from forty to thirty-eight; of Amaziah by eleven years, from twenty-nine to eighteen; and of Azariah by ten years, from fifty-two to forty-two, or a total of twenty-four years.[6]

The revised estimates of Albright, however, present a chronological pattern that differs widely from that constructed in accordance with the biblical data and cannot be viewed as the original chronological and historical pattern of the Hebrew rulers of that time. The recognition of dual dating for the regnal data of Jeroboam II and of Azariah (Uzziah) would have relieved Albright of his perplexities and given him the true pattern.

Oppert and Jacobs also looked on the chronological data of this period as being totally unreliable. It was their view that purposeful altering had been resorted to in an endeavor to cover up certain unpleasant details in Hebrew history. Wrestling with the problem, and highly aggravated, they declared:

> The twenty-seventh year of Jeroboam II King of Israel (II Kings xv. 1), is mentioned as the first year of Uzziah, in flagrant contradiciton to all the statements of the previous chapter, which makes it correspond with the fifteenth or sixteenth year.
>
> Intentional mutilation of the text and suppression of all notice of the temporary suspension of the independence of the kingdom of Israel by the Syrians are the real cause of the larger number (15 or 16) given in ch. xiv: the end of the chapter, and Isa. vii.3, which can not be understood otherwise, indicate clearly that for eleven years Jeroboam II had been expelled from Samaria by the Syrians. The subsequent passages have been ruthlessly altered, in order to obviate the slightest mention of this cessation of Israel's realm. A similar mutilation has been practiced at the end of ch. xv.[7]

Much maligned though these biblical data have been, they are actually amazingly accurate and constitute an extremely valuable source for bringing to light many interesting and important details of Hebrew history.

Beginning a reign of twenty-nine years in 796, the second year of Jehoash in Israel, Amaziah's reign terminates in 767. It will be seen that that date fits in

[5]Frank Knight Sanders, *History of the Hebrews* (New York, 1914), p. 141.
[6]William F. Albright, "The Chronology of the Divided Monarchy of Israel," *Bulletin of the American Schools of Oriental Research* 100 (1945): 21.
[7]*Jewish Encyclopedia* (1903), s.v. "Chronology."

perfectly with the accession of Azariah in the twenty-seventh year of Jeroboam in accord with dual-dating procedure for the data of Jeroboam in Israel and Azariah in Judah.

In the record of Amaziah's reign as given in Kings, there are a number of unusual items that deserve attention. One is the closing formula for the reign of Jehoash at 2 Kings 14:15–16. This is given within the account of Amaziah's reign, although an earlier closing formula for that reign had already been given at 2 Kings 13:12–13. This came at the end of the account of Jehoash where it belonged. Many theories have been advanced for this strange anomaly. The *Seder Olam*, Kimchi, and others concluded that it probably pointed to a co-regency between Jehoash and Jeroboam, whose record follows that of Amaziah, at the time of the interesting events of 2 Kings 14:8–14. They were right. That is the situation revealed by the regnal data.

Another unusual item is the statement at 2 Kings 14:17 that Amaziah lived fifteen years after the death of Jehoash. Why such a statement? It is the only one of its kind in the Book of Kings and must point to some unusual relationship between Amaziah and Jehoash. In all likelihood it points to the fact that Amaziah at the death of Jehoash was released from imprisonment in Israel and outlived his captor by fifteen years. Amaziah returned to Judah but did not reoccupy his throne. In setting forth the length of the reign of Amaziah, however, the record gives the full number of years from the time that he first became king at the death of his father to his own death in a conspiracy fifteen years after Jehoash had taken him captive.

Another unusual item in the account of Amaziah's reign is the statement at 2 Kings 14:21 that "all the people of Judah took Azariah, who was sixteen years old, and made him king in place of his father Amaziah." Why is that statement here? It comes after the report of the death and burial of Amaziah in verses 19 and 20. A crown prince normally comes to the throne at the death of his father and is not placed there by the people. This statement that Azariah was put on the throne by all the people instead of his father clearly points to the fact that Amaziah was still alive when Azariah (Uzziah) was raised to the throne. Some special situation must have called for Azariah's elevation. The chronological evidence points to the fact that Azariah became king only five years after Amaziah had commenced his reign and that this was twenty-four years before Amaziah's death. The place in the biblical record where this took place is in connection with 2 Kings 14:13–14, not after verse 20.

Yet another unusual item in the record of Amaziah is the statement at 2 Kings 14:22 that Azariah "rebuilt Elath and restored it to Judah after Amaziah rested with his fathers." In Kings it is customary to report the name of the successor to the throne at the close of the account of his predecessor, but it is not the custom to report there what the successor did. That comes in his own account. The details of Azariah's rebuilding of Elath must have been found by the final editors of Kings in a record dealing both with Amaziah and Azariah, and we thus have here another indication of the overlapping of these two reigns.

These unusual items are found in the account of Amaziah in 2 Kings 14:1–22 and precede the account of Jeroboam II in verses 23–29. They are all in line with the chronological evidence of the overlap in Judah between Amaziah and Azariah and the coregency in Israel of Jeroboam with Jehoash.

23. Jeroboam II—Israel—793-782—regent
—793-753—total reign

2 Kings 14:23-29
Synchronism: 15th of Amaziah—commencement of sole reign
Length of reign: 41 official years, or 40 actual years

The regnal data for Jeroboam II are in accord with dual-dating procedure. Thus the datum for the length of his reign is the total number of years that he was on the throne, including both his coregency and sole reign. The synchronism of his accession, however, marks the year when his coregency was over and his sole reign began.

The forty-one official years of Jeroboam began in 793/92 when he became coregent with Jehoash. Since the start of the coregency was reckoned as an official first year rather than an accession year, the forty-one official years of Jeroboam are equal to forty actual years—from 793 to 753. Jeroboam was appointed regent when his father, Jehoash, accepted the challenge of Amaziah, invaded Judah, and took Amaziah prisoner.

The reign of Jehoash terminated in 782/81, the fifteenth year of Amaziah. This was the year with which the beginning of Jeroboam's reign was synchronized; in that year Jeroboam began his sole reign.

In Judah the commencement of Azariah's reign was synchronized with the twenty-seventh of Jeroboam. In that year Amaziah died and Azariah began his sole reign, and this was fifteen years after the death of Jehoash (2 Kings 14:17). Since Jeroboam had then reigned twenty-seven years and his father had died fifteen years before, Jeroboam had been on the throne twelve years before the death of Jehoash took place. From the twenty-seventh year of Jeroboam to his death in his forty-first year is fourteen years, and it is then that Jeroboam was

Chart 15
777-766 B.C.

767—Azariah—27th of Jeroboam II—52 years—2 Kings 15:1-2

	777	776	775	774	773	772	771	770	769	768	767	766
JUDAH												
Amaziah after Jehoash	6	7	8	9	10	11	12	13	14	15		
Amaziah	20	21	22	23	24	25	26	27	28	29		
Azariah	15	16	17	18	19	20	21	22	23	24/ac	25	
ISRAEL												
Jeroboam II												
From regency	(17)	(18)	(19)	(20)	(21)	(22)	(23)	(24)	(25)	(26)	(27)	(28)
Sole reign	5	6	7	8	9	10	11	12	13	14	15	16

Tishri years for Judah; Nisan years for Israel.
Accession-year dating for both Judah and Israel.
The years of Jeroboam II from regency are given in parentheses.

succeeded by Zechariah in the thirty-eighth year of Azariah (2 Kings 15:8). That being only fourteen years after the death of Amaziah, Azariah had ruled twenty-four years when Amaziah died.

Chart 16
766–755 B.C.

	766	765	764	763	762	761	760	759	758	757	756	755
JUDAH												
Azariah (Uzziah)	25	26	27	28	29	30	31	32	33	34	35	36
ISRAEL												
Jeroboam II												
From regency	(28)	(29)	(30)	(31)	(32)	(33)	(34)	(35)	(36)	(37)	(38)	(39)
Sole reign	16	17	18	19	20	21	22	23	24	25	26	27

Tishri years for Judah; Nisan years for Israel.
Accession-year dating for both Judah and Israel.
The years of Jeroboam II from regency are given in parentheses.

Chart 17
755–744 B.C.

753—Zechariah—38th year of Azariah (Uzziah)—6 months—
2 Kings 15:8
752—Shallum—39th year of Azariah—1 month—2 Kings 15:13
752—Menahem—39th of Azariah—10 years—2 Kings 15:17
752—Pekah—52nd of Azariah—20 years—2 Kings 15:27
750—Jotham—2d of Pekah—16 years—2 Kings 15:32–33

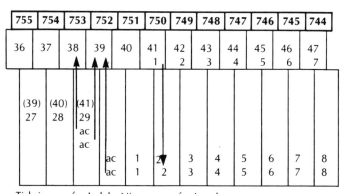

	755	754	753	752	751	750	749	748	747	746	745	744
JUDAH												
Azariah (Uzziah)	36	37	38	39	40	41	42	43	44	45	46	47
Jotham						1	2	3	4	5	6	7
ISRAEL												
Jeroboam II												
From regency	(39)	(40)	(41)									
Sole reign	27	28	29									
Zechariah			ac									
Shallum			ac									
Menahem				ac	1	2	3	4	5	6	7	8
Pekah				ac	1	2	3	4	5	6	7	8

Tishri years for Judah; Nisan years for Israel.
Accession-year reckoning for both Judah and Israel.
The years of Jeroboam II from regency are given in parentheses.
Dual dating was employed for Pekah, with 752 marking the commencement of his overlap with Menahem. Pekah's synchronism denotes the beginning of his sole reign.

The regnal details of these rulers of Israel and Judah for this period are closely intertwined, and unless their meaning is understood they will be regarded as badly confused and erroneous. When understood, however, the basic harmony of these numbers becomes clear and they are seen as correct. With the reign of Azariah there will be a further discussion of these data.

Diagram 16 below sets forth the reigns in Judah and Israel during the period 841–740, beginning with the accession of Athaliah in Judah at the time when Jehu seized the throne in Israel. The period ends in Judah with the termination of Azariah's fifty-two years and in Israel with the end of Pekahiah in the fifty-second year of Azariah.

Diagram 16
841–740 B.C.

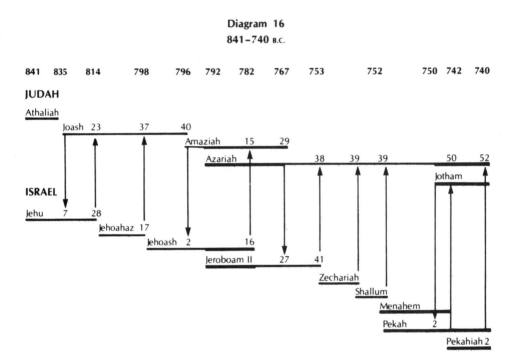

The early rulers of this period, Athaliah and Joash in Judah, and Jehu and Jehoahaz in Israel, used nonaccession-year reckoning; thus the actual totals of their reigns are one year less than their official totals. For the other rulers accession-year reckoning was used in both Israel and Judah. Jeroboam II commenced his coregency with an official first year, not an accession year. Dual dating was used for Azariah in Judah and for Jeroboam II and Pekah in Israel.

24. Azariah (Uzziah)—Judah—792–767—overlap with Amaziah
—792–740—total reign

2 Kings 15:1–7; 2 Chronicles 26:1–23
Synchronism: 27th of Jeroboam, the year of Amaziah's death
Length of reign: 52 years

Chart 18

744–733 B.C.

742—Pekahiah—50th of Azariah—2 years—2 Kings 15:23
740—Pekah—52d of Azariah (Uzziah)—beginning of sole reign—
      2 Kings 15:27
735—Ahaz—17th of Pekah—16 years—2 Kings 16:1–2

	744	743	742	741	740	739	738	737	736	735	734	733
JUDAH												
Azariah (Uzziah)	47	48	49	50	51	52						
Jotham	7	8	9	10	11	12	13	14	15	16	(17)	(18)
Ahaz										ac	(1)	(2)
ISRAEL												
Menahem		8	9	10								
Pekahiah				ac	1	2						
Pekah		8	9	10	11	12	13	14	15	16	17	18	19

Tishri years for Judah; Nisan years for Israel
Accession-year reckoning for both Judah and Israel
Dual dating for Pekah

From a chronological standpoint the long reign of Azariah is of major importance. It provides anchors that fix the dates for a number of difficult reigns in both Judah and Israel.

It is vital to know that the regnal data of Azariah are in accord with dual dating. His length of reign, fifty-two years, includes twenty-four years of overlap with Amaziah and twenty-eight years after Amaziah's death. The synchronism of his accession, the twenty-seventh of Jeroboam, is the year of Amaziah's death in 767. That was fifteen years beyond 782, which marked the death of Jehoash, father of Jeroboam II (2 Kings 14:17; 2 Chron. 25:25).

Amaziah was taken prisoner by Jehoash in 792, and the chronological data show that this year began Azariah's fifty-two-year reign. The details concerning this data have been given in connection with the reigns of Jehoash in Israel and Amaziah in Judah and are set forth in diagram 14 (page 107) and diagram 16 (page 118). With the throne of Judah vacant when Amaziah was taken to Israel as a prisoner, the people made the sixteen-year-old Azariah king. This item is recorded at 2 Kings 14:21 and 2 Chronicles 26:1–3 as a postscript to the account of Amaziah's reign, but it should more properly have been placed immediately after the account of the war of Jehoash with Amaziah at 2 Kings 14:8–14 and 2 Chronicles 25:21–24.

The note of Azariah's restoration of Elath to Judah at 2 Kings 14:22 as a postscript to the account of his father points to a close relationship between the reigns of Azariah and Amaziah, and indicates the overlap here set forth.

The regnal data give positive evidence that this overlap took place. Dual dating for Jeroboam II in Israel and Azariah in Judah is the key. The first twenty-four years of Azariah overlapped the last twenty-four years of Amaziah in a period extending from 792/91 to 767. At the death of Amaziah in 767 the accession of Azariah is synchronized with the twenty-seventh year of Jeroboam

II, who began his forty-one years in 793/92 in a coregency with Jehoash. Jeroboam II's accession (that is, of his sole reign) is synchronized with the fifteenth year of Amaziah at the death of Jehoash in 782/81. The end of Jeroboam II came in 754/53 when he was succeeded by Zechariah in the thirty-eighth year of Azariah (2 Kings 15:8). The end of Azariah's fifty-two years came in 740/39. All these data fit perfectly together when dual-dating procedure is understood, and they provide the correct historical pattern of Hebrew history of that time.

In 752, the thirty-ninth year of Azariah, Menahem began his reign of ten years (2 Kings 15:17). In 742, the fiftieth year of Azariah, Pekahiah succeeded Menahem and began a two-year rule (2 Kings 15:23).

Also in 752 Pekah began a rival reign with Menahem. It is vital that it be understood that his data are given in terms of dual dating. A failure to understand this in ancient times led to serious difficulties with the numbers in Kings of this period. Pekah's twenty years began in 752 and ended in 732, but his accession is synchronized with the fifty-second year of Azariah (2 Kings 15:27). That was in 740 when he took the throne from Pekahiah. The end of Pekah came in 732, the twentieth year of Jotham, when Pekah was slain and succeeded by Hoshea (2 Kings 15:30).

Hoshea ruled nine years (2 Kings 17:1), to 723, when the kingdom of Israel came to its end at the fall of Samaria.

In 750, the second year of Pekah, Jotham began his reign of sixteen official years (fifteen actual years) in a coregency with Azariah (2 Kings 15:32–33). In 735, the end of the sixteen official years of Jotham, Ahaz took the throne of Judah in the seventeenth year of Pekah (2 Kings 16:1). Although not on the throne, Jotham continued to 732, his twentieth year (2 Kings 15:30). Then Ahaz began sixteen years of rule that terminated in 716/15 when Hezekiah came to the throne. That brings us to the fourteenth year of Hezekiah in 701, a date firmly established in Assyrian chronology by the attack of Sennacherib on Hezekiah that year.

All these items will be discussed more fully with the individual reigns. The comprehensive arrangements from 752 to 701 are set forth in diagram 17.

As previously noted the correct dating for Azariah is a matter of vital importance because of the number of Hebrew rulers whose dates are tied in with him.

At this period the Hebrew rulers had many contacts with Assyria. We can expect that correct Hebrew dates will be the same as corresponding Assyrian dates.

Azariah figured prominently in the records of Tiglath-Pileser III, being looked on as a leader among the rulers of the Mediterranean area. Also mentioned by Tiglath-Pileser III are Menahem, Pekah, Hoshea, and Ahaz. Specific years of contact are not given, but some can be determined within narrow limits.

Since the pattern here given terminates the reign of Menahem in 742, it allows no contacts between Tiglath-Pileser III and Menahem after that year. And since Tiglath-Pileser III did not begin till 745, there could have been no contacts before that. That gives 745 to 742 for contacts between Tiglath-Pileser III and Menahem.

Diagram 17
752–701 B.C.

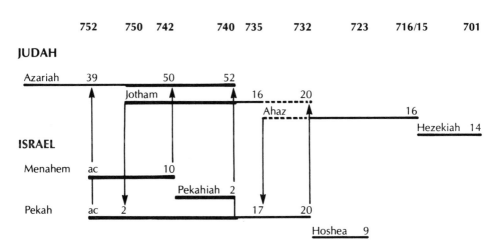

Regnal years in diagram 17 are actual years since the data for both Israel and Judah are in accord with the accession-year system. The data for Pekah are in accord with dual-dating procedure.

But the limits can be reduced still further, for Tiglath-Pileser III in 745 campaigned in Babylonia; and in 744 he was in the area of the Medes. But from 743 to 738 he conducted a great campaign in the Mediterranean area, and it is in the records of that campaign that Menahem and Azariah are mentioned. So according to the pattern of Hebrew years here given, the contact between Tiglath-Pileser III and Menahem has two possibilities: it was either in 743, the year when the western campaign began, or in 742, when Menahem ended his reign.

Any Assyrian records with a bearing on these Hebrew years should be looked at with interest and care. If specific years of Azariah and Menahem could be tied to specific years of Tiglath-Pileser III, it would greatly facilitate our study. But that is not the case. Precise contacts are rare. And even in some cases of seeming precision, there is not always clarity or certainty as to exactly what is involved. Things are not always what they seem.

The dates 792 to 740 here assigned to Azariah are part of a single unit based on an unbroken chain of intertwined Judahite and Israelite years starting at the accessions of Rehoboam and Jeroboam in 930 and extending to 723 for the end of Hoshea in Israel and to 701 as the fourteenth year of Hezekiah in Judah.

Anchor points are as follows: 853, the battle of Qarqar in the sixth year of Shalmaneser III when Ahab fought against Assyria in, according to my pattern, the last year of his reign; 841, the eighteenth year of Shalmaneser III, when he claimed the receipt of tribute from Jehu in, according to my pattern, the year when Jehu began to reign; 723, the last year of Hoshea when Samaria fell to

Assyria; and 701, the fourteenth year of Hezekiah when Sennacherib came against him and the fortified cities of Judah.

One of these dates can give all the others. On my early charts there were no dates. There was simply a pattern of years of Hebrew kings that were arranged in their mutual relationships with each other in accord with the regnal data of Kings as set forth here in the year-by-year charts in this volume. I did not know how far it was from one point to another. I did not know how many years it was on my charts from the beginning of the reigns of Rehoboam and Jeroboam to the end of Hoshea in Israel and the fourteenth year of Hezekiah when the attack of Sennacherib took place. I knew that this must have been several hundred years, but my charts did not tell me exactly how many, for my charts had no dates or numbers giving the overall passage of years. While my pattern was in preparation, I did not want to know. Only when my arrangement was completed would I insert dates that would give me information concerning the overall passage of time. My completed charts thus would give me the test I desired concerning the accuracy of my dates.

If the dates I arrived at for the reigns of the kings were indeed the correct original years of reign, then those years for Judah and Israel would fit in perfectly with the years of contemporary Assyria and Babylon, or any other ancient nation. And then the regnal data in Kings would have proved themselves to be reliable and true. Such a test I planned that my pattern would be, and such a test it has been, with much of interest and delight.

I began the insertion of dates to my chart with 854 as the year for the battle of Qarqar and the death of Ahab, and 842 as the eighteenth year of Shalmaneser III when Jehu paid tribute to him in the year that he killed Joram of Israel and Ahaziah of Judah and took his seat on Israel's throne. Those were the dates that up to that time I had accepted as correct in Assyrian history. From there I went on year by year and reign by reign until I came to 702 as the fourteenth year of Hezekiah and the attack of Sennacherib in his third campaign. That date, however, I knew was one year wrong, for the attack took place in 701, not 702, and that date could not be changed. But neither could the years on my charts be changed. So the conviction came over me that the true date for Qarqar was 853, not 854, and that the correct date for the eighteenth year of Shalmaneser must be 841, not 842. When I approached Prof. George Cameron of the Oriental Institute of the University of Chicago on that point, I learned that German scholars were then using 853 as the date for Qarqar, as against 854 as the date used in America. Careful study showed that 853 was right and that 854 was wrong. That brought a deep conviction that the dates on my charts were right, not only at 853 but also at other points along the line.

This became all the more true when I dealt with my date of 723 for the last year of Hoshea and the fall of Samaria. The almost universally accepted date was 722 as based on Sargon's claim. My chart called for 723 as the year when Samaria fell, but that was a year before Sargon had commenced his reign. That problem was easily and happily solved when I learned that the renowned Assyriologist Prof. A. T. Olmstead of the University of Chicago had, after a careful study of the evidence, shown that Samaria fell in 723, not 722, and that Sargon was not telling the truth when he claimed to have taken Samaria.

Shortly thereafter Prof. Hayim Tadmor of the Hebrew University of Jerusalem presented additional evidence that Samaria fell in 723, not 722.

It can hardly be only a matter of chance that my pattern of Hebrew years calls for 853 as the correct date of Qarqar, a year later than the formerly accepted date of 854, and that for the fall of Samaria it calls for 723, a year earlier than the formerly accepted date. What we have here is historical truth—truth for the Hebrews and truth also for Assyrian years.

In 1944, shortly after I came to the above results concerning the years of reign of the Hebrew kings, my findings were published as an article[8] and a few years later in book form.[9]

The dates I am now presenting are part of my original pattern. All are closely bound together by biblical regnal data of synchronisms and lengths of reign that permit no change. The years I have here given for Jeroboam II, Zechariah, Shallum, Menahem, Pekahiah, Pekah, and Hoshea in Israel, and for Jotham, Ahaz, and Hezekiah in Judah, are all tied in with my dates of 792 to 740 for the fifty-two years of Azariah. They are one unit. If 723 is the correct date for the fall of Samaria in the ninth year of Hoshea, and if 701 is the correct date for Sennacherib's attack on Jerusalem in the fourteenth year of Hezekiah, then 740 is the correct year for the end of Azariah after his fifty-two years on the throne.

Much is involved here for ancient Hebrew history. But also involved are details concerning ancient Assyria and other nearby states. The following chapter, "The Contacts of Tiglath-Pileser III with Azariah and Menahem," will deal particularly with the question of when some of the contacts of Azariah and Menahem with Tiglath-Pileser took place.

25. Zechariah—Israel—753

2 Kings 15:8–12
Synchronism: 38th year of Azariah
Length of reign: 6 months

The synchronism of Zechariah's accession in the thirty-eighth year of Azariah is of major importance, for this synchronism reveals that only fourteen years after the death of Amaziah, the latter's son Azariah had already been on the throne of Judah thirty-eight years.

When in 753 Zechariah came to the throne, his father Jeroboam had ruled forty-one years. It is with the twenty-seventh year of that reign, 767—only fourteen years before 753—that the accession of Azariah is synchronized (2 Kings 15:1). Dual dating for the regnal data of Azariah explains how his accession can be given for a year that is only fourteen years before he had been on the throne thirty-eight years.

The first twenty-four years of Azariah overlapped the last twenty-four of Amaziah's twenty-nine years. Only when Amaziah died and Azariah began his sole reign was his accession synchronized with the twenty-seventh year of

---

[8]Edwin R. Thiele, "The Chronology of the Kings of Judah and Israel," *The Journal of Near Eastern Studies* 3 (1944): 137–86.

[9]Edwin R. Thiele, *The Mysterious Numbers of the Hebrew Kings* (Chicago: University of Chicago Press, 1951).

Jeroboam. But the fifty-two years of Azariah included both his twenty-four years of overlap with Amaziah and his twenty-eight years after Amaziah's death.

An understanding of these points clears up one of the major problems with the mysterious numbers of the Hebrew kings. Dual dating supplies the key.

26. Shallum—Israel—752

2 Kings 15:13–15
Synchronism: 39th year of Azariah (Uzziah)
Length of reign: 1 month

The record calls Shallum the "son of Jabesh." This may mean that he was from Jabesh in Gilead rather than that his father's name was Jabesh. In that case it points to Gileadite aspirations for royal power in Israel at that time. This would help to explain the support that Pekah received from "'fifty men of Gilead" in his overthrow of Pekahiah, son and successor of Menahem who had assassinated Shallum and taken his throne (2 Kings 15:14, 25).

27. Menahem—Israel—752–742

2 Kings 15:16–22
Synchronism: 39th year of Azariah
Length of reign: 10 years, accession-year reckoning = 10 actual years
Paid tribute to Pul (Tiglath-Pileser III) of Assyria (745–727)

Diagram 17 (page 121) for the years 752 to 701 gives the arrangement of Hebrew reigns for this period. Its vital point is 740 for the fifty-second and last year of Azariah of Judah. All the other dates in both Judah and Israel are tied in with that year. That includes the death of Pekahiah and the accession of Pekah in 740, Azariah's fifty-second year (2 Kings 15:27). Pekahiah ruled two years and Menahem ruled ten years before him (2 Kings 15:17, 23), a period overlapped by twelve years of Pekah.

As chapter 8 will show, 723 was the year of Samaria's fall and the end of the nine years of Hoshea. That makes 732 the year when Hoshea began his reign in the twentieth year of Jotham when he assassinated Pekah (2 Kings 15:30). Since Pekah had reigned twenty years (2 Kings 15:27), he began in 752, the same year when Menahem began. That makes two Hebrew nations in the north and one in the south at that time, as it must be in accord with Hosea 5:5.

In this pattern Pekah's first twelve years—from 752 to 740—of his twenty years overlap the ten years of Menahem and the two years of Pekahiah, and the last eight years of Pekah constitute a sole reign from 740 to 732. The synchronism of his accession, however, marks the commencement of his sole reign in 740, the fifty-second year of Azariah (2 Kings 15:27). This is dual dating for Pekah, and it is vital that this be clearly understood; otherwise serious problems in harmonizing the data will arise. That such difficulties did arise when the Masoretic Text came into being will be shown in our discussion of the synchronisms in 2 Kings 17 and 18.

The date of 701 as the fourteenth year of Hezekiah and of the attack of Sennacherib called for in my pattern provides clinching evidence of its correctness. It was by working forward from 853 in accord with the regnal data of Kings that I arrived at 701 as the fourteenth year of Hezekiah. If I had worked backward from 701, I would have secured 853 for the end of Ahab. Both 853 and 701 are correct. The fact that I arrived at these dates shows that all other dates in this arrangement also are correct. The value of the numbers in Kings for the reconstruction of many details of ancient Hebrew history has not yet been fully appreciated.

The years of Assyrian rulers whose reigns overlapped the years of Hebrew rulers from 752–701 (cf. diagram 17, page 121) are as follows:

Ashur-nirari V	755–745
Tiglath-Pileser III	745–727
Shalmaneser V	727–722
Sargon II	722–705
Sennacherib	705–681

A number of these rulers mention contacts with Hebrew kings. Tiglath-Pileser III mentions Azariah and Ahaz of Judah, and Menahem, Pekah, and Hoshea of Israel. Specific years of contact are seldom mentioned, but a careful study of all the available material throws some light on the years involved.

Azariah is mentioned a number of times in connection with Tiglath-Pileser's protracted campaign in the Mediterranean regions from 743 to 738. This is in line with my terminal date of 740 for Azariah.

According to the Assyrian eponym canon there was a campaign against Damascus in 732, and that campaign falls within the reign of Tiglath-Pileser. According to my pattern 732 is the end of a four-year overlap of Ahaz with Jotham, and the commencement of the sixteen-year reign of Ahaz that terminated in 716/15 at the accession of Hezekiah. That brings the fourteenth year of Hezekiah in 701.

Ahaz made a plea to Tiglath-Pileser to deliver him "out of the hand of the king of Aram and of the king of Israel" (2 Kings 16:7). Tiglath-Pileser responded by attacking Damascus and executing its king, Rezin (v. 9). That would be the attack of Tiglath-Pileser in 732.

Tiglath-Pileser in his annals makes the boast that when the people of the "Omri-land" had overthrown Pekah their king, he placed Hoshea over them and received their tribute."[10] That was in 732.

In 2 Kings 15:19 we are told, "Pul king of Assyria invaded the land and Menahem gave him a thousand talents of silver to gain his support and strengthen his own hold on the kingdom." Positive proof that Pul is Tiglath-Pileser III is provided by two Babylonian documents. One of these mentions that Pulu reigned two years in Babylon after a reign of three years by Ukin-zer; the other states that Tiglath-Pileser ruled two years after Ukin-zer had reigned three years. Pul was the Babylonian name of Tiglath-Pileser.

According to his annals Tiglath-Pileser in 743 began a great campaign in the Mediterranean area and received tribute from a large number of its rulers.

---

[10]James B. Pritchard, *Ancient Near Eastern Texts Relating to the Old Testament*, 2nd ed. (Princeton, 1955), pp. 283–84.

Menahem was among these in all probability, willingly paying tribute to Assyria to secure its support in his effort to maintain his hold against the rival rule of Pekah.

The sculptures of Tiglath-Pileser on his palace walls include the name of Menahem in a list of western rulers who paid tribute to him. This list is on a slab where it immediately precedes a mention of the ninth year, 737. On the assumption that the annals constitute an unbroken year-by-year record of events, the conclusion was reached that the tribute list must be dated to 738.

It is extremely rare, however, that an Assyrian inscription provides an account of every year without a gap. The eponym canon deals with every year, and a very few other inscriptions give annual reports; but the usual rule is many omissions in the record. Seldom is there any indication as to just how large or small a gap may be, whether many years or only a few.

In my next chapter on "The Contacts of Tiglath-Pileser III with Azariah and Menahem," I will deal more fully with this subject as it concerns these particular rulers. Here it need only be pointed out that items in a record may often be dated just as accurately by that which precedes them as by what follows. Tiglath-Pileser's annals have come down to us in a very fragmentary state. Careful efforts have been put forth to effect accurate reconstructions, but no amount of effort can always replace what is missing. On the annals as we now have them the section preceding the Menahem list of tribute payers deals with the year 743. In the following chapter I will show that the available evidence points more definitely to 743 as the year when Menahem paid tribute than it does to 738. That fits in with my terminal date of 742 for Menahem.

For many years Prof. Hayim Tadmor, the very able Assyriologist of the Hebrew University of Jerusalem, has been making a particular study of the section of Tiglath-Pileser's annals that deals with Azariah. When completed this will be published, but it is not yet available. So for the time being we must content ourselves with currently available materials.

In addition to the inscriptions of Tiglath-Pileser that have long been available, a new inscription has in recent years come to light on which Menahem is mentioned. Hopefully, this will throw additional light on the time of Menahem's contacts with Assyria. Two brief items about this stele have been published by Louis D. Levine.[11]

The significant item in this inscription for us here is the inclusion of "Menahem of Samaria" in a list of tribute payers to Tiglath-Pileser. This list is almost identical to the one in the annals where Menahem is mentioned. In the annals Hiram is referred to as the king of Tyre, but the new stele has Tubail. The annals also mention Eni-ilu of Hamath, but this name is missing from the new stele.

The mention of Menahem occurs on the upper right side of the new stele. With the front of the stele as its column I, Levine evidently was not certain whether the right side or the left constituted column II. On page 13 of his *Occasional Paper 23* he says, "The text of the front continues on the right side of

---

[11]One was a monograph, *Two Neo-Assyrian Stelae from Iran*, Occasional Paper 23, Royal Ontario Museum, Toronto, 1972; and the other was an article, "Menahem and Tiglath-pileser: A New Synchronism," *Bulletin of the American Schools of Oriental Research* 206 (1972): 40–42.

the stele, where our column II is inscribed." But on page 14 he reverses himself, saying, "It is more than likely, however, that the back of the stele and the left side were columns II and III respectively, and that the preserved right side was originally column IV." If the right side is column IV, the sides of the stele go clockwise, from right to left. If the right side is column II, the sides go counterclockwise, and the reading at the lower front would continue on the upper right side where the name of Menahem is found.

What is at the lower front of the stele and what is on its left side and back may be of considerable importance as regards the light the new stele might give concerning the year when Menahem paid tribute to Tiglath-Pileser. Some information on this should be available when a part of the new stele already at hand is made public, for Levine states, "Further proof of the date will be forthcoming shortly with the publication of another part of the same stele that has just recently come to light. On this new piece the mention immediately preceding the tribute list of column II is devoted to the events of the ninth campaign of 737."[12]

It is regretable this information that in 1972 was to be "forthcoming shortly" has been so long in being made public for wider study. But in the meantime certain facts are definitely known from which clear deductions can be made. First is the fact already published by Levine concerning the front of the stele where after the usual opening formalities these words occur: "In my first regnal year." That was 745 and there were reported the events of that year. There the bottom of that piece is broken off, but one would expect the lower front to go on with the events of the following year, 744, and perhaps also 743. From there the narration would continue to the right side of the stele if that is column II, or to the left side if that is column II.

Another fact is that on a stone slab from Tiglath-Pileser's palace at Calah a parallel list of payers of tribute in which Menahem is included comes immediately before a report of Tiglath-Pileser's ninth year, 737. That, however, would not necessarily date Menahem either to 737 or to the preceding year, for I will point out in the following chapter that there are frequent gaps of years in Assyrian historical inscriptions. But what is altogether clear in the annals account is that the Menahem report of tribute precedes the report of the ninth year. The sequence on the new stele should be the same as in the annals, with Menahem coming before 737, not 737 preceding Menahem.

Inasmuch as the report of the ninth year, 737, comes on the left side of the new stele and the mention of Menahem comes on the right side, then in accord with the sequence in the annals the left side is column IV and the right side is column II. Only thus would the sequence of accounts on the new stele be in agreement with the sequence in the annals. In such a case the reading of the historical items on the new stele would be from left to right, counterclockwise, from the front as column I, to the right side as column II, and terminate with the left side as column IV.

This would be in accord with the regular procedure on Assyrian historical inscriptions, where the normal movement is from left to right, on stelae as well

---

[12]Louis D. Levine, "Menahem," p. 41.

as tablets. So it is on the Black Obelisk of Shalmaneser III, where a single line runs right around the whole stele, with the pictorial views below. On stelae inscribed in separate columns on their sides, such as the stele of Ashurnasirpal II from the Ninurta temple at Nimrud, the movement is likewise from left to right, with the front of the stele constituting column I, and the right side being column II. This same left to right movement is found on the hexagonal prism of Sennacherib now at the Oriental Institute of the University of Chicago, where column I is on the front face, column II is on the next face to the right, and so on to the end of the inscription.

This same left to right movement, counterclockwise, is to be looked for on the new Tiglath-Pileser III stele here under discussion. Toward the lower part of the front already published by Levine is the mention of year one, 745. From there the stele would continue with the events of years two and three, 744 and 743, and that is to be looked for when this new piece is published. From there the presentation should go on to the right side, column II, for events of years three and four, 743 and 742. And it is there that the mention of Menahem is made.

The indication is that when the parts of the stele already available to Levine at his previous writing are made available, they will point to 743 or 742 as the year of Menahem's payment of tribute to Tiglath-Pileser III, and not to 738 as has been proposed from the arrangements on the annals slab, or to 737 as Levine has proposed from his observations of the new stele.

The biblical regnal data give 743 or 742 as the time of Menahem's payment of tribute to Tiglath-Pileser. That testimony is not to be lightly discarded. The regnal data of Kings have proven to be amazingly accurate and worthy of confidence. The ancient Hebrew testimony deserves careful attention.

The arrangement here proposed, with the right side of the stele being column II and reporting the events of years three and four at the top, and with the left side constituting column IV and presenting the events of year nine toward the bottom, the remaining parts of the right side, the rear, and the upper left side would provide the proper space for the presentation of the events of the years between four and nine as they are known from other historical documents and for such other items as the usual maledictions, etc.

There are still numerous questions that remain to be answered about the stele and a number of problems still calling for solution, but from what is now known to me about the stele it is my studied conclusion that when all its available parts are carefully studied in the light of all the evidence available from other Assyrian documents, the testimony will point to the year 743 or 742 as the time when Menahem paid tribute to Tiglath-Pileser III.

Any part of the new stele not yet published should at the earliest possible moment be brought into the open for the most careful study. It will be of major importance to publish what is known of the left side of the stele with its events of the ninth year, 737, and of the years dealt with at the bottom of the front.

28. Pekahiah—Israel—742–740

2 Kings 15:23–26
Synchronism: 50th of Azariah
Length of reign: 2 years

Since Pekahiah began his two years in the fiftieth of Azariah, his years end with 740, Azariah's fifty-second and last year. The accession of Pekah is synchronized with that year. It would thus seem that it is there that the twenty years of Pekah would begin (2 Kings 15:27). And there Jotham should succeed Azariah. Hoshea would take the throne from Pekah in the twentieth year of Jotham (2 Kings 15:30). With Hoshea reigning nine years (2 Kings 17:1), this would work out as follows:

Pekah—740–720

Jotham—740–720

Hoshea—720–711

All these reigns, however, are twelve years beyond their correct positions. In the pages to follow I will discuss just what is involved.

29. Pekah—Israel—752–732

2 Kings 15:27–31

Synchronism: 52nd of Azariah

Length of reign: 20 years

The date 752 for the beginning of Pekah is in accord with dual-dating procedure for the regnal data of Pekah, including both his synchronism and the length of reign.

Pekah began his twenty years in 752 as a rival of Menahem, who also began that year.[13] The first twelve years of Pekah overlapped the ten years of Menahem and the two years of Pekahiah. In 740, the fifty-second and last year of Azariah, Pekah killed Pekahiah and took the throne in Samaria. There he began his sole reign, continuing for eight years—from 740 to 732. In 732, the twentieth year of Jotham, Hoshea assassinated Pekah and succeeded him (2 Kings 15:30). For the details of these arrangements from 752–701 see diagram 17 (page 121).

A number of items point to Gilead as the probable site of Pekah's rival rule against Menahem. When Menahem seized the throne in Samaria, it was by assassinating "Shallum son of Jabesh" (2 Kings 15:13–14). As noted in the discussion of Shallum's reign above, Jabesh may here be a geographical rather than a personal name. The meaning might be that Shallum was from the town of Jabesh.[14] If this refers to Jabesh in Gilead, Pekah would have had strong support there for his stand against Menahem in Samaria.

Exercising jurisdiction in Gilead, Pekah could well have had his eye on Samaria. With the plot in mind of taking over the entire country when the time was ripe, he could have come to terms with Pekahiah by accepting a prominent military post under him. It was with the aid of "fifty men of Gilead" that Pekah was successful in overthrowing Pekahiah and taking his throne in Samaria (2 Kings 15:25).

Pekah allied himself with Rezin of Aram in an attack on Ahaz of Judah and

---

[13]For a good discussion of twelve of the twenty years of Pekah overlapping Menahem and Pekahiah, see H. J. Cook, "Pekah," *Vetus Testamentum* 14 (1964): 121–35.

[14]Cf. "the son of Tabeel" (Isa. 7:6), meaning a person from Tabeel. See also "Shamgar son of Anath" (Judg. 3:31; 5:6), which some scholars believe means "Shamgar of Beth-anath."

planned to replace him with "the son of Tabeel" (2 Kings 16:5; Isa. 7:1–7). This effort struck Ahaz with terror and he appealed to Tiglath-Pileser for aid. "The king of Assyria complied by attacking Damascus and capturing it. He deported its inhabitants to Kir and put Rezin to death" (2 Kings 16:9). According to the Assyrian eponym canon the campaign of 732 was against Damascus.

This date is of interest in connection with the prediction given in Isaiah 8:4 concerning the birth of Isaiah's son Maher-Shalal-Hash-Baz. This prophecy indicates that 732 would be the year of fulfillment (for fuller explanation see page 133–34).

Tiglath-Pileser boasted that when the people of the "Omri-land" had overthrown Pekah, their king, he had placed Hoshea over them and received their tribute.[15]

As has previously been pointed out the overlap between Pekah and Menahem and Pekahiah in Samaria is testified to in the Book of Hosea where two Hebrew kingdoms in the north, Israel and Ephraim, are repeatedly mentioned, in addition to Judah in the south (cf. Hos. 5:5; 11:12 et al.).

A correct interpretation of the data for Pekah is necessary for an understanding of the years that immediately follow for Israel and Judah. If the years of Pekah are not analyzed properly, the regnal data and the years of Hoshea in Israel and of Ahaz and Hezekiah in Judah will not be understood. It is only when dual dating for Pekah is recognized that the entanglements in the regnal data of 2 Kings 17 and 18 can be unraveled.

If dual dating for Pekah is not understood, and if his twenty years are begun in 740, the fifty-second year of Azariah, and if Jotham there follows Azariah, the following pattern results:

Diagram 18

740–710—If Dual Dating for Pekah Is Not Recognized

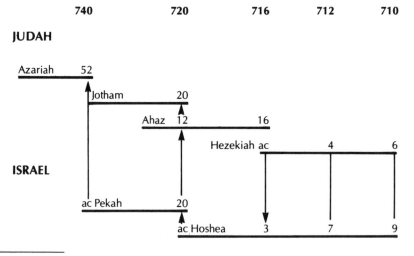

---

[15]Luckenbill, *Ancient Records*, sec. 816.

In this pattern the years of Israel are thrown twelve years in advance of their true position and in their relationship to the kings of Judah. The perplexing synchronisms that result are discussed below in connection with the reigns of Jotham, Ahaz, and Hoshea.

Chart 19
733–721 B.C.

732—Hoshea—20th of Jotham—2 Kings 15:30
     —9 years—2 Kings 17:1
732—Ahaz—16 years—2 Kings 16:2

	733	732	731	730	729	728	727	726	725	724	723	722	721
JUDAH													
Jotham		(19)	(20)										
Ahaz		(3)	▲(4)										
Ahaz			ac	1	2	3	4	5	6	7	8	9	10
ISRAEL													
Pekah		19	20										
Hoshea			ac	1	2	3	4	5	6	7	8	9	

Tishri years for Judah; Nisan years for Israel
Accession-year reckoning for both Judah and Israel
Overlapping years for Jotham and Ahaz in parentheses

Chart 20
721–709 B.C.

715—Hezekiah—29 years—2 Kings 18:2

	721	720	719	718	717	716	715	714	713	712	711	710	709
JUDAH													
Ahaz	11	12	13	14	15	16							
Hezekiah							ac	1	2	3	4	5	6

Regnal years begin with Tishri.
Accession-year reckoning.

30. **Jotham—Judah—750–732**—reign reckoned to his 20th year
       750–740—coregency with Azariah
       750—735—years in accord with the official datum of 16
                years for the length of his reign

2 Kings 15:32–38; 2 Chronicles 27:1–9
Synchronism: 2nd of Pekah
Length of reign: 16 official years = 15 actual years

As shown on diagram 17 (page 121) the accession of Jotham in the second year of Pekah is in accord with the reign of Pekah that commenced in 752 when he was a rival of Menahem. Unless this is understood, no correct dating for Jotham is possible.

While Pekah ruled in Gilead, Menahem was on the throne in Samaria, and Jotham's accession could have been synchronized with him. The reason why Pekah was recognized in the synchronism of Jotham's accession was probably because of his strong anti-Assyrian stand, as against the conciliatory attitude of Menahem. Judah at this time was strongly anti-Assyrian. In the annals of Tiglath-Pileser Azariah stands out as a leader among the anti-Assyrian forces of the west.

Jotham became regent when Azariah was smitten with leprosy (2 Kings 15:5). The year when he became regent was reckoned as his official first year, not as an accession year. This was in accord with the usual procedure in coregencies.

Thus the sixteen official years of Jotham are fifteen actual years, from Pekah's second to his seventeenth years, 750 to 735. Although Ahaz took the throne from Jotham in the seventeenth year of Pekah, he did not then slay him, for Jotham continued to live at least to his twentieth year (2 Kings 15:30). That was 732 and Ahaz then began his own sixteen years. He reigned to 716/15 when Hezekiah began. So the years when Jotham was sole ruler began with the death of Azariah in 740 and continued to 735. From 735 to 732 Ahaz was in control, but Jotham was permitted to live.

For three years during the period when Jotham was sole ruler, the Ammonites paid tribute to him (2 Chron. 27:5). Azariah (Uzziah) had brought the Ammonites under tribute (2 Chron. 26:8), but that probably was broken off at his death. When Jotham was in sole control, he sent his forces against the Ammonites and received tribute from them for three years. The fact that this continued for only three years would indicate that when Ahaz seized the power from Jotham in 735, Ammon again asserted its independence.

The combined attack on Jerusalem by Rezin of Aram and Pekah of Israel is mentioned in the account of Ahaz at 2 Kings 16:5–7 and also in a postscript to the account of Jotham at 2 Kings 15:37. That clearly points to an overlap between Jotham and Ahaz. If the attack had come when Jotham was in full control, it would have been reported only in the account of his reign. But the fact that it comes as a postscript to Jotham's account indicates that he was still alive when the attack was made; and the fact that it comes again in the record of Ahaz points to his being at the helm at that time.

In 2 Kings 15:37 we are told that "the LORD began to send Rezin king of Aram and Pekah son of Remaliah against Judah." Against which ruler of Judah was this attack directed, Jotham or Ahaz? Concerning Jotham the record is that "he did what was right in the eyes of the LORD" (2 Kings 15:34). But of Ahaz it is said that he "did not do what was right in the eyes of the LORD" but that "he walked in the ways of the kings of Israel" (2 Kings 16:2–3). It was because of their evil that the Lord sent judgments upon "Israel; he afflicted them and gave them into the hands of plunderers" (2 Kings 17:20). And it was because of the iniquities of Ahaz that "the LORD his God handed him over to the king of Aram" (2 Chron. 28:5).

It is our privilege to often turn to the regnal data of Kings for otherwise forgotten details of Hebrew history.

31. **Ahaz—Judah—735–715**—total years of rulership
    735–732—overlap with Jotham
    732–715—official reign, after the 20th of Jotham[16]

2 Kings 16:1–20; 2 Chronicles 28:1–27
Synchronism: 17th of Pekah, at the end of Jotham's 16 years
Length of reign: 16 actual years, after the 20th of Jotham

The overlap of Ahaz with Jotham from 735 to 732 has already been mentioned in connection with the reign of Jotham. It is practically certain that Ahaz was raised to the throne in 735 with the aid of a pro-Assyrian faction, that being the seventeenth year of Pekah. Assyria at this time was very active in the Mediterranean area but was facing stiff resistance in many places. Azariah is noted by Tiglath-Pileser as a leader in the resistance. Jotham no doubt was also an active agent in this resistance. Ahaz, however, proved himself to be a collaborationist and was put in power by those who favored conciliation.

In the face of a violent anti-Assyrian atmosphere in western Asia, Ahaz pursued a policy that would bring him into serious difficulties with his neighbors, who assailed him from all quarters. In the southeast Edom attacked Judah (2 Chron. 28:17). In the southwest the Philistines invaded Judah and seized much territory (v. 18). In the northeast Aram attacked Ahaz and took many captives to Damascus, and Pekah of Israel came in from the north (vv. 5–8).

In his terror Ahaz appealed to Tiglath-Pileser for help, saying, "I am your servant and vassal. Come up and save me" (2 Kings 16:7). Tiglath-Pileser responded with the capture of Damascus and the slaying of Rezin, the Aramean king (2 Kings 16:9). This probably was in 732 when the Assyrian campaign was against Damascus.

The name of Ahaz is included in a list of rulers in the Mediterranean area who paid tribute to Tiglath-Pileser.[17]

In the account of Ahaz we are told at 2 Kings 16:5–8 of an attack on him by Rezin of Aram and Pekah of Israel. The mention of this war also in the postscript to the account of Jotham at 2 Kings 15:37 suggests an overlap between Ahaz and Jotham.

Additional light concerning this situation is found in Isaiah 7–8. Ahaz was terrified because the purpose of Pekah and Rezin was to replace him on the throne of Judah by "the son of Tabeel" (Isa. 7:5–6). Albright has identified this name as being typical of the desert fringes of Palestine and Syria.[18] The Lord, however, told Ahaz through Isaiah that this effort would not succeed and that He would give him a sign concerning it. A child would be born who would not be old enough to discern evil from good (Isa. 7:16) or to "say 'My father' or 'My mother'" before the land of the two kings Ahaz feared would be devastated and the "wealth of Damascus and the plunder of Samaria" (8:4) would be taken away

---

[16]The difference in elapsed time between the years given here and the biblical record is due to the variance of calendar years and not an incorrect chronology. See the footnote on pages 87–88 for a fuller discussion of this issue.

[17]Pritchard, *Ancient Near Eastern Texts*, p. 282.

[18]W. F. Albright, "The Son of Tabeel (Isaiah 7:6)," *Bulletin of the American Schools of Oriental Research*, 140 (1955): 34–35.

by the king of Assyria. The child was to be called "Immanuel" (7:14). This was the second son of Isaiah, Maher-Shalal-Hash-Baz ("speed the spoil, hasten the prey"), who was to be a prototype of Christ (cf. Isa. 7:11–16; 8:3–4, 7–10, 18). The invasion would occur before the child had reached the age of two. It was between the years 735 to 732 that this took place.

32. Hoshea—Israel—732–723

2 Kings 17:1–41
Synchronisms: 20th of Jotham, 12th of Ahaz
Length of reign: 9 years

A correct understanding of the regnal data of Hoshea is vital to a correct understanding of the Hebrew history of this important time. Diagram 17 (page 121) gives the correct arrangements of reigns of the period 752–701 B.C.

This arrangement is based on the recognition of dual dating for Pekah. Unless this is understood, and unless it is seen that Pekah began his twenty years in 752, the arrangement in diagram 18 (page 130) is brought into being. That, however, throws Hoshea twelve years beyond his true position in history and twelve years out of line with the rulers of Judah.

When the editors of Kings were bringing that book into its final shape, they did not understand dual dating for Pekah; and this fact was responsible for the synchronisms of 2 Kings 17 and 18. In 2 Kings 17:1 the accession of Hoshea is placed in the twelfth year of Ahaz. That, however, is twelve years out of line with 2 Kings 15:30, where we are told that Hoshea assassinated Pekah and "then succeeded him as king in the twentieth year of Jotham." The synchronism of 2 Kings 17:1, which places the accession of Hoshea in the twelfth year of Ahaz, reveals this twelve-year misplacement of Hoshea.

Hoshea did not begin to rule in 720 but in 732, which was the twentieth year of Jotham and the commencement of the sixteen years of Ahaz. In the key year of 752 two kings began in Israel, Menahem in Samaria and Pekah in Gilead. The first twelve of Pekah's twenty years, from 752 to 740, overlapped the ten years of Menahem and the two years of Pekahiah. From 740 to 732 Pekah had a sole reign of eight years. That began in the fifty-second and last year of Azariah in accord with the synchronism of 2 Kings 15:27. All this is in accord with dual dating for Pekah and with the picture given in Hosea 5:5 (MT).

Only in accord with this arrangement does the accession of Hoshea come in the twentieth year of Jotham in accord with 2 Kings 15:30. And only thus is the true historical situation of that period correctly portrayed.

The twentieth year of Jotham was 732, twelve years before 720. And the beginning of Pekah was 752, twelve years before the fifty-second year of Azariah, 740. Thus also the commencement of Hoshea was 732, twelve years before 720, and his end came in 723. There was no overlap with Hezekiah, who began in 716.

As shown in diagram 18 (page 130) the failure to understand these points brought into being the following synchronisms based on a reign of Hoshea that began twelve years too late:

2 Kings 17:1 —Hoshea accession = 12th year of Ahaz   —720
2 Kings 18:1 —Hoshea 3rd year = accession of Hezekiah —716
2 Kings 18:9 —Hoshea 7th year = 4th year of Hezekiah —712
2 Kings 18:10—Hoshea 9th year = 6th year of Hezekiah —710

A careful survey of the account of Hezekiah's reign shows that when he began his reign Hoshea and the nation of Israel were gone. This will be discussed in connection with the details of Hezekiah's reign and in chapter 8 on "The Siege and Fall of Samaria."

What it was that brought into being the above synchronisms of 2 Kings 17 and 18 may be learned by noticing the order of sequence in which the accounts of the rulers occur in the Book of Kings. As mentioned before the editors followed the rule of placing the accounts in the order in which the rulers began their reigns. If one king began before another, his account preceded the other. If he began after another, his account followed. The sequence of accounts in Kings from Menahem to Hezekiah is as follows:

1. Menahem	—2 Kings 15:16–22
2. Pekahiah	—2 Kings 15:23–26
3. Pekah	—2 Kings 15:27–31
4. Jotham	—2 Kings 15:32–38
5. Ahaz	—2 Kings 16:1–20
6. Hoshea	—2 Kings 17:1–41
7. Hezekiah	—2 Kings 18:1–20:21

The significance of this arrangement is that it reveals what the editor had in mind when he placed the reigns in this order. It is important to notice that Pekah (no. 3) was placed at 2 Kings 15:27–31, following Pekahiah (no. 2) in verses 23–26. This shows that the editor regarded Pekah as having begun his reign after Pekahiah.

The above sequence calls for the following arrangement of years for the beginnings of these reigns (see diagram 19 on the next page).

This is the sequence of reigns as the editors of Kings thought it ought to be when they made the present arrangement. Diagram 19 shows that Menahem ended his ten years in 742, the fiftieth year of Azariah. Pekahiah ended his two years in 740 when Azariah was in his fifty-second and last year. Pekah, in this arrangement, was regarded as having begun his twenty years in 740, the fifty-second year of Azariah, and as having ended them in 720. Jotham followed Azariah at his death in 740 and had his twentieth year in 720. Ahaz had 720 as his twelfth year. Hoshea began in 720 when he slew Pekah in the twentieth year of Jotham (2 Kings 15:30) and had his accession in the twelfth year of Ahaz (2 Kings 17:1). Hezekiah began in 716, the third year of Hoshea, according to this arrangement.

But in this pattern shown by diagram 19 something is seriously wrong, for Hoshea began in 732, twelve years before 720. In 720 Hoshea was dead, Samaria had fallen, and Israel had come to its end. Our task is to find the root of the difficulty.

Diagram 19

**Dates of Reigns According to Sequence
of Reigns in Kings (742–701 B.C.)**

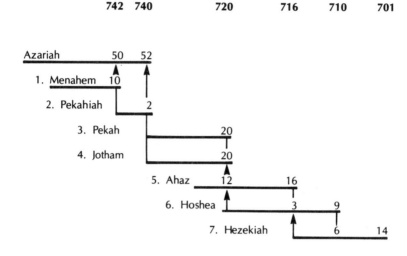

An important clue is found in the two synchronisms for the beginning of Hoshea—in the twentieth year of Jotham and in the twelfth of Ahaz. According to these synchronisms there was an overlap of twelve years between Jotham and Ahaz. Was this artificial or real? If there was no overlap, and if the reign of Jotham were thrust twelve years back, his twentieth year would be 732, not 720 (cf. diagram 17, page 121). In such a case the beginning of Hoshea and the end of Pekah would be in 732. For Hoshea that would be exactly right. And for Pekah it would also be right, for it would fix the commencement of his twenty years in 752, when Menahem also began, taking into account two kingdoms in the north in accord with Hosea 5:5 (MT).

With Pekah beginning in 752, his second year would be 750; and then Jotham began (2 Kings 15:32) as a coregent with Azariah (Uzziah). With 750 as the first year of that coregency, its sixteenth year would be 735 when Ahaz took the throne in the seventeenth year of Pekah in accord with 2 Kings 16:1. The synchronisms for the accessions of Jotham and Ahaz in the second and seventeenth years of Pekah cannot be fitted into a pattern that begins Pekah's reign in 740.

In the pattern that begins Pekah's reign in 740 he is twelve years beyond his true position, and so also are Jotham and Hoshea. When Hoshea is in his true position, his reign is over before that of Hezekiah begins. Also, Hoshea begins his nine years in 732 when the sixteen years of Ahaz begin. Thus it is only when the synchronisms of 2 Kings 17 and 18 are seen as late and artificial that the true picture of Hebrew history of this important time can be reconstructed. Only when it is seen that Pekah began in 752, not in 740, will a picture emerge of three Hebrew kingdoms at the time of Hoshea in accord with Hosea 5:5 (MT). And only thus will the years of Hoshea fall into line with the years of contemporary Assyria.

Failure to recognize dual dating for Pekah threw him and Hoshea twelve years beyond their true positions in history. This misunderstanding was responsible for the synchronisms in 2 Kings 17 and 18.

The original regnal data in Kings were matters of early contemporary recording, not of late calculation. The recorders were extremely careful and accurate. Through the ages they were followed by copyists who were meticulous, honest, and superbly capable as they preserved for us the numbers of the rulers as we now find them in Kings.

Some of these numbers had meanings so difficult to grasp that the numbers were thought to be in error. Efforts were made to correct them as is seen in the variant regnal data in the Septuagint Greek texts. Efforts at amplification are seen in the Hebrew synchronisms of 2 Kings 17 and 18. An examination of the synchronism of 2 Kings 17:1 that placed the accession of Hoshea twelve years beyond his time enabled me to see the solution of the most difficult problem with the regnal data in Kings. This solution was found in an adjustment in these twelve years.

My attitude toward the editor responsible for these synchronisms in 2 Kings 17 and 18, late though he may be, is not one of indignation or disparagement. It was specifically because of what he did that I was finally able to complete my task of weaving together the involved reigns of Israel and Judah into a harmonious whole that sets forth the ancient Hebrew years in their correct alignment with the years of neighboring states. My attitude toward him is not one of censure but of gratefulness and praise. He had a task to perform and he did it with insight, devotion, and courage. His synchronism at 2 Kings 17:1 gave me the key to the solution of the most knotty chronological problem in the Book of Kings.

Another problem concerning the reign of Hoshea is the year when Samaria fell. According to my pattern presented here, Samaria fell in 723 during the reign of Shalmaneser V (727–722). But Sargon II (722–705) claims that he took Samaria. Because of this the year of 722 came to be looked on as the date of Samaria's fall.

As mentioned earlier, a number of outstanding scholars have carefully studied the subject and concluded that Samaria fell in 723. Among these are the renowned Assyriologists Prof. A. T. Olmstead of the University of Chicago and Prof. Hayim Tadmor of the Hebrew University of Jerusalem.

Every Assyriologist knows that Assyrian inscriptions are not always reliable in all details. The account given in one place may vary from that found in another place. An achievement of one king may be claimed by his successor. The specific details of a victory reported in one year may grow in magnitude and splendor in the reports of succeeding years. The fact that Sargon claimed to have captured Samaria does not prove that he did so. This subject is of such major importance that I am devoting to it all of chapter 8, entitled "The Siege and Fall of Samaria."

The fact that my pattern for Hebrew years calls for 723 as the year when

Samaria fell is an important testimony to its accuracy, as will be seen when all the details are carefully considered.

With the end of Hoshea we come to the end of Israel. Thus far we have dealt with the dates of Hebrew rulers in various parts of the north as well as Jerusalem in the south. Henceforth we will deal only with kings in the south.

CHAPTER SEVEN

The Contacts of
Tiglath-Pileser III
With Azariah and Menahem

F THE CHRONOLOGICAL outline that has just been presented is indeed accurate, then we must expect exact synchronisms with the absolute chronology of Assyria at all points at which precise contacts between the two nations can be established. In securing such exact synchronisms, however, we would have to be as certain of the correct chronology of the one nation as of the other. As any date in Hebrew history that might synchronize with any absolute date in Assyrian history would have to be correct, so any date in Assyrian history that would synchronize with any absolute date in Hebrew history would likewise have to be correct.

Accepted dates, however, both in Hebrew and secular history, are not always absolute dates. It is true in every field of endeavor that what has long been accepted as truth is not always truth. In our present quest it must be kept in mind that it is entirely possible we will find dates in both Assyrian and Hebrew history that have long been accepted but fail under careful investigation. Dates that are absolutely accurate will stand the test of the most searching analysis. The more minute and careful the investigation, the more certain and the more voluminous will be the evidence that they are sound.

The well-known contacts of Tiglath-Pileser III with Azariah and Menahem may be of service in testing the accuracy of the biblical and Assyrian dates for this period.

One of the first questions to arise in this connection is the identity of Pul with Tiglath-Pileser III. According to 2 Kings 15:19–20, Menahem paid tribute to Pul, and in 1 Chronicles 5:26 the names of Pul and Tiglath-Pileser are given.

The text in 1 Chronicles 5:26, "And the God of Israel stirred up the spirit of Pul king of Assyria, and the spirit of Tilgath-pilneser king of Assyria, and he carried them away" (KJV) has often been cited as proof that the Bible supports the position that Pul and Tiglath-Pileser III were two individuals. It has been pointed out, however,[1] that inasmuch as the Hebrew verb "carried" is here in

---

[1]Joseph Horner, "Biblical Chronology," *Proceedings of the Society of Biblical Archaeology*, 20 (1898): 237.

the singular, as it is correctly translated with the singular pronoun "he," this verse definitely conveys the idea that Pul and Tiglath-Pileser were one and the same and that the correct translation of the *waw* introducing the epexegetical phrase concerning Tiglath-Pileser should be "even." Thus the verse would read, "And the God of Israel stirred up the spirit of Pul, king of Assyria, even the spirit of Tiglath-Pileser, king of Assyria, and he carried them away." Most recent English translations give this verse correctly, recognizing that Pul and Tiglath-Pileser were the same individual. Among these are NEB, NIV, NASB, MLB, and GNB. As the verse is translated in the KJV, it is ambiguous and grammatically incorrect, for the singular pronoun *he* cannot stand as the antecedent for the plural Pul and Tiglath-Pileser; but if the plural *they* were used, it would not agree with the singular Hebrew verb. Thus this verse, instead of conveying a wrong idea concerning Pul and Tiglath-Pileser, actually becomes a valuable early documentary authority for the identification of Pul with Tiglath-Pileser III.

BABYLONIAN KING LIST A, COL. IV	BABYLONIAN CHRONICLE, COL. I
Line	Line
5. Nabu-shum-ukin his son for 1 month and 12 days.	17. One month and 2 days Shum-ukin reigned in Babylon.
7. Ukin-zer . . . 3 years.	18. Ukin-zer . . . cast him from the throne and seized the throne.
	19. In the 3d year of Ukin-zer, Tiglath-Pileser
	20. When he made a descent against Akkad
	21. Devastated Bit-Amukan and captured Ukin-zer.
	22. Three years Ukin-zer ruled as king of Babylon.
8. Pulu for 2 [years].	23. Tiglath-Pileser seated himself on the throne in Babylon.
	24. The 2d year Tiglath-Pileser died in the month of Tebetu.

Owing to the extreme difficulties met with in the endeavor to synchronize the biblical and Assyrian chronology of this period, certain scholars for a time took the position that Pul and Tiglath-Pileser were two distinct individuals (cf. 1 Chron. 5:26 KJV). With Tiglath-Pileser coming to the throne in 745 and with 761 as the terminal year of Menahem according to the supposed biblical chronology, no contacts, of course, were possible between these two kings. It became necessary, if the dates set forth for Menahem's reign were to stand, to devise the existence of some Assyrian king ruling at the time of the supposed reign of Menahem with whom the latter might have been in contact. The biblical references to a king of Assyria by the name of Pul and the absence of any information concerning a king by such a name in Assyrian inscriptions thus provided opportunity for postulating the reign of a king whose very existence had completely dropped from Assyrian records.

In view of the fact, however, that Tiglath-Pileser in his annals claimed the receipt of tribute from Menahem,[2] it seemed clear that the reigns of these two kings were contemporaneous and that the supposed years of reign of either the one or the other were in error. And in view of the fact that the biblical record states that Menahem paid tribute to a king of Assyria by the name of Pul, there was strong probability that this Pul was the Tiglath-Pileser who claimed the receipt of tribute from Menahem. Many years ago Schrader presented convincing arguments that Pul and Tiglath-Pileser must be the same individual.[3] Indisputable proof of their identity is provided by notations from a Babylonian king list and the Babylonian Chronicle where, in a list of the Babylonian kings, Tiglath-Pileser appears by his usual Assyrian name on the one list and by his name Pulu on the other, as shown in the lists on page 140.[4]

It is quite clear, then, both from the impartial testimony of Babylonian documents already cited and from the evidence of 1 Chronicles 5:26, that Pul and Tiglath-Pileser are two names for the same individual. Pul evidently is the name assumed by Tiglath-Pileser when he took the throne of Babylon, just as Shalmaneser V was known in Babylon as Ululai. Further confirmation is given by Ptolemy's Canon, which for the seventeenth to the twenty-first years of the Nabonassar era (731–727) gives Chinziros and Poros as the Babylonian kings. The latter name is a Persian corruption of Pul, and Chinziros is clearly Ukin-zer.

With such positive proof that Pul and Tiglath-Pileser are names for the same king, it is clear that Menahem and Tiglath-Pileser were contemporaneous and that either the system of biblical chronology that gives the date 761 for the termination of Menahem's reign is wrong, or Assyrian chronology is wrong when it provides the date 745 for Tiglath-Pileser's accession. But Assyrian dates for the years of Tiglath-Pileser's reign are fully established, being verified by the astronomical evidence of the solar eclipse in the eponymy of Bur-Sagale in 763 and the eclipses establishing the years of Ptolemy's Canon. It will be noticed that the dates we have secured for the reign of Menahem as based on the chronological data of the Books of Kings and Chronicles, 752 to 742/41, provide for an overlap of Menahem's reign with that of Tiglath-Pileser III, whose years were 745–727.

Of particular importance to our inquiry is a record of Tiglath-Pileser in which he mentions a campaign to the Mediterranean seacoast and to the land of Hatti to put down an uprising instigated by "Azriau of Yaudi." During the

---

[2]Daniel David Luckenbill, *Ancient Records of Assyria and Babylonia*, vol. 1 (Chicago, 1926), sec. 772.

[3]Eberhard Schrader, *The Cuneiform Inscriptions and the Old Testament*, trans. Owen C. Whitehouse (London, 1885), 1:218ff.

[4]Eduard Meyer, *Geschichte des Altertums*, 5th ed. (Stuttgart, 1926), vol. 1, part 2, 36ff. The cuneiform text of Babylonian King List A was published by P. Rost in *Mitteilungen der vorderasiatischen Gesellschaft*, vol. 2, part 2 (1897), p. 242. A recent translation in English by A. Leo Oppenheim appeared in *Ancient Near Eastern Texts Relating to the Old Testament*, ed. James B. Pritchard (Princeton, 1950), p. 272. The cuneiform text of the Babylonian Chronicle was published by H. Winckler, *Zeitschrift für Assyriologie* 2 (1887): 163–68. An English translation appeared in Robert William Rogers, *Cuneiform Parallels to the Old Testament* (New York, 1926), pp. 208–19. The text here provided was copied from a translation from an unpublished text of the Assyrian Dictionary of the Oriental Institute of Chicago, CT, vol. 34. Pls. 46–47.

course of that campaign he claims to have received tribute from "Menihimmu of Samerina."[5] "Azriau" is Azariah of Judah and "Menihimmu" is certainly Menahem of Samaria or Israel. There are some who believe that the "Azriau" referred to by Tiglath-Pileser was not the Azariah of the Old Testament,[6] but a king of another nation in northern Aram. The present writer believes that the evidence is entirely convincing for the identification of the "Azriau" and the "Yaudi" of this Assyrian inscription with the biblical Azariah (Uzziah) and Judah.[7] It is extremely unlikely that at the very time Judah had such an outstanding king, possessing such marked abilities as a warrior and statesman (2 Chron. 26:6–15), another state of a similar name should possess a king with an almost identical name and with the same outstanding characteristics.

An interesting problem is introduced by the frequently accepted date of 738 for this expedition of Tiglath-Pileser and the terminal dates here presented of 742/41 for Menahem and 740/39 for Azariah. A careful study of all the available evidence should give some indication as to whether or not 738 is sound or whether the chronological pattern presented here is correct in demanding a somewhat earlier date than 738 for Tiglath-Pileser's measures against Azariah and Menahem. The historical records of Tiglath-Pileser[8] were mainly engraved on stone slabs that originally lined the walls of his palace at Calah (Nimrud), but that were later removed by Esarhaddon to be used in his palace in the same city. Here they were found by Layard in his excavations of what he termed "the Southwest Palace of Nimrod." Layard gives a vivid description of the mutilated and disordered condition in which these slabs were found,[9] some sawed in two with only a portion of the original slab remaining, many with the original carvings completely chiseled away to be replaced by new inscriptions, and yet others that had been exposed to fire with the stone nearly reduced to lime and that were too cracked and fragile to permit removal. A number of slabs were still piled on each other in the center of the room and ready to be put in place in the new palace under construction.

In addition to the stone slabs once lining Tiglath-Pileser's palace walls, a number of clay tablets containing important historical information are also available. Some of these, although fragmentary, contain material of great historical value.

With so many of the materials constituting Tiglath-Pileser's annals being in such a ruinous and disordered state, it will be recognized that the correct rearrangement of the remaining fragments to their original order constitutes an exceedingly difficult task. Thanks to the Assyrian custom of producing duplicate

---

[5]Luckenbill, *Ancient Records*, vol. 1, secs. 770, 772.

[6]A. T. Olmstead, *History of Assyria* (New York, 1923), p. 186.

[7]For a discussion of this side of the question see Schrader, *Cuneiform Inscriptions*, 1:208ff.; Howell M. Haydn, "Azariah of Judah and Tiglath-pileser III," *Journal of Biblical Literature* 28 (1909): 182–99; D. D. Luckenbill, "Azariah of Judah," *American Journal of Semitic Languages and Literatures*, 41 (1924–25), 217–32; and Hayim Tadmor, "Azriyau and Yaudi," *Studies in the Bible, Scripta Hierosolymitana* 8 (1961), 232–71. Cf. also H. R. Hall, *The Ancient History of the Near East*, 9th ed. rev. (London, 1936), p. 463.

[8]For a good discussion of these see Abraham S. Anspacher, *Tiglath Pileser III* (New York, 1912), pp. 1–9.

[9]Austen Henry Layard, *Nineveh and Its Remains* (New York, 1850), 2:26ff.

records at different times and in various forms, much more can be done in the way of restoration than at first might seem possible. The piecing together of pictures accompanying the inscriptions is of great assistance in securing the correct order of sequence. The Eponym Chronicle has been of invaluable service to scholars in their endeavor to fit properly together facts gleaned from other sources. But in spite of the splendid work that has already been done, it is admitted by careful historians that future study may indicate the necessity of making some modifications in results already achieved.[10]

With the aid of the Eponym Chronicle and numerous duplicate records, and by fitting together the pieces of available text and their accompanying carvings, restorations have been made that give the main features of Tiglath-Pileser's reign with a high degree of trustworthiness. Here only the items relevant to our inquiry will be considered.

The most recent and doubtless the most thorough work of restoration has been under way for some fifteen years or more by Prof. Hayim Tadmor of the Hebrew University of Jerusalem. When that work is published it should be the chief authority on the annals of Tiglath-Pileser III. But at this writing Prof. Tadmor's work is not yet available and probably will not be for some time to come. So I am using for my main source on Tiglath-Pileser the work of Daniel David Luckenbill, *Ancient Records of Assyria and Babylonia.*

It should be noticed that the section of the palace annals dealing with Menahem's payment of tribute immediately precedes a section denoting the events of Tiglath-Pileser's ninth year,[11] 737. It is therefore presumed that the immediately preceding section of the annals must deal with the immediately preceding year and that 738 must thus be the year of Menahem's payment of tribute. Second, in the section dealing with Azariah of Judah in the midst of a list of places taken by Tiglath-Pileser in this campaign are the badly damaged signs of the name of a site that has generally been restored as "Kullani."[12] And inasmuch as the eponym list with notes gives for the eponymy of Adad-bela-ukin, 738, the capture of Kullani, it is taken for granted that this is additional evidence for 738. Yet a third point seemingly in favor of 738 is that in this same section dealing with Azariah mention is made of the settlement of a number of captives in the land of Ulluba, and this would be a logical procedure for that year inasmuch as the campaign for the previous year, 739, in the eponymy of Sin'taklak, was against Ulluba.

At first sight such evidence might appear to be conclusive and in favor of 738. But let us examine these items a bit more closely. Simply because the section of the annals dealing with Menahem's payment of tribute immediately precedes the section of the annals dealing with Tiglath-Pileser's ninth year, 737, does it necessarily follow that that section must deal with Tiglath-Pileser's eighth year? Such an argument would rest on the assumption that the records from Calah are complete, dealing consecutively with each year of Tiglath-Pileser's reign. That, however, is a mere assumption of which we have no proof. A complete record of events by unbroken, consecutive years is by no means the

---

[10]Luckenbill, *Ancient Records,* 1:269.
[11]Ibid., secs. 772, 773.
[12]Ibid., sec. 770.

invariable rule for Assyrian records. The task of the Assyriologist would be easy indeed if there were such complete records of yearly events in the reigns of all the kings. The Eponym Chronicle with notes does indeed supply such a record, the famous Black Obelisk of Shalmaneser III is of this nature, and so also are the annals of Sargon II engraved on the wall slabs of his palace at Dur-Sharrukin, but there are also notable exceptions. The final edition of the annals of Ashur-nasir-pal II are found on the pavement slabs of the entrance to the temple of Urta at Calah.[13] Here the events for the first six years are dated in terms of the limmu officials, then follow three campaigns undated by years but with the months strangely retained, followed by another campaign in the eponymy of Shamash-nuri, Ashur-nasir-pal's eighteenth year, 866. But who would dare to conclude that because his campaign to the land of Kipani took place in his eighteenth year, 866, the campaign to Mount Lebanon and the Great Sea mentioned in the section immediately preceding must have taken place in his seventeenth year, 867? Who would conclude that his campaign against the lands of Suhi and Lake must have taken place in his seventh year, 877, simply because that record immediately follows the account of his campaign against Karduniash in his sixth year, 878? If such reasoning were sound, then it would be true that his undated campaign against Bit-Adini must have taken place in his eighth year, 876, simply because this account immediately follows the record of the campaigns against Suhi and Lake, and it must also have taken place in his sixteenth year, 868, simply because this same account immediately precedes the record of his campaign against Mount Lebanon and the Great Sea. Obviously position alone means little as to the precise dating of these three campaigns on this important Assyrian document in which the campaigns of seven out of eighteen years are definitely dated but the rest are not.

Another example of an incomplete Assyrian inscription is the Monolith Inscription of Shalmaneser III. This record covers in detail the first four and the sixth years of Shalmaneser's reign, but the record of the fifth year is strangely missing.[14]

Still another example is the gate inscription of Shalmaneser III at Balawat on which are found a few selected events of the first four years of Shalmaneser's reign; however, after these the events of the fifth, sixth, and seventh years are missing, but the record is resumed for the eighth and ninth years.[15]

Yet another example is that of the bull-colossi of Shalmaneser III from Calah, where the record mentions the fourth to the fifteenth years inclusive with their outstanding events, skips the sixteenth and seventeenth years, and goes on again with the eighteenth year.[16]

Also to be noted are the records of Sennacherib in which events are reported, not in terms of years of reign, but according to his eight campaigns during a reign of twenty-four years.

A careful study of the records must determine whether in the case of Tiglath-Pileser III the events of his reign were recorded on the walls of the

---

[13]Ibid., pp. 138–69.
[14]Ibid., pp. 211–23.
[15]Ibid., pp. 227–32.
[16]Ibid., pp. 236–41.

palace at Calah in a complete and unbroken sequence of years, whether there was merely a partial presentation, or whether events were recorded according to the sequence of campaigns. What is the evidence?

The annals open by setting forth what is clearly—though the statement to that effect has not been preserved—an account of Tiglath-Pileser's first year the record of his Babylonian campaign. Then follows the record of his second year, his campaign against the lands of Namri, Bit-Sangi, and other countries of the northeast. Next comes the great campaign of the third year against Sardurri of Urartu and other restless and powerful peoples in the northwest. It is in the course of this campaign that the names of Azariah and Menahem are introduced. Immediately following the section dealing with Menahem comes a section dealing with the ninth year when the focus of attention had swept back to the northeast. The next year, the tenth, is again not expressly mentioned on the records as they now exist, but from that year to the fourteenth we know from the Eponym Chronicle that the campaign was again in the northwest and west, and these are the places that are mentioned in this part of the annals.

In view of the fact that certain sections of the annals are introduced by the mention of specific years, such as the second, the third, and the ninth, the assumption has been that this was originally the case throughout the record. But again it should be pointed out that of this we have no proof. It is true that the annals as they exist today are in a fragmentary state and that in their original form there may have been a more complete mention of events than we find on these records in their present form. But it should be noticed that those sections of the annals in which we do find a specific mention of years are sections introducing campaigns in certain geographical localities. Thus the second year, 744, deals with the campaign in the northeast; the third year, 743, is the year that opened the great campaign in the regions of the northwest and that remained the center of attention for six years, till in the ninth year, 737, the center of action swept back again to the northeast. And that ninth year is again specifically mentioned. The question of interest and importance is whether, outside of the reference to the third year introducing this section, there ever was any mention of specific years from 742 to 738 inclusive. If this were the case, it would have a very definite bearing on the accuracy of certain dates that have up to the present been regarded as settled. Thus the Azariah-Menahem section has been assigned the date of 738 because it immediately precedes the section dated in the ninth year, 737. But if this section is a unit not broken up into individual years, it could just as readily be assigned the date 743, as immediately following or even being a part of the section dealing with the events of 743. Until we are in possession of further evidence concerning the exact nature of Tiglath-Pileser's annals—whether these consisted of annual records in an unbroken sequence of years, or whether they were divided into larger sections dealing with the campaigns as they took place in certain broad geographical areas—we are in no position to say with finality whether the generally accepted date of 738 is correct. The full evidence will first need to be considered.

In regard to the assumed mention of "Kullani" as it has been restored in the section dealing with Azariah, it must be remembered that this restoration may or may not be correct and that any argument based on such a restoration is sound only to the extent that the restoration itself is certain.

It should be noticed, moreover, that even if the restoration of "Kullani" were correct, it would not of itself prove the correctness of the date of 738, for a campaign against Kullani that year would not preclude a campaign against that city some years previous. This is true because Assyrian inscriptions are replete with records of repeated campaigns against certain sites at surprisingly frequent intervals. A brief glimpse at the Eponym Chronicle (pp. 221–26) reveals a frequent repetition of the names of a number of sites as centers of attack by Assyrian arms year after year. The Eponym Chronicle could record only a few of the sites against which the Assyrian armies directed their numerous and repeated assaults. Naturally there would be many other places that repeatedly became the target of Assyrian attacks, and so Kullani might have been attacked not only in 738 but in many another year.

The mention of Ulluba is important, but it must be remembered that this name appears a number of times in the inscriptions of Tiglath-Pileser III,[17] the dates of which are by no means finally settled, and that as early as 830, in the eponymy of Nergal-ilia, the campaign of the year was against Ulluba.[18]

A careful consideration of the various points that in the past have been regarded as positive proof for the accuracy of the date 738 will thus be seen not to constitute conclusive evidence. We have as yet presented no evidence disproving 738, but we have shown that, without further corroborative evidence, the date 738 rests on a basis far from secure. A careful study of all the available evidence might be expected to throw further light on this question. Let us examine the record, the key information of which is listed on the following page in "Targets Under Repeated Assyrian Attack."

Any internal evidence that might link the Azariah-Menahem section of the annals with material that precedes or follows may be of vital importance in dating this section. When we examine the annals, we find that the portion mentioning Azariah and Menahem is more closely connected to the preceding material than to what follows. The section dealing with Azariah begins with the following words: "[In] the course of my campaign, I received the tribute of the kings of the seacoast . . . [Azariah] of Judah, like. . . ."[19] The annalist is here dealing with some definite campaign of Tiglath-Pileser. Which campaign? The natural answer is that campaign that he has just been describing, the campaign of his third year, 743, against Sardurri of Urartu and his sympathizers of the west. From 743 to 738 inclusive, as the notes from the Eponym Chronicle reveal, Tiglath-Pileser was engaged in a tremendous undertaking to bring under control the restless and powerful groups of peoples in the north and west. In 743 he was in Arpad in northern Aram and a struggle took place in Urartu of Armenia. Urartu was now at the height of its power. Sardurri (Sarduish) controlled all the regions of Armenia up toward the Caucasus and had taken to himself the titles of "King of Kings" and "King of Shuraush." If Aram

[17]Ibid., secs. 770, 785, 796, 814; Paul Rost, *Die Keilschrifttexte Tiglat-Pilessers III,* (Leipzig, 1893), 1:23, 47, 53, 67.

[18]*Reallexikon der Assyriologie,* ed. Enrich Ebeling and Bruno Meissner (1938), 2:433.

[19]Luckenbill, *Ancient Records,* vol. 1, sec. 770.

TARGETS UNDER REPEATED ASSYRIAN ATTACK

Hamanu	Bit-Adini	Hatti	Babylonia	Tabali	Ulluba	Damascus	Namri	Urartu
858	857	853	851	837	830	841	843	832
842	856	848	850	720	739	773	835	781
	855	845	811			733	797	780
						732	774	779
						727	749	778
							748	776
							744	774
								743
								735

Madai	Arpad	Itu	Mannai	Karne	Tille	Guzana	Musasir	Hubushkia
821	805	790	829	819	817	808	716	801
809	754	783	806	818	816	759	713	791
800	743	782	718			758		784
799	742	777						
793	741	769						
792	740							
789								
788								
786								
766								
737								

Kue	Der	Hatarika	Arrapha	Dur Iakin	Gananati
840	795	772	761	706	771
834	794	765	760	705	767
833		755			

was to come under Assyrian rather than Haldian power and if Tiglath-Pileser was to be master of the regions from Babylonia to the Mediterranean coast, then Sardurri must be vanquished and these nations of the west must be taught the might of Assyrian arms. The undertaking was not easy and was to keep the Assyrian forces engaged in an unbroken struggle in this region for six years and was to be later renewed after a brief respite. In 743 Tiglath-Pileser claimed the defeat of Sardurri and the receipt of tribute from Pisiris of Carchemish and Hiram of Tyre.[20] The next year, 742, the campaign of the year was against Arpad, evidently now the center of resistance, for thus it was again in 741 and once more in 740. For 739 the Eponym Chronicle cites Ulluba on the Armenian frontier as the center of hostilities, while for 738 it was Kullani, the Calneh (Calno) of the Old Testament (Amos 6:2; Isa. 10:9).

None of the records now available except the Eponym Chronicle breaks up this period into units of individual years. A careful study of the internal evidence points to the fact that the entire period from Tiglath-Pileser's third to his eighth years, following the mention of only a single year, evidently the third, is dealt with as a single unit. The question at issue is: when during this six-year period did Azariah and Menahem enter the picture, as early as 743 or as late as 738?

---

[20]Ibid., sec. 769.

In the section of the annals in which Azariah is introduced is found a long list of cities in the land of Hamath that at that time were brought within the power of Assyria.[21] This list is clearly parallel to a similar list of cities found on a twenty-four-line inscription that contains the names of cities in the lands of Enzi, Urartu, Unki, and Hamath.[22] The following cities of Hamath and the seacoast are found on both lists: Usnu, Siannu, Simirra, Hatarikka, Nukudina, Ara, Ashhani, Iadabi, Ellitarbi, and Zitanu. In the annals these are mentioned as cities that had gone over in revolt to Azariah but had been brought back under Assyrian domination and placed under tribute. The purpose of the parallel list is not stated, but it evidently constitutes a list of cities paying tribute to Assyria. There is no question concerning the parallelism of the two lists. Both constitute a group of cities under Assyrian domination at the same time and at the same period paying tribute to Tiglath-Pileser. The date for the one list would be the date of the other and would help to establish the dates of other events appearing in the same connection. In the annals a list is given of such leaders of the west as Kushtashpi of Kummuhu, Hiram of Tyre, and Pisiris of Carchemish, who paid tribute to Tiglath-Pileser "in Arpad."[23] Among the cities on the parallel list is Arpad.[24] Here we have, then, a time when Tiglath-Pileser was in the city of Arpad. According to the Eponym Chronicle, 743 was such a year, for in that year the king was "in" Arpad, whereas during the next three years the campaign was "against" Arpad.

Also of interest to our inquiry is the fact that shortly before the group of cities in the land of Hamath appearing on the parallel list III R, 10, No. 3, there occurs the name of the city of Kulmadara, and shortly before the same group of cities in the annals' list there occurs a single "Kul" sign that Rost has restored to "Kullani," a restoration that, it will be recalled, has been widely used as evidence that this particular section of the annals should be dated to 738. But if Kulmadara is the name appearing on the one list before the group of Hamath cities, then that is the name that should appear on the other list before the same group of cities. "Kullani" is an erroneous restoration, and the single "Kul" sign should rather have been restored as "Kulmadara."[25]

---

[21]Ibid., sec. 770.

[22]III R, 10, No. 3; Luckenbill, *Ancient Records,* vol. 1, sec. 821; Rost, *Die Keilschrifttexte,* pp. 84–85.

[23]Luckenbill, *Ancient Records,* vol. 1, sec. 769.

[24]Ibid., sec. 821.

[25]It should be noted that in the annals a single sign for "Kul" appears, but on III R, 10, No. 3, two signs are employed, "Ku-ul." Rost in his transliteration has mistakenly written "Kul" instead of "Ku-ul," and in this mistake he has been followed by many writers (cf. Rost, *Die Keilschrifttexte,* vol. 1:85, and ibid., vol. 2, bl. 27). Such a variation could not be urged as a valid objection, however, to the identification of the site intended by the "Kul" sign in the annals with the Kulmadara on the parallel list, for the variant "Ku-ul" for "Kul" would be altogether possible, such variations being a common practice in Assyrian inscriptions, here as well as elsewhere. Still another objection that might be raised is that the spacing on Rost's autographic copy of Layard, between the "Kul" sign and the final "lu" of [Gu-ub]-lu, the following word—a space now a blank—would seem to favor the restoration of five signs rather than the six that would be necessary if "Kulmadara" rather than "Kullani" were to be restored. A careful comparison of Rost's spacing with the spacing of inscriptions still extant shows frequent variations from the original in this regard, and there is thus no certainty that these six signs might not be inserted in the necessary space of the original inscription if that were now available.

An examination of the order of sequence between the items in the annals and list III R, 10, No. 3, will be of interest. This is as follows:[26]

LIST OF CITIES, III R, 10, No. 3	ANNALS
Cities of the lands of Enzi and Urartu	Uratru subjugated
	City of Kukusanshu
Kukusanshu	City of Izzida
Izzida	Receipt of tribute in Arpad
Cities of Bit-Adini	Unki subjugated
Arpadda	Tribute from kings of the seacoast who
Cities of the land of Unki	had gone over to Azariah Kul[lani] or
Kulmadara	Kul[madara]?
Cities of the land of Hamath	Hamath and environs subjugated
Hatarikka	Usnu
Simirra	Siannu
Usnu	Simirra
Sianu	Hatarikka
Ara	Nukudina
Nukudina	Ara
Ashani	Ashhani
Iadabi	Iadabi
Ellitarbi	Ellitarbi
Zitanu	Zitanu

Only the relevant items from the two documents have been listed. The general parallelism in arrangement is striking. On the list of cities there are no comments; only the names of cities are given and the countries in which they are located. Kulmadara appears as one of the cities in the land of Unki. Unki is located on the Mediterranean coast at the extreme north of Aram. Somewhere within that area is the site of Kulmadara. At the southern environs of Unki is Calneh or Kullani. Which city did the Assyrian annalist have in mind when in connection with the discussion of rulers of the westland who had gone over to Azariah, the name of the city of Kul is introduced, Kullani or Kulmadara? In the annals this item appears just before the list of cities on the seacoast and in the environs of Hamath. On list III R, 10, No. 3, Kulmadara appears in the Unki group in the section immediately preceding the same list of cities in the land of Hamath. That position calls for the restoration of "Kulmadara." Kullani is mentioned nowhere else in the Assyrian records except in the Eponym Chronicle, where it appears as the site captured in the campaign of the year 738, in the eponymy of Adad-bel-ukin. Kalmadara appears once more in the annals, in the Menahem section, as one of the cities of Unki where Babylonian captives were placed.[27] There is no question concerning Kulmadara as having been the target of Assyrian attack in 743 when Unki was conquered. Did Kullani also figure prominently at that time in the Assyrian campaign? That is not only possible but

---

[26]Luckenbill, *Ancient Records*, vol. 1, secs. 769–70, 820–21.
[27]Ibid., sec. 772.

probable, for it was in the locale of action in that important year. And if the "Kul" sign in the Azariah section stands for Kullani, we would have evidence that Kullani figured in the Assyrian campaign not only of 738 but also of 743. So whether the restoration is Kulmadara or Kullani would have no bearing on the settlement of the date in question. The occurrence of Kulmadara at the place where it appears on list III R, 10, No. 3, and the occurrence of the "Kul" sign at that identical place in the Azariah section of the annals, points conclusively to Kulmadara as the correct restoration. Thus the "Kul" sign here provides not the slightest evidence for 738 as against 743.

Tiglath-Pileser claims to have inflicted a devastating defeat on Judah's allies in the northwest, and the statement is made that captives from the campaign in which Azariah is mentioned were settled in Ulluba.[28] While it is true that the eponym canon records for the year 739 a campaign against Ulluba, it is also true and possibly significant that the important Nimrud Tablet No. 1 records the capture of Ulluba and Kirhu in the lines immediately preceding those recording the revolt of Sardurri,[29] which took place in Tiglath-Pileser's third year, 743.[30] On Nimrud Slab No. 1, which is probably the earliest inscription extant from Tiglath-Pileser and which Olmstead dates to the year 743,[31] the conquest of Ulluba is once more dealt with in the same section relating the revolt of Sardurri.[32] If this inscription is correctly dated to the year 743, it will thus fix this victory over Ulluba to that year. On yet another document, Nimrud Slab No. 2, the conquest of Ulluba is again closely associated with the conquest of Sardurri.[33]

It should be noticed that while there is no evidence that would exclude Ulluba from the great campaign against Sardurri in Tiglath-Pileser's third year, there is evidence in each of the above-mentioned inscriptions in which Ulluba is named to indicate that that land occupied a part in the campaign of 743. First, the annals in opening the account of the third year report the revolt of Sardurri and his allies and their crushing defeat, with 72,950 captives taken.[34] And it is the very next section opening with the words "in the course of my campaign"—evidently continuing the account of the same campaign—that mentions the settling in Ulluba of 1,223 captives taken from among Azariah's allies.[35]

The point is often stressed that events on inscriptional material of the so-called *Prunkinschriften* group are arranged not in chronological but in geographical order,[36] and on these grounds the effort may be made to rule out any chronological significance of the mention of Ulluba in connection with Sardurri's revolt on the other inscriptions mentioned. But a careful comparison of

---

[28]Ibid., sec. 770; Rost, *Die Keilschrifttexte*, p. 22, 1. 133.
[29]Luckenbill, *Ancient Records*, vol. 1, secs. 796, 797; Rost, *Die Keilschrifttexte*, p. 66, 11. 43ff.
[30]Luckenbill, *Ancient Records*, vol. 1, sec. 769; Rost, *Die Keilschrifttexte*, p. 12, 1. 59.
[31]A. T. Olmstead, *Assyrian Historiography* (Columbia, Mo., 1916), p. 34.
[32]Luckenbill, *Ancient Records*, vol. 1, sec. 785; Rost, *Die Keilschrifttexte*, p. 46, 1. 25.
[33]Luckenbill, *Ancient Records*, vol. 1, secs. 813, 814; Rost, *Die Keilschrifttexte*, p. 53, 1. 41.
[34]Luckenbill, *Ancient Records*, vol. 1, sec. 769; Rost, *Die Keilschrifttexte*, p. 12, 1. 66.
[35]Luckenbill, *Ancient Records*, vol. 1, sec. 770; Rost, *Die Keilschrifttexte* p. 22, 1. 133.
[36]Rost, *Die Keilschrifttexte*. p. 1; Anspacher, *Tiglath Pileser III*, p. 3; Olmstead, *Assyrian Historiography*, pp. 33–34; Bruno Meissner, *Babylonien and Assyrien* (Heidelberg, 1925), 2:371.

these inscriptions with the eponym lists and the annals reveals striking parallels in arrangement on all these accounts. Using the numbers of the sections as they are given by Luckenbill, the arrangement is as follows:

TIGLATH-PILESER III, AZARIAH AND MENAHEM

Year B.C.	Eponym List	Annals Sec. No.	Nimrud Tablet No. 1 Sec. No.	Nimrud Slab No. 1 Sec. No.	Nimrud Slab No. 2 Sec. No.
To Babylonia:					
745 1st year	Between the rivers	762 Chaldea	788 Babylon	782 Til-kamri	809 Uknu
		763 Til-kamri	789 Chaldea	783 Chaldea	810 Babylon
		764 Sippar	790 Tarbasu		811 Chaldea
		765 Babylonia	791 Amlilatu		
			792 Sapie		
			793 Larak		
			794 Sealand		
To the Northeast:					
744 2d year	Against Namri	766 Namri	795 Namri	784 Parsua	812 Medes
		767 Kapsi			
		768 Arazi			
To the Northwest and West:					
743 3d year	In Arpad	769 Urartu	796 Ulluba	785 Urartu	813 Urartu
	Urartu revolt	770 Seacoast	797 Urartu		814 Ulluba
		771 Syria	Break in tablet;		
		772 Unki	about 100		
			lines missing		
742 4th year	Against Arpad				
741 5th year	Against Arpad				
740 6th year	Against Arpad				
738 7th year	Against Ulluba				
738 8th year	Kullani captured				
To the Northeast:					
737 9th year	Against Madai	773 Madai			
		774 Kapsi			
		775a Til-Ashuri			
To the Northwest and West:					
736 10th year	To Mount Nal	775b Na'iri			
735 11th year	Against Urartu	776 Musurni			
734 12th year	Against Pilista	777 Aram	798 Bir'ai		
733 13th year	Against Damascus	778 Arabia	799 Temai		
732 14th year	Against Damascus	779 Ashkelon	800 Egyptian Frontier		
			801 Hamath		
			Iauhazi (Ahaz)		
			of Judah		
To Babylonia:					
731 15th year	Against Sapia				
King in Assyria:					
730 16th year	In the land		802 Rab-shaku to Tabal		
			803 Rab-shaku to Tyre		
			804 Palace built in Calah		

With such a pattern before us it would be difficult to argue that, though the eponym lists and annals are arranged in chronological order, the Nimrud tablet and slabs are not, for the basic order is the same. If one group of these documents may be considered to be chronological in nature, that is also true of the other. And if it is true that the documents of the *Prunkinschriften* group are primarily geographical in nature, then this also holds true of the annals, for they are arranged alike. In fact we may have here the real secret of the arrangement not only of Tiglath-Pileser's annals but of the other documents as well, and that is chronological-geographical for all rather than strictly chronological for some and strictly geographical for others. In other words events were not arranged on the basis of a strict sequence of years but according to a sequence of activities in certain geographical areas, or campaigns. Thus when Azariah and Menahem were introduced into the record, they were not introduced in that section dealing with Tiglath-Pileser's first campaign that took place in Babylonia in his first year, nor in the section dealing with his second campaign that took place in the northeast in his second year, but in that section of the annals dealing with his third campaign that took place in the regions of the northwest and was carried on from his third to his eighth years of reign.

Olmstead and others no doubt perceived the general principles of this basic chronological-geographical arrangement, but assigned the annals to a chronological classification because of the occasional mention in them of certain specific years of the king as beginning certain major campaigns. They assigned other documents to a geographical classification because of the very obvious arrangement by major campaigns. In discussing the Nimrud tablet Olmstead refers to the Tabal and Tyre paragraphs as being "out of the regular geographical order," and being "obvious postscripts."[37] But what he did not see was that we have evidence here of the chronological as well as the geographical arrangement of this tablet, for the Tabal and Tyre activities, together with those involving Iauhazi (Ahaz) of Judah and Hanunu of Gaza belong, without question, at the very place on this tablet where they appear, and that is at the close, for these are events that took place toward the close of Tiglath-Pileser's reign. If the order of the tablet had been strictly geographical rather than chronological, these items would, of course, have appeared in an earlier section where items of an earleir campaign in the west first appear, but this was a new and a later campaign, and as such these items appear toward the end of the tablet, not as "obvious postscripts" but as intrinsic factors of a late campaign. Ahaz is referred to at this time as paying tribute of gold to Tiglath-Pileser because he was king in 732, which was not the case at the time of the previous campaign in the north and west from 743 to 738.

It is particularly unfortunate that there should be such a large break of approximately a hundred lines in the Nimrud tablet and that this break should come just where it does, for the missing sections, as Olmstead has suggested,[38] must have contained most of the Urartu account and an account of the events in Aram during the campaign against Arpad. This document, in the portion still

---

[37]Olmstead, *Assyrian Historiography*, p. 34.
[38]Ibid.

extant, gives a full account of the events of Tiglath-Pileser's campaign in Babylonia during his second year, and the probability is that the portion now missing dealt with the events of the important campaign in the northwest with equal fullness. But enough of the tablet remains to indicate that its essential arrangement, as well as that of the Nimrud slabs, is chronological, if not by individual years at least by major campaigns.[39]

To the extent that these campaigns were geographical in nature, confining the major efforts of Assyrian arms to certain areas for certain longer or shorter periods of time, it might indeed be said that not only the records of the *Prunkinschriften* group but the so-called annals as well were arranged in geographical rather than chronological order.

Although the order of sequence was adhered to in the presentation of the accounts of the major campaigns themselves, and although at times a striking parallelism is found in the sequence followed in the presentation of individual events as they appear on various records of the campaigns, the same order of sequence is not invariable in the case of these individual events. An item that on one account precedes some other item may follow it on another. The arrangement of individual items as recorded for a single campaign will, therefore, not always be strictly according to a chronological sequence. That it is dangerous to be dogmatic concerning the exact order in which events must have happened simply on the basis of the place where they are recorded in the annals is indicated by the fact that according to the Eponym Chronicle the campaign against Philistia appears as the event of the year in Tiglath-Pileser's twelfth year of reign, while the campaign against Damascus was the event of the thirteenth and fourteenth years; but in the annals the campaign against Rezin of Aram precedes the mention of the campaign against Ashkelon in Philistia. Thus the place where an item is mentioned in the annals does not necessarily indicate its exact chronological relationship to some other item. Simply because one event is found recorded immediately preceding or following some other event does not always prove that that is exactly the order in which these events took place. In order to ascertain the exact relationship of one item to some other item, it will be necessary to make a careful study of all the available evidence. Let us notice a number of items concerning Tiglath-Pileser's great campaign against the northwest.

---

[39]The fact that the eponym list mentions a campaign against Sapia for 731 and that the Babylonian Chronicle mentions a march by Tiglath-Pileser against Akkad in the third year of Ukinzer (I:19–21), 729 B.C., may be raised as an argument against a campaign by Tiglath-Pileser in his first year against Sapia, as would be indicated by the mention of Sapia in the first part of the Nimrud tablet if the arrangement of this tablet were on a strictly chronological basis. While the possibility exists that Tiglath-Pileser may have made some move against Amukani as early as the first year of his reign, it could also very well be that the above item has been removed from its correct chronological arrangement although it would lend some force to the argument that other items might also have been removed from their exact chronological setting. Every Assyriologist, however, is aware of the weaknesses inherent in the royal documents of Assyria, including chronological items in the royal annals (cf. A. T. Olmstead, *Western Asia in the Days of Sargon of Assyria, 722–705 B.C.* [New York, 1908], pp. 2ff., and *Assyrian Historiography;* Luckenbill, *Ancient Records,* 1:7). The above tabulation, however, is sufficient proof of the basic chronological arrangement of the items on Nimrud Tablet No. 1 and bears witness to its validity as evidence concerning Ulluba's part in Tiglath-Pileser's great northwestern campaign in his third year.

That Tiglath-Pileser's campaign of his third year against Urartu did indeed cover a large extent of that country can be learned from the names of three cities—Kukusanshu, Harbisina, and Izzeda—evidently conquered by him and that are found in a section of the annals placed by Rost, followed by Luckenbill, immediately after the section giving a description of Sardurri's flight and the capture of his camp.[40] Both Izzeda and Kukusanshu are included in the list of cities (III R, 10, No. 3) of the lands of Enzi and Urartu.[41] An idea of the location of these cities may be gained from the inclusion among them of the city of Parisu, a site that on Nimrud Slab No. 1 is listed as one of the strongholds of Urartu, back of Mount Nal, in the land of Ulluba.[42] Harbisina is included among the strongholds of Urartu listed on Nimrud Slab No. 1 as captured by Tiglath-Pileser.[43] This group of strongholds immediately follows the mention of Ulluba.

If Ulluba figured in the early part of Tiglath-Pileser's campaign against the northwest beginning in 743, and if captives from the campaign in which Azariah is mentioned were settled in Ulluba, this would point to an early dating of the campaign against Azariah and his allies among the events of 743–738.

In brief, a careful survey of the section of the annals dealing with Azariah makes it clear that this section demands a time when the king was present in the west, when his campaign was thought of as an integral part of the campaign of his third year against Urartu, and when Arpad was under Assyrian power. The year 743 meets all these requirements.

It is generally acknowledged that the section of the annals dealing with the payment of tribute from Menahem dates from the same year as the section dealing with Azariah.[44]

Proof that these two sections were very closely associated in Tiglath-Pileser's annals and that the Menahem section immediately followed the Azariah section lies in the fact that the last line of a fragment of one version of the annals that was written across a group of figures, plate XXI in Rost, is the first line of a column of the twelve-line version, plate XV in Rost. This is line 141 of the annals as arranged by Rost. The Azariah-Ulluba campaign is the topic of lines 105–133, and the Menahem-Kulmadara campaign is the subject of lines 144–150.

Yet another indication of the close connection between the Azariah and Menahem sections is found in the fact that the rulers of nearby lands listed in the one section are the same as those listed in the other. Among these are the following: Sulumal of Melid, Tarhulara of Gurgum, Kushtashpi of Kummuhu, Uriak of Kue, Pisiris of Carchemish, Hiram of Tyre, and Rezin of Damascus.[45]

Of interest and importance in the endeavor to secure the correct dating of the Azariah-Menahem sections of the annals is the fact that a number of these

---

[40]Luckenbill, *Ancient Records*, vol. 1, sec. 769; Rost, *Die Keilschrifttexte*, pp. 14ff., ll. 77ff.

[41]Luckenbill, *Ancient Records*, vol. 1, sec. 820; Rost, *Die Keilschrifttexte*, p. 84, ll. 1, 17.

[42]Luckenbill, *Ancient Records*, vol. 1, sec. 785; Rost, *Die Keilschrifttexte*, p. 46, l. 26.

[43]Luckenbill, *Ancient Records*, vol. 1, sec. 785; Rost, *Die Keilschrifttexte*, p. 46, l. 28.

[44]Sidney Smith, *Cambridge Ancient History* (Cambridge, 1929), 3:37; Hall, *Ancient History*, pp. 463–64.

[45]Luckenbill, *Ancient Records*, vol. 1, secs. 769, 770, 772.

rulers, such as Sulumal of Melid, Tarhulara of Gurgum and Kushtashpi of Kummuhu, are named with Sardurri of Urartu in Tiglath-Pileser's account of his great campaign to suppress the revolt in the northwest in 743.[46]

Also of interest in this connection is the list of tribute-paying cities in the land of Hamath[47] that has many parallels to the cities of Hamath listed in the Azariah section.

If the indications are that the Azariah section of the annals should be dated to the year 743, then, if the Menahem section actually constitutes an integral part of the Azariah section, that section too should be dated to the year 743. If our deductions thus far are sound, we should expect a careful examination of the Menahem section likewise to reveal indications of its dating to 743 rather than 738. What is the evidence?

Of great assistance in dating the Menahem section are lists of places from which and to which captives were transported at the time of the Assyrian campaign. Captives were usually transported on the occasion of a conquest or very soon afterward. At the time of the suppression of the uprising of the western allies, Usnu, Siannu, and Simirra are listed among the subdued cities.[48] We have just seen definite indications that this was the year 743. The same three cities are included in a group on the seacoast[49] in which captives were settled at the time of the reception of tribute from Menahem.[50] Among the captives transported were 600 from Amlate of the Damunu area, 5,400 from the city of Dir,[51] and 588 Budeans, Duneans, and others.[52] Tiglath-Pileser's campaign into Babylonia, where these sites were located, took place in his first year, 745, at which time Budu was one of the lands overcome.[53] Three times captives are mentioned from Bit-Sangibuti.[54] Tiglath-Pileser's march to the northeast, where Bit-Sangibuti was located, took place in his second year, in the eponymy of Bel-dan, 744, when the campaign of the year was against the land of Namri.[55] Namri also was located in northeastern Mesopotamia. On Nimrud Tablet No. 1 is a section clearly dealing with the campaign of this second year to the northeast.[56] The land of Namri heads this list and Bit-Sangibuti comes next. Many names on this list, such as Bit-Hamban, Sumurzu, Bit-Zatti, Bit-Abdadani, Bit Kapsi, Bit Sangi, Ariarma, and Tarlugale, are common to a list of places mentioned in the annals as subdued by Tiglath-Pileser in his campaign against the northeast in his second year.[57] With Bit-

---

[46]Ibid., secs. 769, 796–97.

[47]For those who may be using Luckenbill, attention is called to the fact that the list of cities, III R, 10, No. 3, is mistakenly given by him as III R, 10, No. 2 (see Luckenbill, *Ancient Records*, 1: 294; cf. also p. 292).

[48]Rost, *Die Keilschrifttexte*, pp. 20–21; Luckenbill, *Ancient Records*, vol. 1, sec. 770.

[49]Rost, *Die Keilschrifttexte*, pp. 24–25; Luckenbill, *Ancient Records*, vol. 1, sec. 772.

[50]Rost, *Die Keilschrifttexte*, pp. 24–25; Luckenbill, *Ancient Records*, vol. 1, sec. 772.

[51]Rost, *Die Keilschrifttexte*, pp. 24–25; Luckenbill, *Ancient Records*, vol. 1, sec. 772.

[52]Rost, *Die Keilschrifttexte*, pp. 24–25, 1. 146; Luckenbill, *Ancient Records*, vol. 1, sec. 772.

[53]Rost, *Die Keilschrifttexte*, p. 4, 1. 14; Luckenbill, *Ancient Records*, vol. 1, sec. 764.

[54]Rost, *Die Keilschrifttexte*, pp. 24–25, ll. 145, 148–49; Luckenbill, *Ancient Records*, vol. 1, sec. 772.

[55]Luckenbill, *Ancient Records*, vol. 1, sec. 766; 2:436.

[56]Rost, *Die Keilschrifttexte*, p. 62, 1. 29; Luckenbill, *Ancient Records*, vol. 1, sec. 795.

[57]Rost, *Die Keilschrifttexte*, pp. 6–13; Luckenbill, *Ancient Records*, vol. 1, secs. 766–68.

Sangibuti coming into Assyrian hands in Tiglath-Pileser's second year, 744, a logical time for the transfer of these captives to cities of the west would be the following year. And the section of the annals dealing with Menahem, as we have just seen, three times mentions these Bit-Sangibuteans being transported to the cities of the northwest. When would this be, in 743 or in 738? Having conquered Bit-Sangibuti in 744, would he wait six years—till 738—before he transferred these captives to another land? That would be extremely unlikely. We have seen on other grounds that the probable dating of the Azariah section is 743, and not 738, and now we find still further evidence pointing to 743 rather than 738 for the dating of the section dealing with Menahem.

It should be noticed, moreover, that on the badly damaged Nimrud tablet the section dealing with the conquest of Namri and Bit-Sangibuti immediately precedes the section dealing with the campaigns against Ulluba, Kirhu, and Urartu.[58] That is just where this important tablet breaks off and one hundred lines are missing. One can only wonder what items that missing section contained. Perhaps if this tablet, so full in its accounts in the sections still intact, had been preserved in its entirety, we would have a sufficient account of just what took place in connection with Azariah and Menahem to answer the questions that are so troublesome today.

Still more to the point is a list of cities, found in the Menahem section of the annals, in which transported captives were settled. Among these is a group of cities in the land of Unki—Kunalia, Huzarra, Tae, Tarmanazi, Kulmadara, Hatatirra, and Sagillu.[59] The capture of Kunalia, capital of the land of Unki, and the subjugation of that country took place in the third year of Tiglath-Pileser.[60] Mention has already been made above of a list of cities of the west and northwest (III R, 10, No. 3), which on other grounds has been dated to the third year. One group of these cities—in all probability cities that were paying tribute to the Assyrian king—is from the land of Unki.[61] With Unki brought into subjection in the third year of Tiglath-Pileser, it would again be a logical procedure to transport captives there either that year or very soon afterward.

Yet again, among those listed with Menahem as paying tribute to Assyria are the following: Kushtashpi of Kummuhu, Rezin of Damascus, Hiram of Tyre, Uriak of Kue, Pisiris of Carchemish, Tarhulara of Gurgum, and Sulumal of Melid.[62] All of these are likewise listed by Tiglath-Pileser as having been subdued and as paying tribute on the occasion of his campaign against Urartu in his third year.[63] It will be remembered that the reception of tribute from this group of worthies was "in Arpad,"[64] and that the time was 743 when, according to the eponym canon, Tiglath-Pileser was "in Arpad."

Inasmuch, then, as the places from which captives were transported at the

[58]Luckenbill, *Ancient Records*, vol. 1, secs. 795–97.

[59]Rost, *Die Keilschrifttexte*, pp. 24–25, ll. 144–45; Luckenbill, *Ancient Records*, vol. 1, sec. 772.

[60]Rost, *Die Keilschrifttexte*, pp. 16–17, ll. 92ff.; Luckenbill, *Ancient Records*, vol. 1, sec. 769.

[61]Luckenbill, *Ancient Records*, vol. 1, sec. 821; Rost, *Die Keilschrifttexte*, p. 85.

[62]Rost , *Die Keilschrifttexte*, pp. 26–27, ll. 150ff.; Luckenbill, *Ancient Records*, vol. 1, sec. 772.

[63]Rost, *Die Keilschrifttexte*, pp. 12–13, ll. 61ff.; Luckenbill, *Ancient Records*, vol. 1, sec. 769.

[64]Rost, *Die Keilschrifttexte*, p. 16, l. 91; Luckenbill, *Ancient Records*, vol. 1, sec. 769.

time of Menahem's payment of tribute to Tiglath-Pileser were those captured immediately prior to his third year, inasmuch as the places in which these captives were settled were places taken in the great campaign of the third year, and inasmuch as the august group of tribute-payers of that year was the same group that paid tribute "in Arpad" in Tiglath-Pileser's third year, it seems only logical to conclude that this section of the annals dealing with Menahem's payment of tribute must be closely related to the third year. And while there are such definite connections of this section with the third year, the internal evidence shows no such connection with the material of the ninth year, which immediately follows the Menahem section in the Assyrian annals.

It was previously noted that there are indications that the Azariah section of the annals is very closely related to the events of Tiglath-Pileser's third year and that the Azariah-Menahem sections of the annals are very closely related to each other. Now we have seen that there is also strong evidence pointing to a close relationship between the Menahem section of the annals and the events of Tiglath-Pileser's third year—exactly the result that was to be expected if the Azariah-Menahem sections are so closely related to each other.

Just what is the significance of the close interrelationships of the various parts of these materials to each other and of their ties with the events of the years 745 and 744? Careful scrutiny has brought me to the conclusion that we have here a record of events all taking place in the year 743. In other words it is my conclusion that this entire section of Tiglath-Pileser's annals, beginning with the revolt of Sardurri and concluding with the section dealing with Menahem and the receipt of tribute from a large group of Mediterranean states, deals with various phases of the great campaign through Urartu to the coast in 743.

This section dealing with the Urartuan revolt opens with the statement, "[in my third] year of reign." The Eponym Chronicle also reports a revolt in Urartu in that year, 743. The items that follow give details of the course of this campaign through to the Mediterranean coast and of the events that took place there. Parallel items from other documents help to complete the picture. The revolt involved not only Sardurri of Urartu but Mati'-ilu of Arpad, who had been tied to Assyria by a solemn treaty early in the reign of Ashur-nirari V (755–745). Sulumal of Melid, Tarhulara of Gurgum, and Kustashpi of Kummuhu also joined the rebellion. Sufficient details have been preserved to provide a picture of a particularly swift and outstandingly victorious campaign. The initial attack was against Sardurri, whose domain extended from the regions of Ararat and Lake Van westward to the Euphrates bend. Urartu was overrun and Sardurri continued his flight to the west, evidently to take refuge with his coastal allies. Ulluba and Kirhu, districts of Urartu at the foot of Mount Nal, were overrun. At Kummuhu, north of Carchemish, Sardurri was defeated and his camp was taken. In the retribution that followed, mention is made of Kukusanshu, Harbisina, and Izzeda, all cities of Ulluba.

The vigorous pursuit extended west of the Euphrates, to Arpad, which had evidently played a leading role in the revolt. There Tiglath-Pileser established his headquarters and received the submission of many of the coastal lords, including—according to one list—Rezin of Aram, Kushtashpi of Kummuhu,

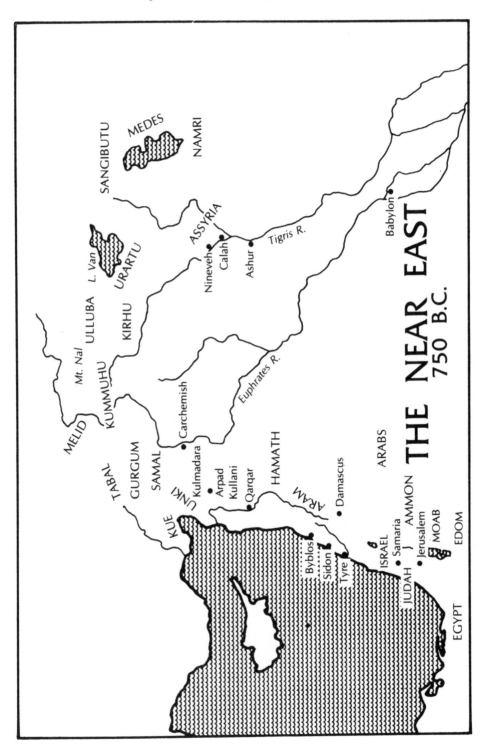

Hiram of Tyre, Uriak of Kue, Pisiris of Carchemish, and Tarhulara of Gurgum, and also—according to another list—Menahem of Samaria, Shiptiba'al of Byblos, Eni-ilu of Hamath, Panammu of Sam'al, and Sulumal of Melid.[65]

In addition to the above group that paid tribute in Arpad, mention is made of the receipt of tribute from nineteen districts of Hamath that had gone over to Azariah and of the settling of many of their captives in Ulluba. This, it will be recalled, was a district of Urartu overrun early in this campaign of 743 in the pursuit of Sardurri.

Attention is given to Tutammu of Unki, an area immediately west of Arpad. The land was subjugated and its capital, Kinalia, was captured. In the cities of Unki were settled many captives from places in Babylonia and Namri, areas that Tiglath-Pileser had conquered during the two previous years. The fact that the transfer of captives subdued in 745 and 744 is mentioned in the Menahem section constitutes convincing evidence that this section of the annals is tied in very closely with the campaigns of those years and that it was in 743 that the submission of Menahem took place, not five years later.

I am not alone in the conclusion that the section of the annals we have here been discussing dates to a single year and that the records of intervening years are not here recorded. Prof. Hayim Tadmor in a careful study of this section has come to a similar conclusion.[66] The omission of the events of a single year or a group of years is nothing strange to Assyrian palace records. The artists who prepared these pictorial inscriptions were not so much interested in providing future historians with year-by-year, blow-by-blow accounts of all the royal encounters as they were with the glorification of the king. If 743 was a year of unusual glory, why not concentrate on it? And if the following years were somewhat lacking in luster, why bother to record them on palace walls? The reports of the events that followed after 743 make it clear that Tiglath-Pileser had greatly overextended himself in his great campaign of that year and paid the price in the ensuing years. This is indicated by the fact that in 742, 741, and 740, Arpad, where submission was made and tribute was received in 743, was the prime target of the year, while in 739 Ulluba necessitated resubjugation.

A careful survey of all the evidence points to 743 as the year of Tiglath-Pileser's great campaign in which mention is made of the subjugation of Azariah's allies and the receipt of Menahem's tribute. That date is in perfect accord with the terminal dates of 742/41 for Menahem and 740/39 for Azariah, as called for by the present reconstruction of the chronology of the Hebrew kings.

---

[65]I am in agreement with Benno Landsberger, ("Sam'al: Studien zur Entdeckung der Ruinenstätte Karatepe," *Veröffentlichungen der Türkischen historischen Gelkschaft* 1 [Ankara, Turkey; 1948], p. 67), and Tadmor ("Azriyau of Yaudi," *Studies in the Bible, Scripta Hierosolymitana* 8 [1961]: 256), that these two lists of tribute payers constitute parallel accounts of the same event. The argument of Saggs ("The Nimrud Letters, 1952—Part II," *Iraq* 17 [1955]: 145), that the additions in the second list provide proof of different dating is hardly sound, for if it were it would require that Assyrian listings of names be identical in all instances, which is not the case.

[66]Tadmor, "Azriyau of Yaudi." I differ, however, with Tadmor regarding the dates involved, my years for the gap being 742 to 738 against his dates 743 to 739. Reasons for my views are found in my arguments throughout this chapter.

PARALLELS IN THE ASSYRIAN
Items as listed follow the order

Annals Luckenbill Secs. 769-70	Annals Section 772	List III R, 10, No. 3 Luckenbill Sec. 821
Third year [743]		
Sardurri revolted in Urartu		
Mati-ilu joined Sardurri		
Sulumal of Melid		
Tarhulara of Gurgum		
Kushtashpi of Kummuhu		
		Cities of Urartu, etc.
Kukusanshu		Kukusanshu, etc.
Harbisina		
Izzeda		Izzeda, etc. ....
Tribute from:	*Tribute from:*	
Rezin of [Aram]	Kushtashpi of Kummuhu	
Kushtashpi of Kummuhu	Rezin of Aram	
[Hiram] of Tyre	MENAHEM of Samaria	
Uriak of [Kue]	Hiram of Tyre	
Pisiris of Carchemish	Shiptiba'al of Byblos	
Tarhulara of Gurgum	Uriak of Kue	
	Pisiris of Carchemish	
	Eni-ilu of Hamath	
	Panammu of Sam'al	
	Tarhulara of Gurgum	
	Sulumal of Melid	
Received in Arpad		Arpad ....
Tutammu of Unki revolted		Cities in Unki
Tribute received from kings who went over to AZARIAH		
City of Kul [madara]		Kulmadara
Hamath subjugated:		*Cities of Hamath:*
Usnu		Hatarikka
Siannu		Gubla
Simirra, etc.		Simirra
Hatarikka		Arka
Nukudina		Usnu
Ara		Siannu
Ashani		Ri'a-sisu
Iadabi		Ri'a-raba
Ellitarbi		Ara
Zitanu, etc.		Nukudina
		Ashani
		Iadabi
		Ellitarbi
		Zitanu
Cities that had gone over to AZARIAH		
Captives settled in Ulluba		

RECORDS OF THE YEAR 743 B.C.
of sequence in the various records

Nimrud Tablet No. 1 Luckenbill Secs. 796-97	Nimrud Slab No. 1 Luckenbill Sec. 785	Nimrud Slab No. 2 Luckenbill Secs. 813-14	Eponym Canon
			. . . Tiglath-Pileser [743]
Ulluba conquered			
Kirhu conquered			
		Sardurri	
Sardurri of Urartu	Sardurri revolt in Urartu . .	revolt in Uratu	Massacre in Urartu
. . . .	Mati-ilu joins Sardurri . . .	Mati-ilu	
Sulumal of Melid			
Tarhulara of Gurgum			
Kushtashpi of Kummuhu . . .	Victorious in Kummuhu . . .	Victorious in Kummuhu	
	Ulluba conquered	Ulluba conquered	
. . . .	Izzeda		
	Harbisina		

. . . . In Arpad

Note: The names of Azariah (col. 1) and Menahem (col. 2) have been capitalized for the sake of emphasis.

Since 743 is such a crucial year in Hebrew and Assyrian relationships, any record that might throw additional light on exactly what took place that year could be highly important. The new Tiglath-Pileser stele, partially published by Levine in 1972 and concerning which he said he had additional materials that would be "forthcoming shortly," might provide information of interest and importance when it is made available. It is sincerely hoped that these will not be delayed much longer.

In the meantime I am here setting forth the biblical pattern of Hebrew reigns as based on the regnal data of Kings. This I have coordinated with the available materials from Assyrian sources. I have shown that the interval of 130 years from the death of Ahab in 853 to the death of Hoshea in 723 is exactly equal to the 130 years in Assyria from the sixth year of Shalmaneser III when in 853 he was engaged in the battle at Qarqar with Ahab to 723 when Samaria fell to Shalmaneser V. And I have shown that the interval of 140 years in Judah from the beginning of Athaliah to the fourteenth year of Hezekiah when Sennacherib came against him is exactly the same as the 140 years in Assyria from the eighteenth year of Shalmaneser III in 841 when Jehu paid tribute to him to the third campaign of Sennacherib in 701 when he went against Hezekiah in Jerusalem. Coordinations with such important years point strongly to similar coordinations at additional points of contact.

From Menahem my chronological pattern as coordinated with Assyria calls for a contact with Tiglath-Pileser III in either 743 or 742. Since Menahem is mentioned on the new stele, that stele is deserving of the fullest study as to the light it might give concerning the precise year in which he paid tribute to Assyria.

Assyrian historical stelae usually record events in sequence, from the early part of a ruler's reign to the time of the stele's erection. Levine says that the new stele was "probably written and erected in the year 737 B.C." In such a case it would be expected that the stele would deal with events from the commencement of Tiglath-Pileser's reign in 745 to the year 737.

Additional details concerning the left and the right sides of the stele are looked forward to with the keenest of interest.

CHAPTER EIGHT

The Siege and Fall
of Samaria

OR MANY YEARS scholars have been concerned with the problems connected with the exact year of the fall of Samaria and the end of the northern kingdom. The siege of Samaria was begun by Shalmaneser V in the seventh year of Hoshea and was continued for three years, to the ninth year of Hoshea, at which time the city fell and Israel was carried captive to Assyria (2 Kings 17:4–6; 18:9–11). Since Hoshea began his reign in 732/31, the seventh to the ninth years of his reign would be from 725/24 to 723/22, and this would mark the period of Samaria's final siege, with the city falling and the northern kingdom coming to its end in 723/22.

It will be remembered that inasmuch as the kings of Israel reckoned their years from Nisan to Nisan, the fall of Samaria must have taken place between Nisan 723 and Nisan 722. The date for the fall of Samaria raises an interesting problem posed by the claim of Sargon II that he captured Samaria at the beginning of his rule.[1] Sargon came to the throne on 12 Tebeth[2] (about the last

---

[1]Daniel David Luckenbill, *Ancient Records of Assyria and Babylonia*, vol. 2, sec. 4. At the beginning of this section of the annals, Luckenbill supplies the following restoration: "At the beginning of my rule, in my first year of reign." Lie, in his translation of the annals of Sargon, words this item as follows: "At the beginning of my government" (A. G. Lie, *The Inscriptions of Sargon II, King of Assyria*, part 1: *The Annals* [Paris, 1929], p. 5). The above statement is of considerable interest, coming as it does in 1. 10 of Lie's text of the recension of Hall II of Sargon's palace, immediately preceding the account of the siege and capture of Samaria that begins in 1. 11. It is not altogether clear just what Sargon has in mind by the statement, "At the beginning of my government," but it evidently is sometime before his first year, for in Olmstead's commentary on Lie's edition of the annals, the section dealing with Sargon's first year does not come until 1. 19 (A. T. Olmstead, "The Text of Sargon's Annals," *American Journal of Semitic Languages and Literatures* 47 [1930–31]: 263). Olmstead omits 1. 10, but he gives the following interesting items from 1. 15–18 regarding Sargon's claims concerning Samaria: "27,290 men who dwelt in it I carried off, fifty chariots for my royal army from among them I selected, and I caused others to take their portion [?]. That city I restored and more than before I made it great; men of the lands, conquered by my hands, in it I made to dwell. My official governor I established, and tribute and tax as upon Assyrians I placed upon them . . . with one another I mixed, and I made the price of silver to be like copper in Assyria." Then Olmstead begins 1. 19 with "In my first year of reign, Humbanigash the Elamite sinned the sin, and became hostile, to make war against me he came." Thus in this translation by Olmstead the section dealing with the siege and capture of Samaria precedes the account of Sargon's first year, when the revolt of Humbanigash took place.

[2]Babylonian Chronicle, 1:31.

of December 722) and his first year began in Nisan 721. The ninth and last year of Hoshea, however, according to our pattern of Hebrew chronology, terminated in Nisan 722, which is some nine months before Sargon came to the throne. It will be seen that if the fall of Samaria took place during the ninth year of Hoshea and if our date for that year is correct, the city must have fallen at least nine months before Sargon began his rule.

In a well-reasoned account concerning the fall of Samaria, Olmstead took the position that all the available evidence points to the fall of Samaria in 723 and that Sargon's claim to have captured the city was not true.[3] It was pointed out that the biblical account of the fall of Samaria makes no mention of Sargon. Shalmaneser is the king who is twice named as having taken punitive measures against Israel's recalcitrant king. In the record of 2 Kings 17:3–9, the account begins with the statement that "Shalmaneser king of Assyria" came up against Hoshea and that Hoshea became his servant. Then the record continues with the words that "the king of Assyria discovered that Hoshea was a traitor" because Hoshea no longer paid tribute to "the king of Assyria," and that thereupon "the king of Assyria" besieged Samaria three years, and that in the ninth year of Hoshea "the king of Assyria captured Samaria and deported the Israelites to Assyria." Which king of Assyria did all this? Or was there more than one king? It was "Shalmaneser king of Assyria" who is mentioned in the opening statement of the account as the king who first came up against Hoshea and placed him under tribute. But from that point on the Assyrian king is not mentioned by name but is always referred to as "the king of Assyria." If it was Shalmaneser who first put Hoshea under tribute, who was "the king of Assyria" against whom Hoshea rebelled? Everyone will admit that that was Shalmaneser. And who was "the king of Assyria" who besieged Samaria three years? Again, it is recognized that this also was Shalmaneser. But who, then, was "the king of Assyria" who in the ninth year of Hoshea captured Samaria and took its people captive to Assyria? If Shalmaneser was "the king of Assyria" in the first instance, if he was "the king of Assyria" in the second instance, and if he was likewise "the king of Assyria" in the third and the fourth instances, then who was "the king of Assyria" in the last instance? Having started the account by naming Shalmaneser as the Assyrian king, was not Shalmaneser the king who is referred to in this account from beginning to end? Why, if a new king came into the picture somewhere along the line, is he not referred to by name? The clear implication of this biblical account, as Olmstead forcibly points out, is that Shalmaneser is the king referred to all the way through. Olmstead notes that the Hebrew account seems to rest on very good sources and that there exists no reason there for any distortion of fact. In contrast, in the Assyrian account the "personal equation" must be taken into consideration; the royal Assyrian scribe would have every reason for carrying over into his master's reign events that took place in the final year of a predecessor.

Another item mentioned by Olmstead pointing to Samaria's capture by Shalmaneser rather than by Sargon is the testimony of the Babylonian Chroni-

[3] A. T. Olmstead, "The Fall of Samaria," *American Journal of Semitic Languages and Literatures* 21 (1904–5): 179–82; and *Western Asia in the Days of Sargon of Assyria 722–705 B.C.* (New York, 1908), pp. 45ff., n. 9.

cle, 1:28, where the only citation given concerning the reign of Shalmaneser is his destruction of the city of Sha-ma-ra-in, which Delitzsch identified as Samaria. If this identification is correct, for which Tadmor has presented strong evidence,[4] then the testimony of this independent and unbiased Babylonian authority would settle the question as to the fall of Samaria in Shalmaneser's reign.

The Eponym Chronicle at this point is not definitive, for the record here is unfortunately badly mutilated. It merely retains the word "against" for the eponymies of Mahdê, Ashur-ishmeani, and Shalmaneser in the years 725, 724, and 723, with the name completely missing for the site against which the campaign for each of those years was directed. The coincidence, however, of these three years with the three years of the Hebrew account of the siege of Samaria by Shalmaneser seems to Olmstead to justify supplying "Samaria" from the Babylonian Chronicle. Luckenbill likewise has restored "Samaria" for these three years in the Eponym Chronicle.[5]

Let us notice the chronicle at this point. For 726, the eponymy of Marduk-bêl-usur, the entry was "in the land." For 722, the eponymy of Urta-ilia, there was a reference, according to Luckenbill's restoration, to the foundation of the temple of Nabu having been torn up for repairs; and for 721, the eponymy of Nabu-târis, of Nabu having entered his new temple. If Sargon had accomplished such an important feat as capturing the city of Samaria in 722 and thus bringing to an end the history of the northern kingdom of Israel—a feat that he so proudly pretended to remember at the close of his reign—why did he not record that capture at the beginning of his reign? Why should not the capture of Samaria have been the event of the year 722 rather than a citation concerning the tearing up of a temple foundation? Or if it was in his first year, 721, that Samaria was taken, why was not that mentioned at least as one of the events of the year together with the entry of Nabu into his new temple? When in 720 he went against Tabala, Sargon recorded that as the event of the year. When in 718 he went against the Mannai, that was the event reported. When in 716 he went against Musasir of Haldia, again that was the event to remember. When in 715 he was in Ellipa, in 713 again went against Musasir, in 711 against Markasa, in 710 against Bet-zernaid, and in 709 took the hand of Bel in Babylon and did not hesitate to tell the world about it, why was he so very modest in 722 as to remember the tearing down of a temple of Nabu but forget the tearing down of the kingdom of Israel?

The biblical record, moreover, tells us that Shalmaneser came against Samaria and that the siege of that city lasted three years. In the Eponym Chronicle no campaign is recorded for 726—the king was in the land. And again, in 722 no campaign was recorded; only the repair of a temple is mentioned. Only three years are left—725, 724, and 723. In 725 Shalmaneser was engaged in a campaign against some city or kingdom the name of which has been lost. Again, for 724, the event of the year was simply "against," with once

---

[4]Hayim Tadmor, "The Campaigns of Sargon II of Assur: A Chronological-Historical Study," *Journal of Cuneiform Studies* 12 (1958): 39. About the only scholars to agree with Delitzsch in this identification were Haupt, Olmstead, and Borée.

[5]Luckenbill, *Ancient Records*, 2:437.

more the name being lost. And for a third successive year, 723, he again went "against," with once more the name being lost. What was the name of the place or places that he went against in 725, 724, and 723? At some time during his reign he went against Samaria. And in 725, 724, 723, he went against some place or places, the names of which have disappeared from the record. According to our reconstructed scheme of Old Testament chronology, Shalmaneser came against Samaria in 725, 724, and 723. So if the entry for those years is to be restored in the Eponym Chronicle, what should that restoration be? We have every reason to agree with Luckenbill and Olmstead that "Samaria" is the correct restoration.

Olmstead further points out that, inasmuch as Sargon came to the throne about the close of December, his accession year would consist of only four months of the worst season of the year, January to April, the rainy season when the Assyrian armies rarely took the field. Sargon's capture of Samaria at such a time would be very improbable.

Still another point of importance is that Sargon's claim to have been responsible for the fall of Samaria is entirely absent from the records that come from his early years; his claim to Samaria's capture is found only in the Khorsabad texts of his fifteenth and sixteenth years. Here in the final series of documents from the closing years of his reign, the capture of Samaria "at the beginning" of Sargon's rule is featured in great prominence for all posterity to remember. Thus it was on the annals appearing on the wall slabs of three of the halls of his newly constructed palace at Khorsabad.[6] Thus also it was on the so-called Display Inscription (German, *Prunkinschrift*) found on the walls of rooms IV, VII, VIII, and X of the palace of Khorsabad,[7] giving a review of the events from Sargon's accession to his fifteenth year. Once more this was the case on the Display Inscription of room XIV, where again Sargon claims to have plundered the city of Samirina (Samaria) and the whole land of Israel.[8] Yet again, on the Bull Inscription where he recounts the building of his famous palace at Dur Sharrukin, he claims Samaria's overthrow.[9] And finally, on the Pavement Inscriptions carved at the base of the palace gates, Sargon in a résumé of the accomplishments of his reign vaunts himself as the conqueror of Samaria and of the whole land of Bit-Humria.[10] If it was indeed a fact that Sargon had captured the city of Samaria at the beginning of his rule, then the question may well be asked why it took him so long to remember this fact. Why, if he captured Samaria so early in his reign, did he not tell of that capture in documents appearing from an earlier year?[11]

To summarize, Olmstead declares that for the capture of Samaria by Sargon we have only his own claim, made in a late series of documents that have

[6]Ibid., sec. 4.
[7]Ibid., sec. 55.
[8]Ibid., sec. 80.
[9]Ibid., sec. 92.
[10]Ibid., sec. 99.
[11]The only reference to Samaria that the writer is acquainted with on any document prior to the Khorsabad texts is Sargon's reference on the Ashur Charter to his gathering together the people of Arpad and Samaria and bringing them to his side (see Luckenbill, *Ancient Records*, vol. 2, sec. 134).

often been proved incorrect. Against this is the silence of Sargon's own earlier accounts and the direct ascription of the capture to Shalmaneser by two separate, independent, unprejudiced authorities—the Hebrew and the Babylonian—while a third, a native Assyrian account, presents data that would fit well into the Hebrew scheme. For the above reasons Olmstead argues for Samaria's capture by Shalmaneser rather than Sargon and places its capture in the year 723,[12] shortly before Sargon came to the throne.

More recently Hayim Tadmor in his brilliant analysis of the chronological and historical details of the records of Sargon II[13] has shown that Sargon did not and could not have captured Samaria at the beginning of his reign, either in the year of his accession or in his first year, 722 or 721, for the simple reason that in those years he was occupied at home in the endeavor to make his position on the throne secure. Not until 720 did he engage in a foreign campaign, first against strong Elamite forces in Babylon, and then against an Aramean-Palestinian coalition in the west headed by Hamath. It was at this time, late in 720, that Sargon first came to Samaria "to deport its people and to rebuild it as the center of a new province 'Samerina.' All references to the conquest of Samaria in Sargon's inscriptions thus refer to the events of 720."[14]

But how was it that Sargon in his annals described these events as taking place "at the beginning of my rule, in my first year of reign"? It was on the wall-slab inscriptions of Sargon's new palace at Khorsabad, dated not before his fifteenth year, 707, that these claims were made. Tadmor discusses at length the conflicting chronological details between events as recorded in the annals of Khorsabad and as they are found on the earlier prism fragments from Nineveh, and he gives the reasons why. It had now become the practice to presuppose "the existence of yearly campaigns. Hence, even into a peaceful year, when the king stayed in Assyria, some military events had to be filled."[15] Since the hero to be glorified at Khorsabad had no military campaigns during his first or his accession years, the royal scribes "attempted to suppress the fact that Sargon did not go to war during his first regnal year," and in the Khorsabad edition of the annals, three years before his death, an "effort was made to 'normalize' the chronology and to glorify Sargon's reign by starting the account of his wars with a major victory: a new passage about the conquest of Samaria was introduced, and the war with Elam and Tu'munu was transferred from his second to his first palu."[16]

Tadmor makes an important point of the fact that whereas "Hannun, the king of Gaza, and Yaubi'di, the king of Hamath, whom Samaria joined in rebellion, are usually referred to by name," in the case of Samaria it is "the 'Samarians' rather than to the '[King of the] Samarians'" that the Assyrian record makes reference, thus seeming to point to the fact that "there was no king in Samaria between 724/3–720."[17]

---

[12]A. T. Olmstead, *History of Assyria* (New York, 1923), p. 205.
[13]Tadmor, "Campaigns of Sargon II," pp. 22–42.
[14]Ibid., p. 38.
[15]Ibid., p. 30.
[16]Ibid., p. 31.
[17]Ibid., pp. 35, 37.

In his masterly analysis of these troublesome records of Sargon, Tadmor has made an important contribution in clearing up the many chronological discrepancies with which scholars have been struggling for years, and placing the events of that reign in their correct historical setting. And he has also gone far in making it clear how Sargon in such important palace inscriptions might claim the capture of Samaria without having been personally involved in the event, although he did quell a later revolt and transferred many of the citizens.

A survey of all the available evidence makes it clear that in spite of the pretentious claims of Sargon, Samaria was not captured by him while he was king, but the city fell while Shalmaneser V was on the throne. After the city fell, Sargon certainly had further contacts with it, such as the suppression of efforts at revolt that took place in his second year[18] and the placing of Arab captives there in his seventh year.[19]

Our discussion of the siege and fall of Samaria will not be complete if it does not include a brief consideration of the synchronisms of 2 Kings 18:9–10 that equate the seventh year of Hoshea with the fourth year of Hezekiah and the ninth year of Hoshea with Hezekiah's sixth year. In those synchronisms the reign of Hoshea was thrust twelve years ahead of its correct position. When that reign is restored to its correct date, the fall of Samaria and the end of Hoshea's rule will be found to have taken place before Hezekiah began his reign (cf. diagram 17, page 121). If that is the true situation, and if Hezekiah and Hoshea did not rule contemporaneously, it is possible that the biblical material concerning these kings might provide some indications to that effect. Let us examine the evidence.

First, let it be noted that the Old Testament is silent about any contacts between Hezekiah and Hoshea. This is unusual, for all through the records of the divided kingdoms we find constant references to the contacts between the contemporaneous rulers of Judah and Israel. Let us go through the list of kings of Judah thus far and notice the evidence in this regard. First, Rehoboam is said to have been at war with his contemporary, Jeroboam, all his days (1 Kings 14:30). Abijah, the next king, publicly upbraided his contemporary, Jeroboam, and engaged in a conflict with him (1 Kings 15:6; 2 Chron. 13:3–20). Judah's third king, Asa, again engaged in war with his contemporary, Baasha of Israel (1 Kings 15:16–22; 2 Chron. 16:1–6). Jehoshaphat, the son of Asa, was friendly with Ahab and accompanied him in a battle against Aram (1 Kings 22:2–37; 2 Chron. 18:1–34). Jehoram, the son and successor of Jehoshaphat, married Athaliah, the daughter of Ahab and Jezebel (2 Kings 8:18, 26; 2 Chron. 21:6). The next king, Ahaziah, went with Joram of Israel against Hazael of Aram and visited Joram in Jezreel (2 Kings 8:28–29; 2 Chron. 22:5–6), and then was slain with Joram by Jehu (2 Kings 9:27; 2 Chron. 22:7–9). Athaliah, the daughter of Ahab and Jezebel (2 Kings 8:18, 26; 2 Chron. 22:2), after her son Ahaziah had been killed by Jehu, attempted to destroy the royal seed and seized the throne of Judah at the same time that Jehu seized the throne in Israel (2 Kings 9:27; 11:1–3). Concerning the following king, Joash, no specific mention is made of

---

[18]Lie, *Inscriptions of Sargon II*, p. 7; Luckenbill, *Ancient Records*, vol. 2, sec. 55.

[19]Lie, *Inscriptions of Sargon II*, p. 23; Luckenbill, *Ancient Records*, vol. 2, sec. 17.

any direct contact. Amaziah, the son of Joash, hired an army from Israel (2 Chron. 25:6–10) and later rashly challenged Jehoash to a war and was disastrously defeated (2 Kings 14:8–14; 2 Chron. 25:17–24). Azariah, the next ruler, is the only other king of Judah till Hezekiah and his successors concerning whom no mention is made of some contact with Israel. At the time of Jotham and Ahaz, Pekah associated with Rezin in a war against Judah (2 Kings 15:37; 16:5; 2 Chron. 28:6; Isa. 7:1–7). When we come to Ahaz's son, Hezekiah, however, there is no reference anywhere in the record of a contact with Hoshea. Such an argument from silence does not alone prove that Israel as a nation was then no longer in existence, for, although the general rule is an account of some contact, we have had two previous kings concerning whom no record of a contact has been preserved. However, if some specific contact between Hezekiah and Hoshea had been mentioned, we would at least be in possession of that definite evidence that these two kings were contemporaneous. But no such evidence exists.

Our next step is to examine the record to see what light can be thrown on conditions then prevailing in the territory to the north. When Hezekiah first came to the throne, one of his first acts in the first month of the first year was to open and repair the temple (2 Chron. 29:3, 17) and to proclaim a solemn Passover that was observed the fourteenth day of the second month (2 Chron. 30:2, 13, 15). Verse 1 of chapter 30 begins with a *waw* conversive, which usually indicates a continuation of the previous narrative. Verse 3 gives as the reason for holding the Passover in the second month rather than the first (as was the usual custom) the fact that the priests had not sanctified themselves sufficiently (which clearly refers back to 29:34) and that the people had not yet gathered at Jerusalem. The main work of cleansing the temple occupied the first eight days of the first month, and the cleansing was not completed until the sixteenth day of the first month (2 Chron. 29:17); hence to hold the Passover in the first month would have been out of the question.

An interesting item concerning the invitations for this Passover was that they were sent not only to places in Judah but also in Israel—to Ephraim and Manasseh and even to Zebulun (2 Chron. 30:1, 6, 10), territory that once had been the domain of the northern kingdom but was now open to the envoys of Judah. When Joash repaired the temple during the period of the divided kingdom, there was no record of invitations having been sent to Israel, but only to Judah and Jerusalem (2 Chron. 24:5, 9). While the northern kingdom was still in existence, it would not, of course, have been possible for the envoys of Judah to pass through the territory of Israel; so we have here a clear indication that it was no longer in existence.[20] Hezekiah sent forth his decree all the way from Beersheba to Dan (2 Chron. 30:5), the latter being the northern limit of the

---

[20]Scholars have long noticed the inconsistencies involved in the attempt to apply the narrative of Hezekiah's first Passover to a period when the northern kingdom was still in existence (see Otto Zöckler, *The Books of the Chronicles*, trans. James G. Murphy, in *A Commentary on the Holy Scriptures: Critical, Doctrinal and Homiletical*, ed. John Peter Lange [New York, 1877], 7:259; Edward Lewis Curtis and Albert Alonzo Madsen, *A Critical and Exegetical Commentary on the Books of Chronicles*, International Critical Commentary [New York, 1910], p. 471; Keil, *Commentary on the Books of Kings*, trans. James Murphy [Edinburgh, 1857], 2:79ff., n. I).

undivided kingdom of David and Solomon (1 Chron. 21:2). At the time when the northern kingdom was still in existence, Jehoshaphat extended his reforms only from Beersheba to the hill country of Ephraim (2 Chron. 19:4).

Hezekiah's admonitions were expressly addressed to a nation that was in deep distress and desolation and whose people had already gone into captivity, for the ones who would now receive his letters were spoken of as those who had escaped out of the hand of the kings of Assyria (2 Chron. 30:6). Their forebears had been made objects of horror (2 Chron. 30:7). If they now turned to the Lord and came to the sanctuary at Jerusalem, their brothers might obtain mercy from the ones who had taken them captive (2 Chron. 30:8–9).

Although these invitations were largely spurned, there was a considerable response from Asher, Manasseh, Ephraim, Issachar, and Zebulun (2 Chron. 30:11, 18). No such Passover had been observed in Jerusalem since the days of Solomon (2 Chron. 30:26), before the nation was divided, when the people from all the land, north as well as south, were accustomed to coming to Jerusalem for worship. When the Passover was over, the people went forth to break the sacred stones, cut down the Asherah poles, and throw down the altars, not only in Judah and Benjamin, but also in Ephraim and Manasseh; and they did not cease "until they had destroyed all of them" (2 Chron. 31:1).

The above description can only apply to one time and condition—a time when there was no longer a tight political separation between Israel and Judah, a time when there was no longer a king in the north who would keep out unwanted intruders from the south, a time when the northern kingdom was no longer in existence. Such things could not have happened while Israel remained a sovereign state. No king of Israel would have permitted envoys from his rival to the south to march through his land inviting his subjects to attend a general festival at the rival capital. Particularly, Israel's last king was not the type to have tolerated such a procedure and then to have watched an iconoclastic crowd from the south move through his kingdom smashing all places of worship that were so far out of harmony with Jerusalem but so much in accord with Bethel and Dan. When the northern nation fell, the reason given is that it had gone over to idolatry (2 Kings 17:6–23). But such a statement would be decidedly out of place if at this time such striking evidence of religious reform and pietistic zeal had manifested itself with the full consent of the king. There was a time when such things could not be and that time continued as long as Hoshea was still on Israel's throne. Once he was gone, the borders were open and the atmosphere again was free, and the holy zeal of Jerusalem and its temple could make its influence felt throughout the length and breadth of the land. No more striking testimony could be desired that the kingdom of Israel had already come to its end at the time of the celebration of the first Passover of Hezekiah in the first year of his reign than is found in 2 Chronicles 30:1–31:1.

We might also ask what the foreign policy of Judah was at the time the armies of Assyria were laying siege to Samaria and bringing the northern nation of Israel to its end. We know well the pro-Assyrian policy of Ahaz and the anti-Assyrian policy of Hezekiah. Whose policy was being followed in Judah during the last years that Hoshea was on the throne of Israel? With Ahaz there would have been conciliation toward Assyria. But with Hezekiah there would have been decided resistance, a policy that might well have left its mark on both the secular and biblical records. Whitehouse has suggested that the year 715, assigned by Kamphausen to the death of Ahaz, is supported by the fact that it affords a clue to the foreign policy of Judah during the siege of Samaria—a policy that could hardly have been anything else than friendly neutrality toward Assyria. Such a policy would have been in keeping with Ahaz but definitely not with Hezekiah. When Hezekiah took the throne, the policy of Isaiah involving resistance to the encroachments of Assyrian power became ascendant.[21] Hoshea clearly was gone when Hezekiah became king.

This completes our discussion of the main chronological and historical details of the period of the Hebrew monarchies. We believe we have set forth a true picture, placing each king of each nation in his proper place in relationship to others of his own nation and to those in the broader world in which he lived. That was a world not of fancy but of fact. Its men often came into contact with the characters of the Bible. We have met some of them in these pages—Tiglath-Pileser III, Shalmaneser V, Sargon II, and Sennacherib. These were men of flesh and blood as were also Pekah, Hoshea, Azariah, Ahaz, and Hezekiah. They moved about in the same world. They had dealings with each other on terms of peace and war—Tiglath-Pileser III with Azariah and Menahem, and with Ahaz, Pekah, and Hoshea; Shalmaneser V with Hoshea of Israel; and Sennacherib with Hezekiah of Judah. The contacts of these men were tangible and took place in a world that was very real. The contacts of Tiglath-Pileser with Azariah and Menahem necessarily occurred while all lived at the same time—not twenty years after Menahem and Azariah were in their graves as some systems of "biblical" chronology require. When Sennacherib came against Hezekiah to drive him from his throne, it was not Sennacherib who became king some seven years after that memorable fourteenth year of Hezekiah in which this conflict took place. Let us remember that if history is to consist of fact rather than fiction, then the men of the world and the men of the Word must move along together in lands where time advances at an even pace. The years of the world in which the Assyrians lived kept constantly in accord with the years of the world in which the Hebrews lived. True biblical chronology moved right along together with the chronology of Aram as well as Assyria, and with Babylon as well as Egypt. If the chronology of the world in which the Assyrians and Babylonians lived moved along in tune with the stars, then the chronology of the world in which the Hebrews lived must likewise have moved along in tune with the same firmament of heaven—not faster or slower, but exactly in accord with the other. And if we find time for the Hebrews going faster or slower than it did for the men of Assyria or Egypt, should we not pause long enough to ask just what the cause might be? If the men of the Bible were real men and if the chronology of the Bible is correct, then that chronology must be in harmony with the chronology of every neighboring state. We cannot have men of Israel and men of Babylon or Assyria looking each other in the face if they lived a score or more years apart. Intelligent Bible students cannot deal with figures for men that constitute pious fancy but historical untruth.

---

[21]Schrader, *Cuneiform Inscriptions;* Notes and Addenda by Whitehouse, 2:322.

What we in these pages have been endeavoring to do is to get down to basic facts for both the men of Israel and Judah and the men of the Assyrian Empire. And when we deal with facts—the facts of the Bible as well as the facts of the Assyrian monuments—all these facts will be found to agree with each other, and the years of the men of Jerusalem and Samaria will move along at exactly the same pace as the years of the men of Calah and Nineveh, of Khorsabad and Ashur.

The history of the northern kingdom is now completed. We have observed striking agreement of the chronology of Israel with that of Assyria at such places where definite contacts between the two nations may be established. This has given us confidence that we are dealing with the absolute chronology of both countries. The use by the Books of Kings, as has been demonstrated, of two diverse systems of chronological reckoning for the Hebrew monarchies and their interweaving in the way we find them, together with the evidence of shifts in the systems of reckoning by both Israel and Judah, demands that the writers had access to official chronicles that were correct and that were cited accurately. It is an interesting aspect of their faithfulness and their competence that within a single passage, as so often happens, they readily and quickly swung from one system to another and back again if need be. In all this complex procedure they were able to keep their bearings and pass on to us a record so straight that we today, once the principles of the system are understood, are able to unravel the seemingly tangled skein and reproduce the original pattern.

CHAPTER NINE

The Chronology of the Kings of Judah (715–561 B.C.)

WITH ISRAEL HAVING come to its end, the task of carrying through the reconstruction of the chronology of Judah to its end must proceed without the aid of cross references to the years of the northern kings. Troublesome though the data at times have been, this complete information made possible the task of reconstructing the chronology without guesswork. Without the synchronisms, we would have had no information concerning the existence of certain coregencies or of the methods of reckoning them. And lacking this information, an exact chronological reconstruction would not have been possible. In the period before us we shall be deprived of the invaluable assistance that these synchronisms have furnished. Not until we reach the time when synchronisms are available with Babylonian kings will we have the certain evidence that we are again on solid ground. If there should be a coregency in the century with which we are about to deal, the only means of ascertaining this fact will be to go on to the next fixed date in the history of Judah and then to compare the number of years in this interval with the recorded years of the kings for the same period.

Such a fixed date at the end of the century is provided by the Babylonian Chronicle, which gives the exact date when Nebuchadnezzar captured Jerusalem and took Jehoiachin prisoner to Babylon.[1] That was 2 Adar (15/16 March), 597 B.C.

From 686, the last year of Hezekiah, to 597 is eighty-nine years. The Hebrew rulers during this interval are as follows:

Manasseh	55 years	
Amon	2 years	
Josiah	31 years	
Jehoahaz		3 months
Jehoiakim	11 years	
Jehoiachin		3 months
Total:	99 years,	6 months

---

[1] D. J. Wiseman, *Chronicles of Chaldaean Kings* (London, 1956), p. 33.

To fit ninety-nine years and six months of Hebrew regnal time into eighty-nine years of contemporary time calls for a coregency of ten or eleven years among the above rulers. If we still had such a valuable source as the synchronisms between Israel and Judah proved to be, we would know exactly where that coregency took place. Now, however, we must search the available evidence. The task is not difficult. Three of the rulers eliminate themselves because they were not placed on the throne by their predecessors. Josiah at the age of eight was placed on the throne by the people after Amon was slain by his servants. Jehoahaz was placed on the throne by the people after Josiah lost his life at the hands of Neco. And Jehoiakim was placed on the throne by Neco, who had deposed Jehoahaz. Amon spent two years on the throne, but that was not while Manasseh was king, for "unlike his father Manasseh, he did not humble himself before the LORD" (2 Chron. 33:23). Jehoiachin reigned only three months, and that would not take up much of the ten or eleven years for a coregency.

That leaves only Manasseh, and everything points to his having spent ten or eleven of his fifty-five years on the throne as coregent with Hezekiah.

In 701 Hezekiah faced death with a serious illness. He was told by Isaiah to set his house in order, for he would die. But after an earnest petition to God he was granted an additional fifteen years of life (2 Kings 20:1-7). With that knowledge Hezekiah would lose little time before placing his son on the throne with himself to give him all possible training in leadership.

It is on the basis of a coregency of Manasseh with Hezekiah from 696 to 686 that we will proceed with the dates of Judah's kings for the last century of Judah's history.

33. Hezekiah—Judah—715–686

2 Kings 18:1–20:21; 2 Chronicles 29:1–32:33
Synchronisms: late and artificial accession = 3d of Hoshea
                              4th year = 7th of Hoshea
                              6th year = 9th of Hoshea
Length of reign: 29 years
14th year—701—attack by Sennacherib on Jerusalem

The date of 701 for the attack of Sennacherib in the fourteenth year of Hezekiah is a key point in my chronological pattern for the Hebrew rulers. This is a precise date from which we may go forward or backward on the basis of the regnal data to all other dates in our pattern. Full confidence can be placed in 701 as the fourteenth year of Hezekiah, and complete confidence can be placed in any other dates for either Israel or Judah reckoned from that date in accord with the requirements of the numbers in Kings.

In a discussion of the regnal data of Hezekiah, it is of paramount importance that the synchronisms between him and Hoshea be recognized as late and artificial. These synchronisms came into being because the final editor of Kings did not understand dual dating for Pekah. Because of this he began the twenty years of Pekah in 740, the fifty-second year of Azariah (see diagram 18, page 130). But the twenty years actually began in 752. This was the same year when Menahem began. Having thrust the commencement of Pekah twelve years ahead, from 752 to 740, the editor also thrust the beginning of Hoshea twelve years ahead, from 732 to 720. In such a case the nine years of Hoshea would terminate in 711, not in 723 as they actually did. But with Hoshea being given the terminal date of 711 his years would overlap those of Hezekiah, who began in 715. This brought into being the synchronisms of 2 Kings 17 and 18.

There was no overlap between Hoshea and Hezekiah. Hoshea was dead and the kingdom of Israel was no longer in existence when Hezekiah took the throne. The siege of Samaria ended in 723 and Hezekiah did not begin till 716/15.

There is solid evidence for 723 as the year when Samaria fell. Such outstanding Assyriologists as Olmstead and Tadmor have presented the facts in this regard. And there is no question concerning 701 as the fourteenth year of Hezekiah when Sennacherib came against him.

The biblical records of Hezekiah's reign in Chronicles and Kings make it clear that the nation of Israel was no longer in existence and that Hoshea was gone when Hezekiah began his reign. The main details in this regard have been presented in chapter 8 on "The Siege and Fall of Samaria." Here I will present only a few of the outstanding details. It is important to notice what the Scriptures say concerning Hezekiah's first year on the throne.

In his first year Hezekiah engaged in an earnest work of religious reform. Under Ahaz the temple had been defiled, its religious services had been disrupted, and gross idolatry had been practiced throughout the land (2 Kings 16:4, 10–18; 2 Chron. 28:3–4, 23–25). But Hezekiah reestablished the temple services, cleansed the temple of its defilements, and issued a solemn proclamation for all the people of both Israel and Judah to attend a great Passover service at Jerusalem. Concerning this the Book of Chronicles gives the following report:

> Hezekiah sent word to all Israel and Judah and also wrote letters to Ephraim and Manasseh, inviting them to come to the temple of the LORD in Jerusalem and celebrate the Passover to the LORD, the God of Israel. . . . They decided to send a proclamation throughout Israel, from Beersheba to Dan, calling the people to come to Jerusalem and celebrate the Passover to the LORD, the God of Israel. It had not been celebrated in large numbers according to what was written.
>
> At the king's command, couriers went throughout Israel and Judah with letters from the king and from his officials, which read: "People of Israel, return to the LORD, the God of Abraham, Isaac and Israel, that he may return to you who are left, who have escaped from the hand of the kings of Assyria. Do not be like your fathers and brothers, who were unfaithful to the LORD, the God of their fathers, so that he made them an object of horror, as you see. . . ."
>
> The couriers went from town to town in Ephraim and Manasseh, as far as Zebulun, but the people scorned and ridiculed them. Nevertheless, some men of Asher, Manasseh and Zebulun humbled themselves and went to Jerusalem. . . .

The entire assembly of Judah rejoiced, along with the priests and Levites and all who had assembled from Israel, including the aliens who had come from Israel and those who lived in Judah. There was great joy in Jerusalem, for since the days of Solomon son of David king of Israel there had been nothing like this in Jerusalem.[2]

This account makes it clear that when Hezekiah in the first year of his reign issued this decree for "all Israel and Judah," from "Beersheba to Dan" (1 Chron. 30:1, 5), he was treating the Hebrews as one state, north as well as south, under his jurisdiction. That would not have been possible if Hoshea had still been king. A remnant remained who had "escaped from the hand of the kings of Assyria" (v. 6). Some had become "an object of horror" (v. 7). Many were in captivity (v. 9). Hoshea was gone when Hezekiah began.

Nowhere in the record of Hezekiah's reign is mention made of any contact by him with Hoshea. In less serious times there was almost always a mention in the account of a king of Judah of some contact with the corresponding king of Israel, but none is found here. If it had been during the days of the God-fearing Hezekiah that Assyria was bringing Israel to its end, it is almost certain that Hezekiah would have had some contact with Hoshea and mentioned that contact. The deafening silence in this regard is a clear indication that Hoshea and his kingdom were no more when Hezekiah began.

The time when Merodach-Baladan, "king of Babylon," sent envoys to congratulate Hezekiah on his recent recovery (2 Kings 20:12; Isa. 39:1) must have been shortly after Hezekiah's illness in 701. At that time, however, Merodach-Baladan was no longer on the throne in Babylon, having lost his throne to Assyria a few years before. Bel-ibni, a native Chaldean and probably a member of the family of Merodach-Baladan, had been made king by the Assyrians and ruled from 702 to 700. During this period Merodach-Baladan was a king in exile and was openly active against Assyria. Hearing of Hezekiah's bold and successful stand against Sennacherib, the erstwhile Babylonian monarch might have thought of Hezekiah as a valuable ally against Assyria. The moment was opportune for such an embassy.

During his last ten years (696–686), Hezekiah associated Manasseh with him as regent.

34. Manasseh—Judah—regent—696–686
—696–642—total reign

2 Kings 21:1–18; 2 Chronicles 33:1–20
Length of reign: 55 years[3]
Taken in shackles to Babylon by the king of Assyria

The details of the coregency of Manasseh as regent with Hezekiah from 696 to 686 have been discussed in the opening part of this chapter. Such a

---

[2] 2 Chronicles 30:1, 5–7, 10–11, 25–26.

[3] The difference in elapsed time between the years given here and the biblical record is due to the variance of calendar years and not an incorrect chronology. See footnote on page 87 for a fuller discussion of this issue.

coregency is called for by the excess of ten years in the reigns of the kings of Judah from the death of Hezekiah in 686 to the accession of Jehoiachin in 597.

Chart 21
709–697 B.C.

	709	708	707	706	705	704	703	702	701	700	699	698	697
JUDAH													
Hezekiah	7	8	9	10	11	12	13	14	15	16	17	18	

Regnal years begin with Tishri.
Accession-year reckoning.

Chart 22
697–685 B.C.

697—Manasseh—55 years—2 Kings 21:1

	697	696	695	694	693	692	691	690	689	688	687	686	685
JUDAH													
Hezekiah	19	20	21	22	23	24	25	26	27	28	29		
Manasseh (regent)	1	2	3	4	5	6	7	8	9	10	11	12	

Regnal years begin with Tishri.
Accession-year reckoning.
Manasseh was coregent with Hezekiah from 696 to 686.
The regency of Manasseh begins with an official first year.

Stricken with a serious illness in 701 from which it seemed certain that he was about to die, Hezekiah offered earnest petitions to God and was told by Isaiah that the Lord had granted him an additional fifteen years of life (2 Kings 20:1–6; Isa. 38:1–6). With this message from God, Hezekiah at the earliest opportunity associated Manasseh with himself on the throne to give him every possible training in carrying on the affairs of state. This was when Manasseh was twelve (2 Kings 21:1), when he had become *gadol*. Recall that when Jesus was twelve He reminded His parents that He had reached the time when He should be about His Father's business (Luke 2:42, 49).

Chart 23
685–674 B.C.

	685	684	683	682	681	680	679	678	677	676	675	674
JUDAH												
Manasseh	12	13	14	15	16	17	18	19	20	21	22	23

Regnal years begin with Tishri.
Accession-year reckoning.
The years of Manasseh are reckoned from the start of his coregency.

Chart 24
674–663 B.C.

	674	673	672	671	670	669	668	667	666	665	664	663
JUDAH Manasseh	23	24	25	26	27	28	29	30	31	32	33	34

Regnal years begin with Tishri.
Accession-year reckoning.
The years of Manasseh are reckoned from the start of his coregency.

Chart 25
663–652 B.C.

	663	662	661	660	659	658	657	656	655	654	653	652
JUDAH Manasseh	34	35	36	37	38	39	40	41	42	43	44	45

Regnal years begin with Tishri.
Accession-year reckoning.
The years of Manasseh are reckoned from the start of his coregency.

Chart 26
652–641 B.C.

642—Amon—2 years—2 Kings 21:19

	652	651	650	649	648	647	646	645	644	643	642	641
JUDAH Manasseh	45	46	47	48	49	50	51	52	53	54	55	
Amon											ac	1

Regnal years begin with Tishri.
Accession-year reckoning.
The years of Manasseh are reckoned from the start of his coregency.

The army commander of an Assyrian king took Manasseh in shackles to Babylon (2 Chron. 33:11). There is no mention, however, of who this king was. Two Assyrian monarchs, Esarhaddon (681–669) and Ashurbanipal (669–633) said Manasseh paid tribute to them.[4]

35. Amon—Judah—642–640

2 Kings 21:19–26; 2 Chronicles 33:21–25
Length of reign: 2 years

----

[4]Pritchard, *Ancient Near Eastern Texts*, pp. 291, 294.

Chart 27
641–630 B.C.

640—Josiah—31 years—2 Kings 22:1

JUDAH
Amon
Josiah

	641	640	639	638	637	636	635	634	633	632	631	630
Amon	1	2										
Josiah		ac	1	2	3	4	5	6	7	8	9	10

Regnal years begin with Tishri.
Accession-year reckoning.

Chart 28
630–619 B.C.

13th year of Josiah—Jeremiah begins his warnings—23 years to
the 4th year of Jehoiakim—Jer. 25:1–3

JUDAH
Josiah
BABYLON
Nabopolassar

JEREMIAH'S WARNINGS

	630	629	628	627	626	625	624	623	622	621	620	619
Josiah	10	11	12	13	14	15	16	17	18	19	20	21
Nabopolassar					ac	1	2	3	4	5*	6	7
Jeremiah's warnings				1	2	3	4	5	6	7	8	9

*Lunar eclipse—5th year of Nabopolassar—22 April 621 B.C.
Nabopolassar ruled 21 years.
Judah: Tishri years.
Babylon: Nisan years.
Accession-year reckoning for both Judah and Babylon.

The period before us is in some respects the most interesting and fruitful of all for biblical chronological study. For no other period is there such a wealth of detailed chronological information, both biblical and extrabiblical. These ancient contemporary historical data make it possible to know what was going on in the important nations roundabout Israel; thus at a very critical period of Hebrew history, we have light available concerning exactly what was happening in Babylon and Egypt. There are frequent cross references between Hebrew and Babylonian kings that facilitate the precise and certain dating of events. Dates are now expressed not only in terms of years but at times in terms of months or days.

Babylonian tablets in the British Museum now provide records for the following years in the period here under review:

King	Regnal Years	Dates B.C.	Tablet Number
Nabopolassar	ac- 3	626-23	B.M. 25127
Nabopolassar	10-17	616-9	B.M. 21901
Nabopolassar	18-20	608-6	B.M. 22047
Nabopolassar	21	605	B.M. 21946
Nebuchadnezzar	ac-11	605-594	B.M. 21946
Neriglissar	3	556	B.M. 25124
Nabonidus	ac-17	555-39	B.M. 35382

Although there are certain important periods not represented, such as the twelfth year of Nebuchadnezzar to the close of his reign, there is material of great importance to the period under review.

Babylonian tablets provide, among others, the following fixed dates for the period we are about to discuss:

Egyptian campaign to the Euphrates, against Haran		609 B.C.
Babylonian victory at Carchemish, Hatti-land taken		605
Death of Nabopolassar	16 August	605
Accession of Nebuchadnezzar	7 September	605
Jerusalem taken by Nebuchadnezzar	16 March	597
Jehoiachin captured; Zedekiah made king		597

But numerous difficulties must be faced. If harmony is to be achieved in bringing together the many data left by the various biblical writers, it is necessary to understand how each dealt with the reigns under discussion.

A careful examination indicates that all biblical writers of this period used the accession-year system for Hebrew, Babylonian, and Persian kings.

But there were wide diversities concerning the months with which regnal years began. The recorders in Kings continued to use Tishri years for Hebrew kings and apparently also for Babylonian rulers. Ezra-Nehemiah used Hebrew Tishri years for Persia, although Persia itself had Nisan years. The evidence for Tishri reckoning is found in Nehemiah 1:1 and 2:1, for Nehemiah was in the palace with Artaxerxes in Kislev of the twentieth year, and the following Nisan was still in the twentieth year. That would have been the twenty-first year if the regnal year had been reckoned from Nisan. Such writers as Jeremiah, Ezekiel, Haggai, and Zechariah used Nisan years for Hebrew kings and also for the rulers of Babylon and Persia. Daniel used Tishri years for Hebrew kings. The accompanying charts should be consulted to note the details in individual cases. Only when the above points are understood will the data of the biblical writers of this period fit harmoniously together.

36. Josiah—Judah—640–609

2 Kings 22:1–23:30; 2 Chronicles 34:1–35:27

Length of reign: 31 years

627—13th year of Josiah; Jeremiah began his warnings (Jer. 25:3)

Jeremiah continued his warnings for 23 years to the 4th of Jehoiakim (Jer. 25:1, 3)

609—Josiah slain at Megiddo by Neco of Egypt (2 Kings 23:29)

Chart 29
619–608 B.C.

609—Jehoahaz—3 months—2 Kings 23:31
609—Jehoiakim—11 years—2 Kings 23:36

		619	618	617	616	615	614	613	612	611	610	609	608
Tishri years	**JUDAH**												
	{ Josiah	21	22	23	24	25	26	27	28	29	30	31	
	Jehoahaz											ac	
	Jehoiakim												ac
Nisan years	{ Josiah		21	22	23	24	25	26	27	28	29	30	31
	Jehoahaz												ac
	Jehoiakim												ac |1
	BABYLON												
	Nabopolassar	7	8	9	10	11	12	13	14	15	16	17	18
	JEREMIAH'S WARNINGS	9	10	11	12	13	14	15	16	17	18	19	20

Judah: Tishri years in Kings and Daniel
        Nisan years in Jeremiah
Babylon: Nisan years

With the close of Josiah's reign we find positive contacts with established Babylonian years. Nabonassar was then on the throne in Babylon, and his years have been confirmed by an eclipse of the moon that took place in the fifth year of his reign on 22 April 621 B.C. The 621 anchor date enables us to arrive at 605 as the twenty-first and last year of Nabopolassar and the accession of Nebuchadnezzar. This also provides fixed dates for the remaining rulers of Babylon and for any Hebrew rulers with whom precise contacts with Babylon took place.

The chronological details concerning the death of Josiah at the hands of Neco of Egypt and his succession by Jehoahaz in 609 can now be set forth with clarity and certainty. In Tammuz of 609 (25 June to 23 July) the Assyrian king Ashur-uballit, accompanied by a large Egyptian army, crossed the Euphrates and engaged a Babylonian garrison stationed in Haran. The attack continued to the month of Elul (22 Aug. to 20 Sept.). This was the Egyptian army under Neco that Josiah tried to stop at Megiddo, resulting in his death (2 Kings 23:29–30). Jehoahaz was then placed on the throne by the people and, after a reign of only three months, was replaced by Jehoiakim, who was put on the throne by Neco on his return from the north (2 Kings 23:30–35). With the aid of the Babylonian material the chronology of this period can now be established. Diagram 20 shows the details.

The end of Josiah's thirty-one years took place during Tammuz of 609 B.C. when Jehoahaz began his reign of three months. Since Josiah terminated his reign in 609, his accession took place in 641/40.

Diagram 20

609 B.C.

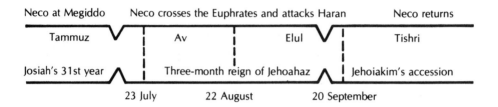

Neco at Megiddo	Neco crosses the Euphrates and attacks Haran	Neco returns
Tammuz	Av	Elul	Tishri
Josiah's 31st year	Three-month reign of Jehoahaz	Jehoiakim's accession
23 July	22 August	20 September

37. Jehoahaz—Judah—609

2 Kings 23:31–35; 2 Chronicles 36:1–4
Length of reign: 3 months
609—deposed by Neco of Egypt and replaced by Jehoiakim (2 Kings 23:33–34)

The circumstances of the three-month reign of Jehoahaz are set forth in diagram 20 above and were noted in the discussion of Josiah's reign. When Neco returned from Megiddo, he deposed Jehoahaz and took him as a prisoner to Egypt. Neco then put Jehoiakim, another son of Josiah, on the throne.

The reign of Jehoahaz began in Tammuz (25 June to 23 July) of 609 and terminated three months later in September or October.

38. Jehoiakim—Judah—609–598

2 Kings 23:36–24:7; 2 Chronicles 36:5–8
Length of reign: 11 years
605—3d year of Jehoiakim; Nebuchadnezzar came against Jerusalem (Dan. 1:1)
605—4th year of Jehoiakim; 23d year of Jeremiah's warnings (Jer. 25:1, 3)

Jehoiakim became king of Judah when he was placed on the throne by Neco of Egypt, who deposed Jehoahaz and took him prisoner to Egypt. Judah was placed under tribute to Egypt.

Egyptian domination of Palestine was not to continue long, for Babylon was at this time making a strong drive to control the Mediterranean coastlands. Almost every year during this period a Babylonian army under the command of Nabopolassar or his son Nebuchadnezzar drove westward from Babylon toward the Mediterranean coast and then southward toward Judah and Egypt.

In the eighteenth year of Nabopolassar (608 B.C. according to the Babylonian Chronicle), the campaign was up the Tigris in the mountainous area of Urartu. The next year, 607, there was a campaign in which Nebuchadnezzar is specifically mentioned as having commanded part of the Babylonian army. Later that year Nabopolassar crossed the Euphrates and seized the city of Kimuhu, located close to the Egyptian stronghold of Carchemish, and left a garrison there as a guard against the forces of Egypt. The following year, 606, the Egyptians attacked Kimuhu and after a four-month siege captured the city.

Chart 30
608–597 B.C.

1st of Nebuchadnezzar—4th of Jehoiakim—23 years of warnings by
Jeremiah—Jer. 25:1, 3
8th of Nebuchadnezzar—Jehoiachin taken to Babylon—
2 Kings 24:12
605—3d of Jehoiakim—Nebuchadnezzar at Jerusalem—Dan. 1:1
597—Jehoachin—3 months—2 Kings 24:8
597—Zedekiah—11 years—2 Kings 24:18

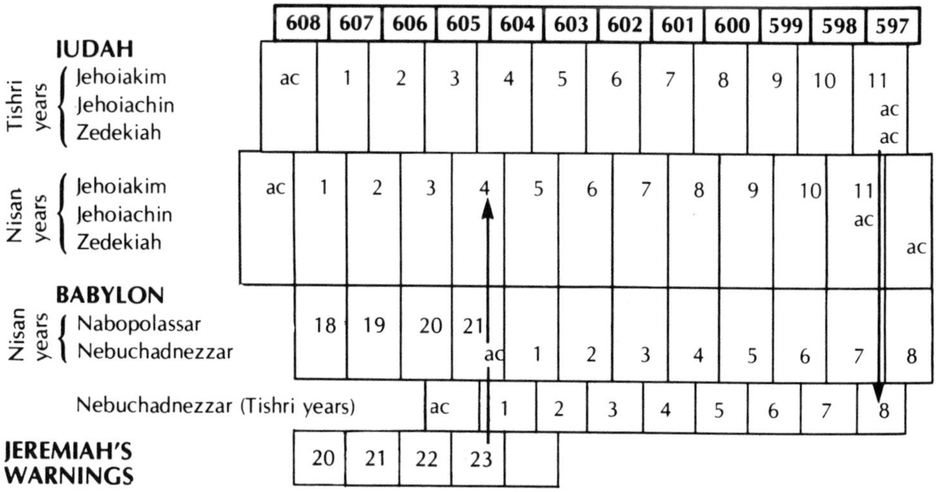

		608	607	606	605	604	603	602	601	600	599	598	597
IUDAH													
Tishri years	Jehoiakim	ac	1	2	3	4	5	6	7	8	9	10	11
	Jehoiachin												ac
	Zedekiah												ac
Nisan years	Jehoiakim	ac	1	2	3	4	5	6	7	8	9	10	11
	Jehoiachin											ac	
	Zedekiah												ac
BABYLON													
Nisan years	Nabopolassar	18	19	20	21								
	Nebuchadnezzar				ac	1	2	3	4	5	6	7	8
Nebuchadnezzar (Tishri years)			ac		1	2	3	4	5	6	7		8
JEREMIAH'S WARNINGS		20	21	22	23								

Judah: Tishri years in Kings and Daniel
Nisan years in Jeremiah and Ezekiel
Babylon: Nisan years in Babylonian records
Tishri years in Daniel

Nabopolassar responded by establishing a garrison at Quramati on the east bank of the Euphrates. Early in 605 the Egyptians crossed the Euphrates and drove the Babylonians from Quramati.

Nabopolassar stayed at home in his twenty-first year, beginning with Nisan, 605, but sent Nebuchadnezzar with the army against Carchemish. A disastrous defeat was inflicted on the Egyptians. A remnant that fled to Hamath was wiped out with the result that "Nebuchadnezzar conquered the whole area of the Hatti-country." This includes all of Aram and the territory south to the borders of Egypt. Babylon rather than Egypt was now the master in Palestine. This was the attack mentioned in Daniel 1:1 that took place in the third year of Jehoiakim and in which Daniel and his companions were taken to Babylon. It should be noticed that this was the third year of Jehoiakim according to Tishri reckoning, but the fourth year according to Nisan years as mentioned in Jeremiah 46:2.

The prophet Jeremiah indicated that Egypt was to suffer serious vengeance from God inflicted through the agency of Nebuchadnezzar. "This is the message against the army of Pharaoh Neco king of Egypt, which was defeated at Carchemish on the Euphrates River by Nebuchadnezzar king of Babylon in the fourth year of Jehoiakim. . . . But that day belongs to the LORD, the LORD Almighty—a day of vengeance, for vengeance on his foes. . . . I will hand them over to those who seek their lives, to Nebuchadnezzar king of Babylon" (Jer. 46:2, 10, 26).

Chart 31
597–585 B.C.

597—Jehoiachin—3 months—2 Kings 24:8
597—Zedekiah—11 years—2 Kings 24:18
597—8th of Nebuchadnezzar—Jehoiachin exiled to Babylon—
    2 Kings 24:12–14
593—31 July—Ezekiel has vision on 4/5/5—Ezek. 1:1–2
592—17 Sept.—elders see Ezekiel on 6/5/6—Ezek. 8:1
591—14 Aug.—elders rebuked on 5/10/7—Ezek. 20:1–3
588—15 Jan.—siege of Jerusalem begun on 10/10/9—2 Kings 25:1;
    Ezek. 24:1–2
587—10th of Zedekiah—18th of Nebuchadnezzar—Jeremiah in prison—
    Jer. 32:1–2
586—19 July—Jerusalem taken on 4/9/11—2 Kings 25:2–3
586—15 Aug.—19th of Nebuchadnezzar—temple burned on 5/7/19—
    2 Kings 25:8–9
585—8 Jan.—on 10/5/12 exiles hear Jerusalem is taken—Ezek. 33:21

		597	596	595	594	593	592	591	590	589	588	587	586	585
JUDAH														
Tishri years	Jehoiakim	11												
	Jehoiachin	ac												
	Exile	1	2	3	4	5	6	7	8	9	10	11	12	13
	Zedekiah	ac	1	2	3	4	5	6	7	8	9	10	11	
Nisan years	Jehoiakim	11												
	Jehoiachin	ac												
	Exile		1	2	3	4	5	6	7	8	9	10	11	12
	Zedekiah		ac	1	2	3	4	5	6	7	8	9	10	11
BABYLON														
	Nebuchadnezzar	8	9	10	11	12	13	14	15	16	17	18	19	20

Judah: Tishri years in Kings
Nisan years in Jeremiah and Ezekiel
Babylon: Nisan years

The battle of Carchemish at the Euphrates in the fourth year of Jehoiakim is now definitely dated by Babylonian evidence (B.M. 21946) in the twenty-first year of Nabopolassar, 605 B.C. In Jeremiah 25:1 the fourth year of Jehoiakim is equated with "the first year of Nebuchadnezzar king of Babylon."

Tadmor has pointed out that this השכה הראשכיח of Nebuchadnezzar refers not to his official first year but to his initial year on the throne, the year of his accession.[5] On chart 30 (page 183), this year, 605 B.C., will be seen to be the twenty-third year from the thirteenth year of Josiah, 627 (Jer. 25:3). Cf. chart 28 (page 179).

The year 605 B.C., when Nebuchadnezzar first came against Jerusalem and took Daniel and others captive to Babylon, marked the beginning of the end for Judah. Mentioned in Jeremiah 25:1, 3, this was the fourth year of Jehoiakim and the twenty-third year that Jeremiah had been giving stern warnings about the doom awaiting Judah if that nation continued to defy God and pursue a course of evil. The specific message was given:

> "I will summon all the peoples of the north and my servant Nebuchadnezzar king of Babylon," declares the LORD, "and I will bring them against this land. . . . This whole country will become a desolate wasteland, and these nations will serve the king of Babylon seventy years. But when the seventy years are fulfilled, I will punish the king of Babylon and his nation, the land of the Babylonians, for their guilt," declares the LORD, "and will make it desolate forever."[6]

While Nebuchadnezzar was engaged in his conquest of Hatti-country, the death of Nabopolassar took place on 8 Av (16 Aug.) 605 after he had reigned twenty-one years. On hearing the news Nebuchadnezzar immediately returned to Babylon, evidently by a rapid ride across the desert; and he took the throne on 1 Elul (7 Sept.). The fact that he reached the capital and was on the throne twenty-one days after his father's death provides an interesting confirmation of Berosus's account, preserved by Josephus. The account of Nebuchadnezzar's victorious Palestinian campaign in the year in which his father died, and his speedy return to Babylon to take the crown, reads as follows:

> Meanwhile, as it happened, his father Nabopolassar sickened and died in the city of Babylon, after a reign of twenty-one years. Being informed ere long of his father's death, Nabuchodonosor settled the affairs of Egypt and the other countries. The prisoners—Jews, Phoenicians, Syrians, and those of Egyptian nationality—were consigned to some of his friends, with orders to conduct them to Babylonia, along with the heavy troops and the rest of the spoils; while he himself, with a small escort, pushed across the desert to Babylon. There he found the administration in the hands of the Chaldaeans and the throne reserved for him by their chief nobleman. Being now master of his father's entire realm, he gave orders to allot the captives, on their arrival, settlements in the most suitable districts of Babylonia. He then magnificently

---

[5]Hayim Tadmor, "Chronology of the Last Kings of Judah," *Journal of Near Eastern Studies* 15 (1956): 227.

[6]Jer. 25:9, 11–12.

decorated the temple of Bel and the other temples with the spoils of war. [7]

The following year, 604, Nebuchadnezzar was back again in the Hatti-territory to receive tribute from all its kings. This no doubt included Jehoiakim. At that time the march went as far south as Askelon, which was captured in the month of Kislev. The next three years found Nebuchadnezzar again campaigning in Hatti-country. In 601 a great battle with Egypt took place, concerning which we are told that "they smote the breast (of) each other and inflicted great havoc on each other. The king of Akkad and his troops turned back and returned to Babylon." [8] This is a frank acknowledgment of a Babylonian defeat, as is confirmed by the record of the following year, 600 B.C.: "In the fifth year the king of Akkad (stayed) in his own land." [9] The next year, 599, the campaign was once more to the Hatti-land, with much plunder taken from the desert Arabs.

39. Jehoiachin—Judah—598–597

2 Kings 24:8–17; 25:27–30; 2 Chronicles 36:9–10
Length of reign: 3 months
597—taken to Babylon in the 8th year of Nebuchadnezzar (2 Kings 24:12)
561—released in the accession year of Evil-Merodach (Amel-Marduk), 37th year of his exile (2 Kings 25:27)

Although the reign of Jehoiachin lasted only three months, certain items about it are unique and important. Its date has been fully established by a Babylonian tablet that gives interesting details parallel to the biblical account. The Babylonian tablet states that Nebuchadnezzar in the seventh year of his reign made an expedition to the Hatti-land in the month of Kislev (17 December 598 to 15 January 597). He besieged Jerusalem and captured the city on 2 Adar (Saturday, 16 March) 597. The king of Jerusalem was taken prisoner and a new king was placed on the throne.

According to the biblical account the captured king was Jehoiachin and the king placed on the throne was Zedekiah.

The biblical account places the capture of Jerusalem in the eighth year of Nebuchadnezzar (2 Kings 24:12), but the Babylonian account places it in the seventh year. The Babylonian account is in accord with Nisan regnal years and the biblical account starts the years of Nebuchadnezzar with Tishri. Chart 30 (page 183) makes the details clear. The last half of the Babylonian Nisan year overlaps the first half of the Hebrew Tishri year. Thus Jerusalem fell to Nebuchadnezzar in his seventh year according to his own reckoning but in his eighth year according to the reckoning in Kings. The overlap was from Tishri in the fall of 598 to Nisan in the spring of 597. Since Jerusalem fell in Adar, the last month of the Babylonian year, this was in the spring of 597.

As to the season of the year of Jerusalem's final fall, the chronicler said that it was "at the turn of the year" (2 Chron. 36:10). It is debatable whether *lithsubathhassānāh* indicates the spring or fall turn of the year. In 2 Samuel

---

[7]Josephus, *Against Apion*, 1.19.136–39; *Antiquities* 10.221–24.
[8]Wiseman, *Chronicles*, p. 33.
[9]Ibid.

11:1 the phrase clearly means the spring, Nisan, for it is here qualified as *le't ṣe't hamal^e'kim*, "at the time when kings go off to war." In Ezekiel 40:1 the vision of the temple is dated in "the beginning of the year," the tenth day of the month, "in the twenty-fifth year of our exile," "on that very day," the four-teenth year after Jerusalem fell. The phrase "on that very day" is significant for it settles the question as to the exact year involved in many of the problematical dates in this period of Hebrew history.[10] Ezekiel 40:1 is closely related to Ezekiel 33:21, as has been pointed out by Irwin,[11] and in that reference the tenth month and the fifth day of the twelfth year of the captivity comes at some time after the fall of Jerusalem. Jerusalem fell on the ninth day of the fourth month of the eleventh year of Zedekiah (Jer. 39:2; 52:5–6; 2 Kings 25:2–3), which is 18 July 586. If Jerusalem fell in the fourth month of a Nisan-to-Nisan year in 586, then the tenth month of the twelfth year of the captivity referred to in Ezekiel 33:21 must also be a Nisan-to-Nisan year, and the same must be true of the twenty-fifth year of the captivity of Ezekiel 40:1, for that is the fourteenth year since the city fell in the Nisan-to-Nisan year of 586. It is clear from the numerical sequence involved that the writer of Ezekiel 40:1 has in mind a Nisan-to-Nisan year; "that very day" of the month marking the beginning of the year when Jehoiachin was deported to Babylon was 10 Nisan. This would be 22 April 597 B.C. That the captivity of Jehoiachin began in Nisan is confirmed by the statement in 2 Chronicles 36:10 that "At the turn of the year, King Nebuchadnezzar sent for him and brought him to Babylon, together with arti-cles of value from the temple of the LORD, and he made Jehoiachin's uncle, Zedekiah, king over Judah and Jerusalem." Nisan 597 is thus the time when Jehoiachin's deportation to Babylon took place and when Zedekiah was placed on the throne of Judah. Since Jerusalem was taken on 2 Adar and since the departure for Babylon began on 10 Nisan, this would allow a little over a month, from 16 March to 22 April, for the bringing together of the spoils of war and the gathering of the captives prior to the trek to Babylon.

The exact length of Jehoiachin's reign is given in 2 Chronicles 36:9 as three months and ten days, which would be from 21 Marcheswan to 10 Nisan, or 9 December 598 to 22 April 597. Jeremiah had made the prediction that Jehoiakim's body would be cast beyond the gates of Jerusalem (Jer. 22:19) and was to be exposed to the heat of the day and the frost of the night (Jer. 36:30). The month of December in Jerusalem would be in full accord with this predic-tion. On the basis of the Babylonian evidence regarding the date of Jerusalem's fall, 9 December 598 may thus be given as the date when Jehoiakim terminated his reign and Jehoiachin was elevated to the throne.

After Jehoiachin and a number of his compatriots were taken captive to Babylon in 597, they numbered their years there in accord with their period of exile. The first year of that period began in Nisan 597, and its thirty-seventh and last year was 561 when Jehoiachin was released from imprisonment.

The prophet Ezekiel was among the exiles taken to Babylon in 597. He

---

[10]For a study of the complicated chronological items in the final years of Judah's history, see Alberto R. Green, "The Chronology of the Last Days of Judah: Two Apparent Discrepancies" *Journal of Biblical Literature* 101 (1982) 57–73.

[11]William A. Irwin, *The Problem of Ezekiel* (Chicago, 1943), pp. 256f.

made a great contribution to the chronology of that period by dating his experiences and visions in terms of the day, month, and year of the Exile. As a result we now know the exact time when many events took place. In Ezekiel 1:1–3 is found the first recorded item: "In the thirtieth year, in the fourth month on the fifth day, while I was among the exiles by the Kebar River, the heavens were opened and I saw visions of God. On the fifth of the month—it was the fifth year of the exile of King Jehoiachin—the word of the LORD came to Ezekiel the priest."

This was 31 July 593.

Chart 32
585–573 B.C.

573—28 April—1/10/25—14th year from fall of Jerusalem to 25th year of exile—Ezek. 40:1

	585	584	583	582	581	580	579	578	577	576	575	574	573
JUDAH Exile (Tishri years)	13	14	15	16	17	18	19	20	21	22	23	24	25	
Exile (Nisan years)		13	14	15	16	17	18	19	20	21	22	23	24	25
BABYLON Nebuchadnezzar		20	21	22	23	24	25	26	27	28	29	30	31	32
JERUSALEM SMITTEN	1	2	3	4	5	6	7	8	9	10	11	12	13	14

Judah: Tishri years in Kings
        Nisan years in Jeremiah and Ezekiel
Babylon: Nisan years

Chart 33
573–561 B.C.

571—26 April—1/1/27—Egypt promised to Nebuchadnezzar as reward for service against Tyre—Ezek. 29:17–19
561—2 April—12/27/37—Jehoiachin released in 37th of his captivity; ac of Evil-Merodach (Amel-Marduk)—2 Kings 25:27

	573	572	571	570	569	568	567	566	565	564	563	562	561
JUDAH Exile (Tishri years)	25	26	27	28	29	30	31	32	33	34	35	36	37
Exile (Nisan years)		25	26	27	28	29	30	31	32	33	34	35	36
BABYLON Nebuchadnezzar		32	33	34	35	36	37	39	38	40	41	42	43
Evil-Merodach (Amel-Marduk)													ac

Judah: Tishri years in Kings
        Nisan years in Jeremiah and Ezekiel
Babylon: Nisan years

On the fifth day of the sixth month of the sixth year (17 Sept. 592) as Ezekiel was in his house and the elders sat before him (Ezek. 8:1), he had a vision in which he saw the gross iniquities going on at the temple gate in Jerusalem. He saw "women . . . mourning for Tammuz" and a group of men "with their backs toward the temple of the LORD and their faces toward the east, and they were bowing down to the sun in the east" (vv. 14, 16).

On the tenth day of the fifth month of the seventh year (14 Aug. 591), "some of the elders of Israel came to inquire of the LORD" but received the following stern words from God: "I will not let you inquire of me" (Ezek. 20:1, 3).

On the tenth day of the tenth month of the ninth year (15 Jan. 588), a solemn message came from God: "Son of man, record this date, this very date, because the king of Babylon has laid siege to Jerusalem this very date. . . . Woe to the city of bloodshed" (Ezek. 24:1–2, 6). Thus on the very day that the final siege of Jerusalem began, the exiles in Babylon had word of that event. "In the ninth year" of Zedekiah, "on the tenth day of the tenth month, Nebuchadnezzar king of Babylon marched against Jerusalem with his whole army. He encamped outside the city and built siege works all around it" (2 Kings 25:1).

Jerusalem fell on the ninth day of the fourth month of the eleventh year of Zedekiah, the nineteenth year of Nebuchadnezzar (2 Kings 25:2–3, 8), that is, on 18 July 586 B.C. On 8 January 585, the fifth day of the tenth month of the twelfth year of Jehoiachin's exile, Ezekiel says that "a man who had escaped from Jerusalem" came to him with the message, "The city has fallen" (Ezek. 33:21).

On the first day of the first month of the twenty-seventh year, 26 April 571, the word of the Lord came to Ezekiel that God would give Egypt to Nebuchadnezzar in return for "a hard campaign against Tyre" that his army had performed (Ezek. 29:17–20). This was after Nebuchadnezzar had besieged the island city without success for thirteen years.

Jehoiachin was eighteen years of age at his accession and the beginning of his captivity in Babylon (2 Kings 24:8; cf. 2 Chron. 36:9 where his age is given as eight in most Hebrew manuscripts). His lot, at least during the early years of his captivity, could not have been very trying, for a tablet dated in 592, listing payments of rations in oil, barley, etc., to captives and skilled workmen in and around Babylon, includes the name of Yaukin, king of Judah, and five of his sons.[12] Later he must have been placed under more restricted custody, for after the death of Nebuchadnezzar he was released from prison by Evil-Merodach (Amel-Marduk) (2 Kings 25:27–30; Jer. 52:31–34). The last dates for Nebuchadnezzar on available tablets are 6/21/43 (3 Oct. 562) and 6/26/43 (8 Oct. 562), and the first dates for Evil-Merodach are 6/26/acc. (8 Oct. 562) and 7/19/acc. (31 Oct. 562).[13] The release of Jehoiachin occurred on the twenty-

---

[12]W. F. Albright, "King Joiachin in Exile," *Biblical Archaeologist* 5 (1942): 49ff.; Ernst F. Weidner, "Joiachin, Koenig von Juda, in babylonischen Keilschrifttexten." *Mélanges Syriens offerts à Monsieur René Dussaud* (Paris, 1939), I: 923–35.

[13]Richard A. Parker and W. H. Dubberstein, *Babylonian Chronology, 626 B.C.–A.D. 75,* (Providence, 1975), p. 12; Albrecht Goetze, "Additions to Parker and Dubberstein's *Babylonian Chronology," Journal of Near Eastern Studies* 3 (1944): 43–46.

seventh day of the twelfth month of the thirty-seventh year of his captivity,[14] in the year that Amel-Marduk began to reign (2 Kings 25:27), or 2 April 561. This was just before the first celebration of the New Year festivities on the part of the new king—a fitting time for the release of political prisoners.

40. Zedekiah—Judah—597–586

2 Kings 24:18–25:26; 2 Chronicles 36:11–21
Length of reign: 11 years
588—9th of Zedekiah; siege of Jerusalem began (2 Kings 25:1)
586—11th year of Zedekiah; Jerusalem taken by Nebuchadnezzar (2 Kings 25:2–4)
586—19th year of Nebuchadnezzar; temple burned (2 Kings 25:8–9)

Certain details concerning the reign of Zedekiah have already been discussed in connection with the reign of Jehoiachin. The Babylonian account that parallels the biblical account concerning these two reigns has been preserved. It mentions that Nebuchadnezzar in his seventh year, in the month of Kislev, 17 December 598 to 15 January 597, made an expedition to the Hatti-land. On 2 Adar (16 March) 597, Jerusalem was taken. Its king was captured and taken prisoner to Babylon and a new king was placed on the throne of Judah. This was Zedekiah according to the biblical account.

In 2 Chronicles 36:10 we are told that it was "at the turn of the year" that Nebuchadnezzar took Jehoiachin captive to Babylon and "made Jehoiachin's uncle, Zedekiah, king over Judah." As has already been pointed out, this was the spring turn of the year. Zedekiah thus began his reign in Nisan of 597 B.C.

In the Books of Jeremiah and Ezekiel the regnal years of the Hebrew as well as Babylonian kings are reckoned as beginning in Nisan. In Jeremiah 32:1 the tenth year of Zedekiah is equated with the eighteenth year of Nebuchadnezzar. This is in accord with an accession year of Zedekiah commencing in Nisan 597, and his tenth year commencing in Nisan 587, which synchronized with the eighteenth year of Nebuchadnezzar that began in Nisan 587. See chart 31 (page 184).

The last event in the checkered history of the southern kingdom was the siege and destruction of Jerusalem by Nebuchadnezzar. This siege began on the tenth day of the tenth month of Zedekiah's ninth year (2 Kings 25:1; Jer. 39:1; 52:4; cf. Ezek. 24:1–2), 15 January 588.[15] The next year, in the midst of the siege, Jeremiah was imprisoned, this being the tenth year of Zedekiah and synchronizing with the eighteenth year of Nebuchadnezzar (Jer. 32:1), 587. Famine prevailed, the city was broken, and the king fled, on the ninth day of the fourth month of Zedekiah's eleventh year (2 Kings 25:2–3; Jer. 39:2; 52:5–7), 18 July 586. On the seventh day of the fifth month the final destruction of the city began (2 Kings 25:8–10), 14 August 586. This was the nineteenth year of Nebuchadnezzar (2 Kings 25:8; Jer. 52:12), which was from Nisan 586 to

[14]It should be noted that, according to the reckoning of Kings, the thirty-seventh year of Jehoiachin's captivity was from Tishri 562, to Tishri 561. But according to Ezekiel's and Jeremiah's method of reckoning, the thirty-seventh year of the captivity would not begin until Nisan 561.

[15]Parker and Dubberstein, *Babylonian Chronology*, p. 28. All Julian dates given here are based on the tables of Parker and Dubberstein.

Nisan 585, Babylonian reckoning, or Tishri 587 to Tishri 586, Judean years. Gedaliah, who had been appointed by Nebuchadnezzar as governor of the land, was slain in the seventh month (2 Kings 25:22–25; Jer. 41:1–2). The month of Tishri began on 7 October 586. It must have been shortly after that, that the remnant left by Nebuzaradan with Gedaliah took Jeremiah and forced him to accompany them to Egypt (Jer. 43:2–7). Word of the fall of Jerusalem reached the captives in Babylon on the fifth day of the tenth month of the twelfth year of their captivity (Ezek. 33:21), 8 January 585. Zedekiah's reign thus was from 597 to 586.

Although the Babylonian tablets dealing with the final fall and destruction of Jerusalem have not been found, it should be noticed that the testimony of Ezekiel 40:1 is definitive in regard to the year 586. Since Ezekiel had his vision of the temple on the twenty-fifth anniversary of his and Jehoiachin's captivity (28 April 573), and since this was the fourteenth year after Jerusalem's fall, the city must have fallen eleven years after the captivity. Eleven years after 597 is 586. Any attempt to date the fall of Jerusalem earlier than 586 would call for an earlier date than 597 for Jehoiachin's captivity; but that is not possible, for that date has been fixed by contemporary Babylonian evidence. Word concerning Jerusalem's fall reached the captives in Babylon the fifth day of the tenth month of the twelfth year of the captivity (Ezek. 33:21), 8 January 585. Diagram 21, on page 192, will clarify the various dates involved. All these details point conclusively to 586 as the year when Jerusalem fell and the nation of Judah came to its end.

The study of the chronological material of the Hebrew kings as recorded in the Masoretic Text has now been completed. Other chronological items besides those discussed, some of great historical and exegetical importance, are to be found in various books of the Old Testament. But these lie outside of the main field we have marked out for our present discussion—the establishment of the chronology of the period of the kings.

Diagram 21
The Fall of Jerusalem in 586 B.C.

Nisan years for Nebuchadnezzar and the kings of Judah according to Jeremiah and Ezekiel

	598	597	596	595	594	593	592	591	590	589	588	587	586	585	584	583	582	581	580	579	578	577	576	575	574	573
Nebuchadnezzar	7	8	9	10	11	12	13	14	15	16	17	18	19	20	21	22	23	24	25	26	27	28	29	30	31	32
Jehoiachin	ac	1	2	3	4	5	6	7	8	9	10	11	12	13	14	15	16	17	18	19	20	21	22	23	24	25
Zedekiah		ac	1	2	3	4	5	6	7	8	9	10	11													
Years since Jerusalem was smitten													1	2	3	4	5	6	7	8	9	10	11	12	13	14

Jehoiakim 11

597, 16 March—2 Adar—Jerusalem taken

597, 22 April—10 Nisan—Jehoiachin deported (Ezek. 40:1)

587, 10th of Zedekiah = 18th of Nebuchadnezzar (Jer. 32:1)

586, July 18—4th month, 9th day of the 11th year of Zedekiah, the 19th year of Nebuchadnezzar, Jerusalem fell (2 Kings 25:2–7; Jer. 39:2; 52:5–6)

585, January 8—10th month, 5th day, 12th year of the captivity, captives in Babylon hear that Jerusalem has fallen (Ezek. 33:21)

573, 28 April—10 Nisan, 25th year of captivity, 14th year after Jerusalem's fall—Ezekiel has vision of the temple (Ezek. 40:1–2)

CHAPTER TEN

The Origin of the Book of Kings

T WOULD BE INTERESTING to know the story of how and where the records of the Hebrew rulers were originally kept, how the tales of people, prophets, and kings were brought together and developed into their present form as now found in the Book of Kings, and how the chronological details of the various rulers were brought into the records of individual reigns. The story of how they were kept with such precision and passed on to posterity with such amazing accuracy would be interesting indeed if it could be learned. The full details of the story will never be known, but our account of these mysterious numbers would hardly be complete if we did not touch on this phase of the question, however lightly that must necessarily be.

One thing we may be certain of is that these materials had a long and complicated history and passed through many hands before assuming their final form. From the very beginning of the Hebrew kingdoms there must have been men who had in mind passing on to the future an accurate, detailed, and orderly account of the rulers of both Israel and Judah that might be read with interest and profit.

A record was kept of every reign in each nation in the order of sequence with which the rulers came to the throne. From first to last, particular emphasis was placed on chronological details, and these details were recorded exactly and accurately. In spite of varied methods of chronological reckoning employed in Israel and Judah, in spite of changes in method that took place from time to time, and in spite of different methods of procedure on the part of individual scribes in recording the varied details of reigns, we are able today to work out the chronology of both nations from the time of the disruption to the end.

A religious evaluation was an important item in the opening formula of the final account of every ruler's reign. The king was good or bad, depending on how he related himself to the worship of Jahweh and led—or failed to lead—the people in pathways of rectitude that alone could insure individual well-being and national prosperity. The Hebrews were God's people. The prophets were His spokesmen. The temple at Jerusalem was His house, and the Hebrew realm was His particular preserve. Rulers were blessed to the degree that they continued faithful to God, or cursed to the degree that they departed from the distinctive features of religious faith and practice.

Distinctly religious history was recorded in the Book of Kings. Such history could have been written only by religious men. In Israel and Judah, as in other nations, there were official court reporters who kept formal records of state. But the more closely we examine the accounts in Kings, the more clear it is that the royal scribes had little if anything to do with most of this material as it has come down to us. There is in these books too much of severe indictment of the wicked ways of individual kings, too much pronouncement of divine doom on the heads of recalcitrant rulers, to believe that royal scribes played any significant part in the production of Kings as the book exists today. What member of a royal court would have dared to record the stories of Ahab and Naboth, of Jezebel's violence against the prophets, of the abominations and sodomies during the reign of Rehoboam, of Ahaz's defilement of the altar, or of Manasseh's dealings with wizards and familiar spirits?

These records were written by men who knew the details of the evil deeds of kings and were willing to report them. They were written by men who thought of kings as individuals who were to be lauded for their virtues but rebuked for their misdeeds. The authors of these volumes were as interested in telling the tale of the calves of gold placed at Dan and Bethel as they were in the story of Hezekiah's removal of the high places and his cleansing of the temple. They were as interested in presenting the details of the three-year drought in the days of Ahab and Elijah the Tishbite and the reason that brought it about as they were in the prophetic rebukes administered to Ahab and Jehoash for their ill-advised clemency to Aram after victories on fields of battle.

These records were written by men who had access to the bed chambers of kings (1 Kings 1:1–4) and were acquainted with the secret connivings that went on in the inner chambers of royal courts. The prophets of Israel found themselves in just such categories (1 Kings 1:11–27). The more carefully these records are examined, the more clear it is that prophets played a major role in their production. Only prophets could have produced many of the most characteristic items that form so basic a part of our present Book of Kings.

Throughout Hebrew history prophets played an important role in the life of the realm. Before either Saul or David had any intimation of ever sitting on a royal throne, they were anointed by Samuel the prophet (1 Sam. 10:1; 16:12–13). When Adonijah conspired to take the throne, Nathan the prophet planned a course of action that was to give Solomon the crown (1 Kings 1:11–27). The anointing of Solomon took place at the hands of Nathan the prophet and Zadok the priest (1 Kings 1:34). The prophet Ahijah informed Jeroboam that ten tribes were to be ruled by him (1 Kings 11:29–38). Jehu the prophet was sent to pronounce doom on Baasha and his house (1 Kings 16:1–4, 7). Elisha sent a young man from one of the prophetic establishments to anoint Jehu and inform him that he was to wear the royal crown (2 Kings 9:1–12).

In the case of the most iniquitous rulers of Israelite history, such as Ahab and his sons Ahaziah and Jehoram, the records are the most replete with tales of a religious interest and accounts of the words and works of prophets and sons of the prophets. The prophet Elijah pronounced the fearful doom that was to fall on Ahab and all his house (1 Kings 21:21–25). To the bed chamber of Ahaziah, Elijah was sent to inform him of his impending death because of his concourse with Baal-Zebub, the god of Ekron (2 Kings 1:15–17).

Who would be in possession of such detailed information concerning prophetic activity? Who would be most apt to pass it on to posterity? Certainly not the official annalists in court employ. And who would be in a better position to know and record the words and thoughts and rebukes of the prophets than the prophets themselves?

We know prophets played an important part in keeping records of the kings, for of David we are told that his deeds were written "in the records of Samuel the seer, the records of Nathan the prophet and the records of Gad the seer" (1 Chron. 29:29). The account of Solomon's reign concludes with the statement that his acts were "written in the records of Nathan the prophet, in the prophecy of Ahijah the Shilonite and in the visions of Iddo the seer" (2 Chron. 9:29). Likewise, we are told that the events of the reign of Rehoboam are in "the records of Shemaiah the prophet and of Iddo the seer" (2 Chron. 12:15). Of Abijah we are informed that his ways and sayings were written in "the annotations of the prophet Iddo" (2 Chron. 13:22). And of Uzziah (Azariah) the report is that his acts "from beginning to end, are recorded by the prophet Isaiah son of Amoz" (2 Chron. 26:22).

In the Hebrew Scriptures the Book of Kings has its place among the "former prophets." This points definitely to the prophetic origin of these writings.

Throughout the books themselves are found constant indications of their prophetic stamp. In Kings is found a striking unity of words and spirit. There is a constant recurrence of phrases that to Burney are characteristic "of one prophetic school of thought, i.e., the Deuteronomic."[1] Burney provides a helpful list of the Deuteronomic phrases so characteristic of Kings and so much in line with a particular manner of prophetic thinking and expression.[2] The unusual type of religious history in Kings certainly expresses Hebrew prophetic ways of thought and action. The same spirit of admonishment and exhortation, of encouragement and reproof, so essentially a part of the homilies of Isaiah, Jeremiah, and the Deuteronomist, permeates Kings from end to end. The similarity of words and phrases, however, together with the thoughts and spirit to which they give voice, need not be attributed solely or primarily to a late editor or a group of redactors, but could well go back to the early and original documents themselves as they came from the hands of a closely knit group of original authors. These people, I would suggest, were members of the ancient prophetic schools.

That there were such establishments is well attested in the Old Testament record. Samuel made an annual circuit to such centers as Bethel, Gilgal, and Mizpah (1 Sam. 7:16). Elisha made visits to Gilgal, Bethel, and Jericho where groups of prophets were located (2 Kings 2:1–7). These were centers of educational and cultural, as well as religious interests. The people who conducted

---

[1] C.F. Burney, *Notes on the Hebrew Text of the Books of Kings* (Oxford, 1903), p. 331.
[2] Ibid., p. xiii.

them had in mind the present material and intellectual welfare of the individual, as well as the good of the soul and the preservation of the state. They were the forerunners of the cloisters of the early Christian and medieval periods.

Attention has recently been called to the important part such organizations of prophets played in the later as well as the earlier periods of Hebrew history. We have also noted the rich opportunities they might have afforded to great prophetic teachers who wished to insure the impact of their teaching on both their contemporaries and posterity.[3]

The Hebrew prophetic societies would provide natural centers for the production and preservation of such records as ultimately developed into the Book of Kings. Prophets would be in possession of this type of information, and it would be their wish to pass it on to posterity. These continuous records covered the history of the rulers of both Judah and Israel from beginning to end. Efforts to produce such writings could not have been fitful or haphazard, dependent on individual whims, but were part of a constant and concerted project that went on from reign to reign, regardless of the religious or political complex of the times, and that knew no end until long after the nations that were their main concern had passed away. All this calls for some sort of religious establishment that would continue the project through the long and colorful history of the northern and southern kingdoms. Individual prophets might come and go, but the connecting links went on that tied together the records of the various kings.

Such information as is available concerning the location of certain of these prophetic establishments indicates that some of them were in the southern area of Israel and others in the northern part of Judah. Here they were in a position to keep in close touch with each other, with a school in Judah centering its attention on Judean kings, and a school in Israel keeping the records of the Israelite rulers.

The content of these records shows they were not kept in a single center and that the reports on the kings of Israel and Judah were not products of the same hands. The records of Israel were written with the interests and customs of Israel always to the front, but with Judah by no means forgotten. The reports of Judah kept first in mind the rulers and customs of Judah, but with Israel still in the picture.

In each nation chronology played an important part. There were both a synchronism with the year of the neighboring king and a record of the time each ruler was on his throne. In each nation there was a strict adherence to the method of chronological procedure there, and then, in force. But neither nation was slavishly dependent on the other. When Menahem came to the throne in Israel, the beginning of his reign was synchronized with Azariah of Judah. But when Jotham was crowned coregent in Judah during the second year of Menahem, it was not Menahem who was recognized but his rival Pekah in Gilead. And when Jotham was displaced by Ahaz, the reign of Ahaz was not

[3]J. H. Eaton, "The Origin of the Book of Isaiah," *Vetus Testamentum* 9 (1959), 139ff. Cf. Robert T. Anderson, "Was Isaiah a Scribe?" *Journal of Biblical Literature* 79 (1960): 57ff.

synchronized with the year that Menahem had been reigning as king of Israel in Samaria, but with the year since the commencement of the rival reign of Pekah in Gilead.

The synchronisms with which these reigns are introduced constitute clear-cut evidence that these journals were not the products of palace recorders but must have come from some source such as the prophetic schools. It is inconceivable that through the long history of Israel the accession of each king would be synchronized with a king of Judah by a royal recorder. One ruler might have had such an idea, but the next might have had an idea that would be totally different. Can we think of a king of Israel at war with Judah synchronizing his accession with the year of reign of an enemy king? Yet this practice was continued throughout the history of both nations, regardless of the political situation. And in Judah, often at war with Israel, it is inconceivable that each time a new ruler came to the throne the palace scribes were under orders to synchronize the accession with the year of the Israelite king. Such synchronisms could come only from the hands of people who were interested in both Israel and Judah, people who kept in mind the fact that the inhabitants of the north as well as the south were Hebrews and descendants of Abraham.

When in either Israel or Judah a new ruler came to the throne, the entry was made in a journal of that nation. In Judah it was "the book of the annals of the kings of Judah," and in Israel it was "the book of the annals of the kings of Israel." In each case the record was an annalistic scroll, a sort of national diary or journal of "words of days," דברי הימים (1 Kings 14:19, 29 et al.) This must have been for each nation a running record in which events were recorded day by day and year by year as they took place. It was the beginning of a national history, with reports of words and deeds, of people, prophets, and kings. There were in these early original records no formal openings and closings of reigns such as we find today. The account of one king flowed into that of another, as one ruler terminated his reign and another took his place. Events in both nations were reported as they occurred.

On these early informal recordings, the closing item of one reign might constitute the opening item of the next. When the death of a ruler took place, a note was made of the termination of the old ruler and of the accession of the new ruler in terms of the year in the neighboring state. The number of years or months or days that the king had reigned was necessarily recorded at the close of the reign. In the records as they have been preserved, we still find indications that these were the ways in which the records were originally kept. Synchronistic citations are still found at the close of the records of Baasha (1 Kings 15:28), Elah (1 Kings 16:10), Ahaziah (2 Kings 1:17), and Pekah (2 Kings 15:30). The length of reign is still found at the close of the records of David (1 Kings 2:11), Solomon (1 Kings 11:42), and Jeroboam (1 Kings 14:20). When the records were reduced to their final forms, we find such entries transferred by the late editors or compilers to the formal opening formulas for the individual reigns.

While on the whole the notations of the contemporary recorders were clear to the editors of a later age, there were times when the historical arrangements were so involved or the recorded data were of so unusual or individualistic a nature that the original meaning was not always grasped. In the earlier pages of this volume, we have had occasion, here and there to refer to items of this nature. We will now briefly review some of these numbers that gave rise to late misunderstandings. An example of this is found in the data of 2 Chronicles 15:19 and 16:1. We know from 2 Chronicles 15:10 that Asa held a great victory celebration in Jerusalem in the fifteenth year of his reign, after his triumphant return from the repulse of the invading forces of Zerah. Yet according to the Hebrew reading of 2 Chronicles 15:19 "there was no war until the five and thirtieth year of the reign of Asa" (KJV). The word "more" is not found in the Hebrew text and was supplied by translators so that verse 19 might not contradict verse 10. Likewise, the statement in 2 Chronicles 16:1 that Baasha built Ramah in the thirty-sixth year of Asa cannot be correct, for Baasha had died and was succeeded by Elah in Asa's twenty-sixth year (1 Kings 16:8). Since the fifteenth year of Asa was the thirty-fifth year from the beginning of the nation of Judah, and since Asa's sixteenth year was the thirty-sixth year from when Rehoboam began his reign, it is clear that an early Hebrew scribe from the time of Asa began to date events in terms of an era beginning with the year when Judah itself began. The following diagram will clarify the years involved:

Diagram 22
Years of Rehoboam, Abijah, and Asa

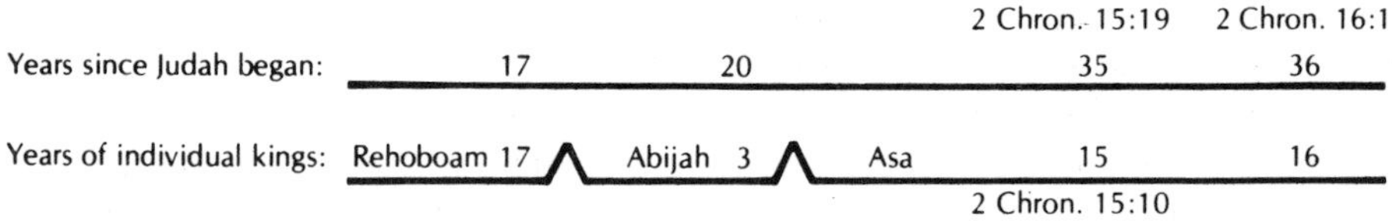

			2 Chron. 15:19	2 Chron. 16:1
Years since Judah began:	17	20	35	36

Years of individual kings:	Rehoboam 17 ⋀	Abijah 3 ⋀	Asa	15	16
			2 Chron. 15:10		

It is unfortunate that later scribes did not continue this early innovation, with an era for Judah beginning with Rehoboam's accession. Certainly, the tasks of later editors, chronologists, and historians would have been greatly facilitated had Hebrew scribal recorders continued with such a practice. The synchronisms of 2 Chronicles 15:19 and 16:1 give evidence that when later editors came across these original citations, they failed to recognize their meaning and interpreted them as the years of Asa rather than the years of the monarchy of Judah.

A good example of the manner in which a notation was made in Israel's journalistic scroll is found in 2 Kings 15:30. There, at the close of the record of Pekah's reign, appears the statement that Hoshea made a conspiracy against Pekah, "and assassinated him, and then succeeded him as king in the twentieth year of Jotham." This citation has all the earmarks of being genuine and of appearing in the context in which it originally occurred. Certainly, in such a setting there was no occasion to introduce a synchronism that might be late and artificial, but the scribe simply passed on an item of information exactly as it was found in the original record of Israelite reigns. As events took place during Pekah's reign, they were duly recorded, including the notation in 2 Kings 15:29 of Tiglath-Pileser's seizure of Gilead and Galilee that took place in 734. Then in

732 a notation was entered of Hoshea's conspiracy against Pekah, his slaying of Pekah, and his taking the throne in Jotham's twentieth year. Next, without further formalities, the original journal undoubtedly went on with entries of events as they took place in Hoshea's reign, concluding with the capture of Samaria in Hoshea's ninth year (2 Kings 17:6). At the occasion of the final compilation of Kings, when the stereotyped opening formula for Hoshea's reign was being prepared, the notation of 2 Kings 15:30 was permitted to remain in the record of Pekah's reign. However, the new calculated synchronism that threw back the reign of Ahaz twelve years and caused his twelfth year to coincide with Jotham's twentieth year was entered in 2 Kings 17:1 as the official synchronism of Hoshea's accession.

Yet another instance involving a late editorial misunderstanding of a chronological datum is found in the insertion in 2 Kings 8:16 of the statement "when Jehoshaphat was king of Judah." It was not at that time that Jehoshaphat was king of Judah, for that was the year of his death and the commencement of Jehoram's sole reign in the fifth year of Joram of Israel. The statement "when Jehoshaphat was king of Judah" should properly have gone with a synchronism of the commencement of Jehoram's coregency, which began before Joram's accession in Israel. Joram took the throne of Israel in the second year of Jehoram's coregency (2 Kings 1:17) and in the eighteenth year of Jehoshaphat's reign (2 Kings 3:1).

Another example of a misplaced datum is the citation in 2 Kings 14:21 and 2 Chronicles 26:1, 3 of the people of Judah placing the sixteen-year-old Azariah on the throne after the burial of Amaziah. This incident took place, not after the slaying of Amaziah at Lachish, fifteen years after the death of Jehoash (2 Kings 14:17–20; 2 Chron. 25:25–28) in 768/67 B.C., but at the time of Amaziah's capture by Jehoash twenty-four years before in 792/91. It is in connection with the events of 2 Kings 14:13–14 and 2 Chronicles 25:22–24 that the incident of Azariah's elevation to the throne as a lad of sixteen should have been noted.

Another instance of a misunderstanding of chronological data is that involved in placing the reigns of Pekah and Jotham (2 Kings 15:27–38) after the reign of Pekahiah (vv. 23–26) rather than preceding Pekahiah's reign where they properly belong and in the creation by late redactors of the synchronisms of 2 Kings 17:1 and 18:1, 9–10. These synchronisms call for the accession of Hoshea in the twelfth year of Ahaz and for an overlap between the reigns of Hoshea and Hezekiah. The correct arrangement of reigns of that period as previously ascertained is shown in Diagram 23 on page 200.

Let us notice how the details of this period were handled by contemporary recorders and the problems they brought to late editorial revisers. Menahem became king in Samaria in 752/51, the thirty-ninth year of Azariah, and a notation to that effect was entered in the Israelite journal. That same year Pekah commenced his rule in Gilead. When Jotham became coregent in Judah in 751/50, his coronation was synchronized, not with the reign of Menahem in Samaria, but with that of Pekah in Gilead, this being the second year of that reign. In Israel, Menahem, after a reign of ten years was succeeded by Pekahiah in the fiftieth year of Azariah, and that fact was again duly recorded on the Israelite scroll. When two years later Pekahiah was slain and succeeded by

Diagram 23
Arrangement of Reigns from 752–686 B.C.[4]

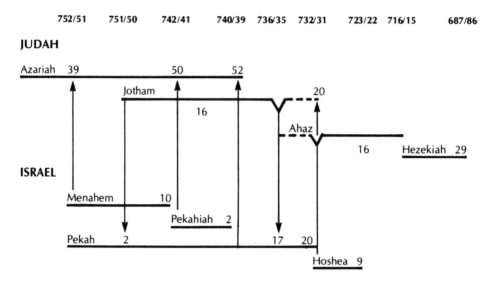

Pekah in the fifty-second year of Azariah, the fact of Pekah's accession to the throne in Samaria was entered in the Israelite record. A notation to the effect that he had previously reigned in Gilead would have been of service, but such does not seem to have been made. When his reign terminated, however, the scribes gave him full credit for all the time he had been on the throne, beginning with his rival reign in Gilead twenty years before.

Jotham was deposed by Ahaz after sixteen years, in the seventeenth year of Pekah—the seventeenth year since the commencement of his reign in Gilead but not since the beginning of his reign in Samaria in Azariah's fifty-second year. All these details were perfectly in order and all were clear at the time of their recording, but these details were no longer understood at the time of the final redaction of Kings.

No additional chronological data of Ahaz seem to have been recorded in the journal of Judah until his death in 716/15, and then he was given credit for a reign of sixteen years. But that was sixteen years from the death of Jotham, not sixteen years since Ahaz took the crown from Jotham.

Following the citation of Pekah's reign of twenty years and his death at the hands of Hoshea in Jotham's twentieth year, the Israelite journal continued with the details of Hoshea's tragic reign, including the three-year siege of Samaria and its fall in the ninth and last year of Hoshea (2 Kings 17:5–6). This brought an end to the Israelite journal, which was kept for so many years in some prophetic establishment of the northern kingdom. It is entirely possible,

---

[4]Because of the complexity of coordinating the modern Julian calendar with the beginning of the ancient years it is necessary to list both of the Julian years that span the ancient year under discussion in this chapter. See pages 87–88, n., for a fuller discussion of this issue.

however, that during the last critical days of Samaria's final siege, the prophetic recorders of Israel made their escape to Judah with their vital chronological documents. The final details of Israel's history could have been added to this journal while it was at a prophetic society in Judah rather than Israel.

The Judean journal, after a notation of the death of Ahaz (716/15), continued with an account of Hezekiah's reign. No synchronism of his accession appeared on the original record kept by contemporary scribes, for none was needed—the northern kingdom had come to its end some years before Hezekiah first came to the throne. To an editor of a later day unaware of the exact historical situation during the closing years of Israel's history, it must have seemed strange to find a king of Judah without a synchronism. And in view of the evidence we have of the late interpretation that was placed on the data preserved, we can conclude that a final redactor felt it his duty to supply the synchronism, which he regarded as in need of restoration.

The account of Hezekiah's reign reported the reform of the first year. The envoys of Judah passed throughout Israel extending their invitations to attend the Jerusalem Passover festival and mentioned a favorable response from many throughout the northern tribes (2 Chron. 29:3; 30:1, 5–7, 10–11, 18, 25). If there had been a king in Israel in this first year of Hezekiah and if he had opened his country to envoys from the south and given his blessing to those who decided to go to Jerusalem to worship, he would have been quite a different ruler from those before him. Shrines had been established at Dan and Bethel to keep Israel away from Jerusalem (1 Kings 12:26–29), and Ramah had been fortified in order to "prevent anyone from leaving or entering the territory of" Judah (2 Chron. 16:1). The characterization accorded Hoshea was not the same as that given to all preceding rulers, for although he was acknowledged as evil it was "not like the kings of Israel who preceded him" (2 Kings 17:2). If it had been thought that Hoshea was a contemporary of Hezekiah and that he had given so favorable a response to Judah's reformatory king by permitting his envoys to pass throughout the northern tribes with their invitations to resume worship at the Jerusalem shrine, and then had given his permission to all who chose to respond, we would find a valid reason for the comparatively favorable evaluation granted the last Israelite king.

The account of Hezekiah's reign on the Judean scroll included a notation of Sennacherib's campaign in the fourteenth year of Hezekiah and closed with the statement that he had reigned twenty-nine years.

Such were certain of the annalistic notations in the journals kept by prophetic recorders in Israel and Judah. These original records were to pass through many hands and undergo much editorial work before they took on their final form, but they constituted material of the highest value. The final editorial work on the Judean record was not completed until after the exile, for of Hezekiah we are told, "There was no one like him among all the kings of Judah" (2 Kings 18:5). Such a statement could not have been made until the last Judean king had been on his throne and the exile to Babylon had taken place. Nor was the record of Hoshea in Israel completed until after the Exile, for in 2 Kings 17:18–20 we read that after the removal of Israel, only Judah remained, but that Judah also turned from the Lord: "Therefore the LORD rejected all the people of Israel; he afflicted them and gave them into the hands of plunderers, until he thrust them from his presence." The citations of "and they are still there" (2 Kings 17:23) and "to this day" (vv. 34, 41) in Hoshea's record appear to hail from the period of Babylonian exile.

When Israel and Judah had met their doom and the northern and southern kingdoms were only a memory, the time had come to bring together the records of both nations into one combined history of the Hebrew kingdoms. No such history would have been possible without records of the type we have been discussing here.

Most of the source material could not be used, but the main source for each nation is distinctly mentioned. For Judah it was "the book of the annals of the kings of Judah" (1 Kings 14:29; 15:7, 23; 22:45; 2 Kings 8:23; 12:19; 14:18; 15:6, 36; 16:19; 20:20; 21:17, 25; 23:28; 24:5). For Israel it was "the book of the annals of the kings of Israel" (1 Kings 14:19; 15:31; 16:5, 14, 20, 27; 22:39; 2 Kings 1:18; 10:34; 13:8, 12; 14:15, 28; 15:11, 15, 21, 26, 31). These are the journals here under discussion, the "words of days" of the prophetic societies—the national diaries containing the day-by-day, year-by-year entries of happenings in Israel and Judah.

With such journals the basic materials were at hand for the composition of the Book of Kings. There still remained the task of final selection, interpretation, evaluation, and arrangement. Many items were used as they were found, preserving the flavor of the original recorders. Others were reworked and given the impress of the editorial revisers. Personal opinions were expressed, summaries were supplied, and words of admonition, commendation, or reproof were added. Our major concern here is the use that was made of the chronological data.

Inasmuch as the reigns of the kings of Israel and Judah were already arranged in their separate journals in the order in which the various rulers had commenced their reigns, and since the reigns of both nations were duly synchronized with each other, the production of a combined volume for Israel and Judah with all rulers arranged in the order of sequence with which they had commenced their reigns was a comparatively simple matter. In the Pekah-Jotham period, however, a situation existed that if not correctly understood, might lead to trouble. There, as we have learned, four Hebrew kings for a period reigned simultaneously—Menahem in Samaria, his rival Pekah in Gilead, Azariah in Judah, and his son Jotham as coregent.

We now know that the final redactors of Kings did not understand the chronological data of those years. The redactors got the impression that both Pekah and Jotham commenced their reigns, not as overlapping those of Menahem and Azariah, but as commencing in 740/39. The data called for twenty official years for each king, commencing, as it seemed, in Azariah's fifty-second and last year, 740/39, and terminating twenty years later, 720/19, in the twentieth year of Jotham when Hoshea slew Pekah and took his crown (2 Kings 15:27, 30).

The following is the order of sequence in which the rulers involved would commence their reigns according to this arrangement:

A. Menahem	752/51
B. Pekahiah	742/41
C. Pekah	740/39
D. Jotham	740/39
E. Ahaz	732/31
F. Hoshea	720/19
G. Hezekiah	716/15

This is the order in which these reigns now appear in Kings:

A. Menahem	2 Kings 15:16–22
B. Pekahiah	2 Kings 15:23–26
C. Pekah	2 Kings 15:27–31
D. Jotham	2 Kings 15:32–38
E. Ahaz	2 Kings 16:1–20
F. Hoshea	2 Kings 17:1–41
G. Hezekiah	2 Kings 18:1–20:21

The fact that the final redactor of Kings placed these reigns in this order makes it clear that this is the order in which they were regarded as having commenced their reigns. It is to be particularly noticed that in the above order the reigns of Pekah and Jotham are placed after Pekahiah. This gives evidence that Pekah and Jotham were considered to have commenced after 742/41 when Pekahiah began, namely, in 740/39. This arrangement would be as follows:

Diagram 24
Apparent Order of Sequence from Menahem to Hezekiah

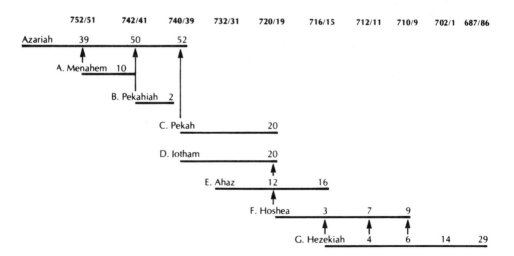

This is the arrangement we now find in the Book of Kings. This is the pattern that is called for by the synchronisms of 2 Kings 17 and 18. When the Old Testament canon was brought to its present form, the final redactors of

Kings were of the view that both Pekah and Jotham commenced their reigns in 740/39 and terminated them in 720/19, the year in which Hoshea would thus have commenced his reign. They were, however, in possession of information that showed them that the reign of Ahaz could not terminate later, nor the reign of Hezekiah begin earlier, than 716/15; so the reigns of these kings were placed in their present position in Kings. This brought the accession of Hoshea to the twelfth year of Ahaz as well as the twentieth year of Jotham as required by the synchronism of 2 Kings 15:30, and it was thus that the synchronism of 2 Kings 17:1 came into being. This also brought about the accession of Hezekiah in the third year of Hoshea and the synchronization of his fourth and sixth years with the seventh and ninth years of Hoshea. And it was thus that the synchronisms of 2 Kings 18:1, 9–10 had their origin. These synchronisms were then added to the records of Hezekiah and Hoshea by the final redactor of Kings.

The indications are that it was about the middle of the sixth century B.C. that these steps were taken. The last date given in Kings is the release of Jehoiachin in the thirty-seventh year of his captivity and the year of the accession of Evil-Merodach (Amel-Marduk) (2 Kings 25:27), 561 B.C.

When the chronicler did his work toward the end of the fifth century, the combined volume of the Kings of Israel and Judah was in existence. This is known from the fact that the sources there cited are no longer the separate journals of days of the kings of Israel or those of Judah as cited in Kings, but a combined "book of kings of Judah and Israel" (2 Chron. 16:11; 25:26; 27:7; 28:26; 32:32; 35:27; 36:8).

The absolutely perfect reconstruction of the past is by no means easy, particularly when it involves so much complexity as is found in the chronological data of Kings. If, however, these data had not been accurately recorded and preserved, those who brought into being our present Book of Kings would have been in no position to produce a volume of such marvelous accuracy as that book is today. So exact are these data that we can use them for the reconstruction of the original pattern of reigns of all the rulers of the divided monarchies. Even in the most difficult area where late misunderstandings arose, we can now complete a task that was then left undone. For the task which they performed so well we cannot but be highly grateful.

CHAPTER ELEVEN

In Conclusion

HE VITAL QUESTION concerning the chronological scheme set forth in these pages is whether or not it is the true arrangement of reigns of the Hebrew kings. Certainly, this system has brought harmony out of what was once regarded as hopeless confusion. But is it necessarily the true restoration of the original pattern of reigns? At the least this research shows that such a restoration is possible. However, we must accept the premise of an original reckoning of reigns in Israel according to the nonaccession-year system with a later shift to the accession-year method; of the early use in Judah of accession-year reckoning, a shift to the nonaccession-year system, and then a return to the original accession-year method; of the need to begin the regnal year in Israel with Nisan and with Tishri in Judah; of the existence of a number of coregencies; and of the fact that at some late date—long after the original records of the kings had been set in order and when the true arrangement of the reigns had been forgotten—certain synchronisms in 2 Kings 17 and 18 were introduced by some late hand twelve years out of harmony with the original pattern of reigns. When all this is understood, we see that it is possible to set forth an arrangement of reigns for the Hebrew kings in which there are both internal harmony and agreement with contemporary history.

Since the first publication of this volume in 1951, a number of tablets have come to light providing additional chronological information concerning the ancient East. One of these is an Assyrian king list tablet that was brought to the United States in 1953 by a student from Iraq. Called to the attention of the Oriental Institute of Chicago, the tablet was found to be similar to the famous Khorsabad King List, but extending two reigns beyond—to the end of Shalmaneser V in 722 B.C. These tablets give the lengths of reign of the Assyrian kings back to the middle of the second millennium B.C. The new tablet was designated the SDAS King List and, together with the Khorsabad King List, was given a preliminary publication by I. J. Gelb.[1]

---

[1] I. J. Gelb, "Two Assyrian King Lists," *Journal of Near Eastern Studies* 13 (1954): 209–30.

Of greater relevance to the period of Old Testament chronology here under discussion were a number of tablets brought to light in the British Museum. In 1923 C. J. Gadd had published tablet B.M. 21901 under the title *The Fall of Nineveh*. The tablet gave a year-by-year account of Assyrian and Babylonian affairs from 616 to 609 B.C. In connection with the closing "catchline" of this tablet that introduced the events of the following year to be described on the next succeeding tablet, Gadd expressed his view that "we might have expected, were the text still before us, to have obtained interesting details of the conflict, which probably occurred in 608, between Nabopolassar and his allies on one side, and on the other Neco II of Egypt, fresh from his victory over Josiah, king of Judah, who had endeavoured to oppose his march into Syria. No livelier wish could be expressed than that this succeeding chapter may some day be discovered."[2]

That wish has now been realized and the tablet has been found, not in ancient Mesopotamian sands but in the British Museum. This is tablet B.M. 22047, covering the years 608–606 B.C., one of a group of tablets published in 1956 by D. J. Wiseman in his *Chronicles of Chaldaean Kings (626–556 B.C.) in the British Museum.* It appears that these tablets had been arranged for publication by Prof. L. W. King, formerly assistant keeper in the Department of Egyptian and Assyrian Antiquities of the British Museum, but whose early demise prevented the project from being carried out. Its recent completion by Wiseman has been of unusual value to all who have an interest in the history of the Neo-Babylonian period, especially to Bible students who are concerned with the closing years of Judean history and the commencement of the Babylonian exile. These newly published tablets have fixed beyond question such dates as 609 for the death of Josiah, 605 for the battle of Carchemish, and 597 for the captivity of Jehoiachin and the accession of Zedekiah.

These Neo-Babylonian tablets are part of a long line of historical records from the hands of detached contemporary observers who narrated events in what appears to be an unbiased and impersonal style. The object seems to have been the presentation of a straightforward account of events strictly as they took place, year by year. As far as we can tell, these chronicles go back with certainty to the Kassite period of the sixteenth to the fourteenth centuries B.C., and with a more limited degree of accuracy to the rulers of Agade in the third millennium B.C. and the earlier Sumerian dynasts and their gods. Incomplete and sometimes inaccurate though the records for the earlier periods might be, for the later periods they provide accurate and detailed sources of the highest importance. Were it not for these chronicles we would have little knowledge of many details concerning events in Babylon and among nations with whom Babylon had contacts, including Assyria, Elam, and such more distant places as the lands of Hatti, Judea, and Egypt.

The extant tablets from the late Babylonian and Persian periods give evidence of a keen historical interest in current events and of a desire to pass on information concerning such events to posterity.

The Neo-Babylonian prisms consist of strict year-by-year records of events

---

[2] C. J. Gadd, *The Fall of Nineveh* (London, 1923), p. 23.

written in a small script in closely packed columns. There are breaks between the various regnal years, marked by lines across the tablet. The record of each year opens with a statement identifying that year, followed by an account of the events of the year. For the final year of Nabopolassar the record reads: "In the twenty-first year (605 B.C.) the king of Akkad stayed in his own land, Nebuchadrezzar his eldest son, the crown-prince, mustered [the Babylonian army] and took command of his troops; he marched to Carchemish which is on the bank of the Euphrates, and crossed the river [to go] against the Egyptian army which lay in Carchemish . . . fought with each other and the Egyptian army withdrew before him. He accomplished their defeat and to non-existence (beat?) them. As for the rest of the Egyptian army which had escaped from the defeat [so quickly that] no weapon had reached them in the district of Hamath the Babylonian troops overtook and defeated them so that not a single man escaped to his own country. At that time Nebuchadrezzar conquered the whole area of the Hatti-country. For twenty-one years Nabopolassar had been king of Babylon. On the 8th of the month of Ab (Aug. 16, 605) he died (literally, 'the fates'); in the month of Elul Nebuchadrezzar returned to Babylon and on the first day of the month of Elul (Sept. 7, 605) he sat on the royal throne in Babylon."[3] The value of such material will be immediately apparent to every student of the Bible or of ancient Near Eastern history.

The account of Nebuchadnezzar goes on as follows: "In the 'accession year' Nebuchadrezzar went back again to the Hatti-land and until the month of Sebat marched unopposed through the Hatti-land; in the month of Sebat he took the heavy tribute of the Hatti-territory to Babylon." "In the first year of Nebuchadrezzar in the month of Sivan he mustered his army and went to the Hatti-territory, he marched about unopposed in the Hatti-territory until the month of Kislev. All the kings of the Hatti-land came before him and he received their heavy tribute. He marched to the city of Askelon and captured it in the month of Kislev. He captured its king and plundered it and carried off [spoil from it . . . .] He turned the city into a mound and heaps of ruins and then in the month of Sebat he marched back to Babylon."

In the second, third, and fourth years there were further campaigns in the Hatti-land. The record of the fourth year reads: "In the fourth year the king of Akkad mustered his army and marched to the Hatti-land. In the Hatti-land they marched unopposed. In the month of Kislev he took the lead of his army and marched to Egypt. The king of Egypt heard [it] and mustered his army. In open battle they smote the breast [of] each other and inflicted great havoc on each other. The king of Akkad and his troops turned back and returned to Babylon." This indicates a Babylonian defeat, as is evidenced by the record of the following year: "In the fifth year the king of Akkad [stayed] in his own land and gathered together his chariots and horses in great numbers."

The sixth year Nebuchadnezzar was once more in the Hatti-country "scouring the desert" and taking plunder from the Arabs. The record of the next year is of unusual interest to Bible students and those interested in Old Testa-

---

[3]D. J. Wiseman, *Chronicles of Chaldaean Kings (626–556 B.C.) in the British Museum* (London, 1956), pp. 67ff.

ment chronology: "In the seventh year, the month of Kislev, the king of Akkad mustered his troops, marched to the Hatti-land, and encamped against (i.e., besieged) the city of Judah and on the second day of the month of Adar (March 16, 597) he seized the city and captured the king. He appointed there a king of his own choice (literally, 'heart'), received its heavy tribute and sent [them] to Babylon."[4] This is the account of the capture of Jehoiachin and the establishment of Zedekiah on the throne.

In his eighth year Nebuchadnezzar went as far as Carchemish. In the ninth year there was a march against Elam, and in the tenth year a rebellion was put down in Akkad, after which there was another campaign to the Hatti-land. The tablet ends with the record of the eleventh year, 594, when the campaign was once more to the Hatti-land. Evidently Palestine was much to the front in Babylonian interests throughout this period. It is to be hoped that the tablet or tablets carrying the record down to Nebuchadnezzar's nineteenth year, when the final fall of Jerusalem took place, may someday be recovered.

With such chronicles the ancient East springs back to life. Rulers live again, battles are fought, cities are built or demolished, rebellions are crushed, and kingdoms are brought to glorious or inglorious ends. And all this is done within an exact chronological framework that is a historian's delight.

These records make it abundantly clear that in ancient times there was a high degree of interest in chronological details. Events were set within their exact historical framework, year by year and month by month, and at times even to the very day. Thus it is that we can now say with certainty that Jerusalem was taken in the spring of 597 B.C. on Saturday, 16 March.

That there were chronologically minded scribes in Babylonia, the chronicles of the Chaldean kings make abundantly clear. That there were such scribes in Israel and Judah is abundantly attested by the interesting and troublesome numbers of the Hebrew kings. To the recorders in the Hebrew prophetic cloisters we owe a debt of gratitude for the vision, devotion, and care that characterized their work. They have at times been accused of negligence and gross inaccuracy, but such charges are without foundation in fact. To say that in their recordings "passages have been ruthlessly altered" is to lay ourselves open to charges of inaccuracy rather than to discredit their work. What these scribes saw or heard or thought, they wrote with a high regard for accuracy and detail. When copies were made of what others had written, the work was done with the utmost fidelity.

The original chronicles of the kings of Israel and Judah were contemporary productions in full accord with the facts of the times. During the period of exile the records from north and south were brought together in a single book. The facts we have set forth here in the restoration of the chronological patterns of the individual reigns give evidence that the work from beginning to end was done with great devotion and almost unbelievable accuracy.

And what are we to say if, here and there, an indication of some misunderstanding may come to light? This work was done by people, not God. These people spoke for God, but they were not divine. God alone is infallible. Has

---

any person ever lived who could make no mistake? That the original records were exact in detail we have no reason to doubt. And that they were copied again and again with an almost uncanny degree of accuracy is altogether clear. But it is likewise clear that in connection with later editorial work on the involved chronological data, misunderstandings could and did take place. Such we have noted in 2 Chronicles 15:19 and 16:1; in 2 Kings 8:16 and 14:21; in the order of sequence in which the reigns were placed in 2 Kings 15:23–38; and in the synchronisms of 2 Kings 17:1 and 18:1, 9–10.

In view of the problems that the complexities of Hebrew chronological data have raised for scholars of our modern age, it is a matter of amazement that the misunderstandings found in the Masoretic Text are so very few. Scholars today have found difficulties that have baffled them all the way along the line. What about ancient times? Were all details always altogether clear to the editors responsible for the later renditions of the Old Testament text? In the synchronisms of 2 Kings 17 and 18 we have seen that this was not the case. Even before the Old Testament canon closed we have evidence that problems existed and that efforts were being made to solve them.

Additional evidence of the difficulties with which early biblical scholars were struggling in their dealings with the chronological data of Kings is found in variations in the Greek texts from the data in the Hebrew. Below is a summary of these variations as brought together by Burney.[5] It must not be thought that all the variations in the Septuagint were the original productions of those who first translated Kings from Hebrew into Greek in the third century B.C., for they could have been found in some earlier Hebrew text not now extant.

VARIANT NUMBERS IN THE GREEK TEXTS

1 KINGS		MASORETIC TEXT	SEPTUAGINT	LUCIAN
15:9	Asa	20th of Jeroboam	24th of Jeroboam	24th of Jeroboam
16:8	Elah	26th of Asa	20th of Asa	20th of Asa
16:15	Zimri	27th of Asa	wanting	22d of Asa
16:29	Ahab	38th of Asa	2d of Jehoshaphat	2d of Jehoshaphat
22:41	Jehoshaphat	4th of Ahab	11th of Omri	11th of Omri
22:52	Ahaziah Is	17th of Jehoshaphat	17th of Jehoshaphat	24th of Jehoshaphat

2 KINGS				
1:17	Joram	2d of Jehoram	18th of Jehoshaphat	2d of Jehoram
3:1	Joram	18th of Jehoshaphat	18th of Jehoshaphat	wanting
8:16	Jehoram	8 years	40 years	8 years
8:25	Ahaziah Ju	12th of Joram	12th of Joram	11th of Joram
9:29	Ahaziah Ju	11th of Joram	11th of Joram	11th of Joram
15:23	Pekahiah	2 years	2 years	10 years

A careful study of these variations reveals that they are not the result of scribal errors but constitute editorial changes made with the object of correcting what were regarded as errors in the early Hebrew text. Thus where the

---

[5]C. F. Burney, *Notes on the Hebrew Text of the Books of Kings* (Oxford: Clarendon, 1903), pp. xliff.

Masoretic Text gives two synchronisms for the accession of Joram in Isarel—in the second year of Jehoram (2 Kings 1:17) and in the eighteenth year of Jehoshaphat (2 Kings 3:1)—the Septuagint gives both of these as the eighteenth year of Jehoshaphat, while Lucian gives the second year of Jehoram in 2 Kings 1:17 but omits the synchronism in 2 Kings 3:1. Thus the Greek translations have lost this valuable indication that there was a coregency between Jehoram and Jehoshaphat and the precise information regarding the year when it began. The substitution of the round number forty for the exact number eight by the Septuagint in 2 Kings 8:16 gives evidence of the uncertainty regarding the exact length of Jehoram's reign. It is only when the number eight is recognized as the length of Jehoram's sole reign, rather than the total including his coregency, that harmony in the chronological data of this period is possible and that the original pattern may be restored, but the Septuagint evidently failed to perceive the existence of this coregency. In the Masoretic Text two synchronisms are given for the accession of Ahaziah in Judah, in the eleventh year of Joram (2 Kings 9:29) and also in the twelfth year (2 Kings 8:25). Lucian gives both of these as the eleventh year. In this obvious endeavor to correct what was regarded as a contradiction in the data, Lucian lost the valuable clue that at this time a shift had been made in Judah from accession- to nonaccession-year reckoning.

It will not be our province here to provide a detailed explanation of just how each of the above variations in the Greek texts arose.[6] However, it is interesting to note the specific details of the struggles early students of the Old Testament were having with the data of the Hebrew kings only a few centuries after the kingdoms had ended and very shortly after the Old Testament canon had been brought into being. In no instance is a Greek variation an improvement over the Hebrew. The fallacies of the Greek innovations may be proved by the wide divergence of the patterns of reigns they call for from the years of contemporary chronology.

In Josephus' *Antiquities* a number of variations also are found from the data of the kings in the Hebrew text. These are as follows:

	MASORETIC TEXT	JOSEPHUS
Omri	31st of Asa	30th of Asa (8.12.5)
Jehu	28 years	27 years (9.8.1)
Jehoahaz	23d of Joash	21st of Joash (9.8.5)
Azariah	27th of Jeroboam	14th of Jeroboam (9.10.3–4)
Jeroboam II	41 years	40 years (9.10.1, 3)
Hezekiah	3d of Hoshea	4th of Hoshea (9.13.1; 10.3.1)
Fall of Samaria	6th of Hezekiah	7th of Hezekiah (9.14.1)
Jehoahaz	3 months	3 months and 10 days (10.5.2)

It will be noticed that none of Josephus' variations is the same as any in the Septuagint. It can be shown that these variations are not the result of scribal

---

[6]A detailed discussion of these individual variations is found in Chapter 9, "The Variant Figures of the Greek Texts," pp. 167–203, of the first edition of my book *The Mysterious Numbers of the Hebrew Kings* (Chicago: University of Chicago Press, 1951, 1955).

errors but fit into an explicit pattern of reigns.[7] Josephus' length of the reign of Jehoahaz, three months and ten days, is obviously an error, taken from the datum for Jehoiachin in 2 Chronicles 36:9. None of the variations of Josephus is an improvement over any datum in the Masoretic Text. The inaccuracy of his pattern is proved by its divergence from the years of contemporary chronology all the way along the line.

Every serious student of the Old Testament is acquainted with the struggles that modern scholars have had with the perplexing numbers of the Hebrew kings and with the numerous systems of Old Testament chronology that have been produced.[8] For many years the conviction has been held that these chronological data provide positive mathematical evidence of the unreliability of the Hebrew text. Today, however, it is evident that such a judgment is not valid. The once ambiguous and confusing numbers of the Hebrew kings have taken on new value and meaning. Bewilderment and doubt have been replaced by certainty and assurance. In these numbers we now know that we are dealing not with fancy but fact. The true meanings of these once seemingly irreconcilable data have been clarified and we are in a position to appreciate their value in the fields of biblical scholarship and ancient historical research. With these synchronisms and lengths of reign as building blocks, we are now in a position to construct an edifice of Hebrew history chronologically sound in the area of the kingdoms of Israel and Judah.

There are four sets of chronological data for the period of the divided monarchy: (1) the lengths of reign of the kings of Judah, (2) the lengths of reign of the kings of Israel, (3) the Judean synchronisms with Israel, and (4) the Israelite synchronisms with Judah. These data provide four distinct chronological yardsticks so precise and so demanding as to call for an historical framework of exact dimensions—the original pattern of reigns of the Hebrew rulers.

In our work with these data we did not begin with the assumption that they were largely in error, whether because of mistakes in original recordings, scribal corruptions that crept in along the way, or editorial misjudgments of some late day. But we did begin on a quest to ascertain whether there might not be some basic chronological pattern into which these numbers would fit, a pattern not heretofore constructed because the true meaning of the data was not understood.

That project has now been completed and the results are here set forth. In the pages of this volume are found the links of a chain of chronological evidence extending from Rehoboam to Hezekiah in Judah and from Jeroboam to Hoshea in Israel. The reigns of both nations are constantly interwoven with each other in strict accord with the requirements of the data provided by the original Hebrew recorders. This chain we believe to be complete, sound, and capable of withstanding any challenge that historical evidence may bring to it.

It is only proper that the dates we have given here for the rulers of Israel

---

[7]It will not be our province here to set forth the specific details of Josephus' arrangement as called for by these variations. For these details see Chapter 10, "The Variant Figures of Josephus," pp. 204–27, of the first edition of *The Mysterious Numbers of the Hebrew Kings*.

[8]A survey of a number of these systems is found in Chapter 11, "Modern Chronological Systems," pp. 228–67, of the first edition of *The Mysterious Numbers of the Hebrew Kings*.

and Judah should be subjected to every possible test. If these dates are final and absolute, they have nothing to fear from the most careful and exhaustive research. The kings of Judah and Israel have in the years gone by had part in many a chronological fray. We have every reason to believe that their days of such conflict are almost over. Our hope is that when the smoke of the battle clears and the din of the final conflict has subsided, each of these valiant stalwarts of old may occupy his rightful place in history.

Appendixes

THE CHRONOLOGICAL DATA OF THE KINGS

JUDAH

Data according to the accession-year system

King	Synchronism	Length of Reign	Reference	
Rehoboam		17 years	1 Kings 14:21	2 Chron. 12:13
Abijah	18th of Jeroboam	3 years	1 Kings 15:1, 2	2 Chron. 13:1, 2
Asa	20th of Jeroboam	41 years	1 Kings 15:9, 10	2 Chron. 16:13
Jehoshaphat	4th of Ahab	25 years	1 Kings 22:41, 42	2 Chron. 20:31

Data according to the nonaccession-year system

King	Synchronism	Length of Reign	Reference	
Jehoram	5th of Joram	8 years	2 Kings 8:16, 17	2 Chron. 21:5, 20
Ahaziah	12th of Joram	1 year	2 Kings 8:25, 26	2 Chron. 22:2
Ahaziah	11th of Joram*		2 Kings 9:29	
Athaliah			2 Kings 11:3, 4	2 Chron. 22:12
Joash	7th of Jehu	40 years	2 Kings 12:1	2 Chron. 24:1

Data according to the accession-year system

King	Synchronism	Length of Reign	Reference	
Amaziah	2nd of Jehoash	29 years	2 Kings 14:1, 2	2 Chron. 25:1
Azariah (Uzziah)	27th of Jeroboam	52 years	2 Kings 15:1, 2	2 Chron. 26:3
Jotham	2d of Pekah	16 years	2 Kings 15:32, 33	2 Chron. 27:1, 8
Ahaz	17th of Pekah	16 years	2 Kings 16:1, 2	2 Chron. 28:1
Hezekiah	3d of Hoshea	29 years	2 Kings 18;1, 2	2 Chron. 29:1
Manasseh		55 years	2 Kings 21:1	2 Chron. 33:1
Amon		2 years	2 Kings 21:19	2 Chron. 33:21
Josiah		31 years	2 Kings 22:1	2 Chron. 34:1
Jehoahaz		3 months	2 Kings 23:31	2 Chron. 36:2
Jehoiakim		11 years	2 Kings 23:36	2 Chron. 36:5
Jehoiachin		3 months	2 Kings 24:8	
Jehoiachin		3 months, 10 days		2 Chron. 36:9 .
Zedekiah		11 years	2 Kings 24:18	2 Chron. 36:11

*This synchronism is according to the accession-year system.

ISRAEL

Data according to the nonaccession-year system

King	Synchronism	Length of Reign	Reference
Jeroboam I		22 years	1 Kings 14:20
Nadab	2d of Asa	2 years	1 Kings 15:25
Baasha	3d of Asa	24 years	1 Kings 15:28, 33
Elah	26th of Asa	2 years	1 Kings 16:8
Zimri	27th of Asa	7 days	1 Kings 16:10, 15
Tibni			1 Kings 16:21, 22
Omri	31st of Asa	12 years	1 Kings 16:23
Ahab	38th of Asa	22 years	1 Kings 16:29
Ahaziah	17th of Jehoshaphat	2 years	1 Kings 22:51
Joram	18th of Jehoshaphat	12 years	2 Kings 3:1
Joram	2d of Jehoram		2 Kings 1:17
Jehu		28 years	2 Kings 10:36
Jehoahaz	23d of Joash	17 years	2 Kings 13:1

Data according to accession-year system

King	Synchronism	Length of Reign	Reference
Jehoash	37th of Joash	16 years	2 Kings 13:10
Jeroboam II	15th of Amaziah	41 years	2 Kings 14:23
Zechariah	38th of Azariah (Uzziah)	6 months	2 Kings 15:8
Shallum	39th of Azariah	1 month	2 Kings 15:13
Menahem	39th of Azariah	10 years	2 Kings 15:17
Pekahiah	50th of Azariah	2 years	2 Kings 15:23
Pekah	52nd of Azariah	20 years	2 Kings 15:27
Hoshea	20th of Jotham		2 Kings 15:30
Hoshea	12th of Ahaz	9 years	2 Kings 17:1

THE DATES OF THE KINGS OF ISRAEL AND JUDAH

ISRAEL			JUDAH		
King	Overlapping Reigns	Reign	King	Coregency	Reign
Jeroboam I		931/30—910/9	Rehoboam		931/30—913
			Abijah		913　—911/10
Nadab		910/9 —909/8	Asa		911/10—870/69
Baasha		909/8 —886/85			
Elah		886/85—885/84			
Zimri		885/84			
Tibni		885/84—880			
Omri	885/84—880	880　—874/73	Jehoshaphat	872/71—870/69	870/69—848
Ahab		874/73—853	Jehoram	853　—848	848　—841
Ahaziah		853　—852	Ahaziah		841
Joram		852　—841	Athaliah		841　—835
Jehu		841　—814/13	Joash		835　—796
Jehoahaz		814/13—798	Amaziah		796　—767
Jehoash		798　—782/81	Azariah (Uzziah)	792/91—767	767　—740/39
Jeroboam II	793/92—782/81	782/81—753			
Zechariah		753　—752			
Shallum		752			
Menahem		752　—742/41	Jotham	750　—740/39	740/39—732/31
Pekahiah		742/41—740/39			
Pekah	752　—740/39	740/39—732/31	Ahaz	735　—732/31	732/31—716/15
Hoshea		732/31—723/22			
			Hezekiah		716/15—687/86
			Manasseh	697/96—687/86	687/86—643/42
			Amon		643/42—641/40
			Josiah		641/40—609
			Jehoahaz		609
			Jehoiakim		609　—598
			Jehoiachin		598　—597
			Zedekiah		597　—586

THE AGES OF THE KINGS OF JUDAH

King	Father	Age at Accession as Coregent	Age at Beginning of Sole Reign	Age at Birth of Successor	Age at Association of Son as Coregent	Age at Death
Rehoboam	Solomon		41			59
Abijah	Rehoboam					
Asa	Abijah					
Jehoshaphat	Asa	35	38	23	54	59
Jehoram	Jehoshaphat	32	37	23		44
Ahaziah	Jehoram		22(42)	22		22
Athaliah	Ahab					
Joash	Ahaziah		7	22		46
Amaziah	Joash		25	15	30	54
Azariah	Amaziah	16	39	33	57	68
Jotham	Azariah	25	36	21		44
Ahaz	Jotham		20	16		40
Hezekiah	Ahaz		25	33	44	54
Manasseh	Hezekiah	12	22	45		66
Amon	Manasseh		22	17		24
Josiah	Amon		8	17 Jehoahaz		39
				16 Jehoiakim		
				31 Zedekiah		
Jehoahaz	Josiah		23			
Jehoiakim	Josiah		25	19		36
Jehoiachin	Jehoiakim		18(8)			
Zedekiah	Josiah		21			

COREGENCIES AND RIVAL REIGNS IN ISRAEL AND JUDAH

	Years Recorded	Years of Coregency or Overlapping Reign
Coregency Included in the Total Years of Reign		
Judah:		
Jehoshaphat	25	4
Azariah	52	24
Jotham	16(20)	12
Manasseh	55	10
Israel:		
Jeroboam II	41	12
Coregency Not Included in the Total Years of Reign		
Judah:		
Jehoram	8	6
Ahaz	16	4
Recorded Reign Partially Overlapping the Reign of a Rival King		
Israel:		
Omri	12	6
Pekah	20	12

HEBREW AND BABYLONIAN MONTHS

Babylonian	Hebrew	Approximate Modern Equivalent
1. Nisanu	Nisan	Middle of March to middle of April
2. Aiaru	Iyyar	Middle of April to middle of May
3. Simanu	Sivan	Middle of May to middle of June
4. Duzu	Tammuz	Middle of June to middle of July
5. Abu	Ab	Middle of July to middle of August
6. Ululu	Elul	Middle of August to middle of September
7. Tashritu	Tishri	Middle of September to middle of October
8. Arahsmnu	Heshvan	Middle of October to middle of November
9. Kislimu	Kislev	Middle of November to middle of December
10. Tebetu	Tebeth	Middle of December to middle of January
11. Shabatu	Shebat	Middle of January to middle of February
12. Addaru	Adar	Middle of February to middle of March

THE ASSYRIAN EPONYM LIST

[NOTE: This list of the Assyrian eponyms is based on the list of Daniel David Luckenbill, *Ancient Records of Assyria and Babylonia*, 2 (Chicago, 1927), 430ff. From 648 to 783 the dates are the same. Nabu-shar-usur has been transferred from 784 to 786 where he occupies the same eponym year with Balatu, thus reducing each eponym beyond 786 by one year.]

892 .... shar ....
891 Urta-zarme
890 Tâb-êtir-Ashur
889 Ashur la-Kînu
888 Tukulti-Urta, the king
887 Tak-lak-ana-bêl-ia
886 Abi-ili-a-a
885 Ilu-milki
884 Iari
883 Ashur-shezibani
882 Ashur-nasir-apli, the king
881 Ashur-iddin
880 Shumutti-adur
879 Sha-ilima-damka
878 Dagan-bêl-nasir
877 Urta-pia-usur
876 Urta-bêl-usur
875 Shangu-Ashur-lilbur
874 Shamash-upahir (var., ub-la)
873 Nergal-bêl-kumua
872 Kurdi-Ashur
871 Ashur-li'
870 Ashur-natkil
869 Bêl-mudammik
868 Daiân-Urta
867 Ishtar-emukâia
866 Shamash-nuri
865 Mannu-dân-ana-ili
864 Shamash-bêl-usur
863 Urta-iliai
862 Urta-etiranni
861 Urta (var., Ashur)-iliai
860 Nergal-iska-danin

859	Tâb-bêl when Shulman-asharidu (Shalmaneser) son of Ashurnasirpal [took his seat on the throne]		
858	Sharru-baltu-nishê		[against Hamanu]
857	Shulman-asharid (Shalmaneser)	king of Ashur	[against Bit-Adini]
856	Ashur-bêl-ukin	field-marshal	[against Bit-Adini]
855	Ashur-bunaia-usur	chief cup-bearer	[against Bit-Adini]
854	Abu-ina-ekalli-lilbur	high chamberlain	....
853	Daiân-Ashur	field-marshal	[against Hatte]
852	Shamash-abua	governor of Nasibina	[against Til-Abni]
851	Shamash-bêl-usur	(governor) of Calah	[against Babylonia]
850	Bêl-bunaia	high chamberlain	[against Babylonia]
849	Hadi-lipushu	(governor) of	[against Carchemish]
848	Nergal-alik-pani	(governor) of	[against Hatte]
847	Bir-Ramana	(governor) of	[against Pakarhubuna]
846	Urta-mukîn-nishê	[(governor) of	against Iaeti]
845	Urta-nâdin-shum	[(governor) of	against Hatte]
844	Ashur-bunua	[(governor) of	against Nairî]
843	Tâb-Urta	[(governor) of	against Namri]
842	Taklak-ana-sharri (var., -Ashur)	[(governor) of	against Hamanu]
841	Adad-rimani	[(governor) of	against Damascus]
840	Bêl-abua (var., Shamash-)	[(governor) of Ahi-[Suhina]	[against Kue]
839	Shulmu-bêl-lumur	(governor) of Rasappa	against [Kumuhi]
838	Urta-kibsi-usur	(governor) of Ahi-Suhina	against Danabi
837	Urta-ilia	(governor) of Salmat	against Tabali
836	Kurdi-Ashur	(governor) of [Kirruri]	against Melidi
835	Shêpâ-sharri	(governor) of Nineveh	against Namri
834	Nergal-mudammik	the abarakku	against Kue
833	Iahalu	(governor) of [Kakzi] against Kue	against Kue The great god went out from Dêr
832	Ululâia	(governor) of [Nasibina]	against Urartu (Armenia)
831	Nishpatî Bêl	(governor) of [Calah]	against Unki
830	Nergal-ilia	(governor) of Arrapha	against Ulluba
829	Hubâia	(governor) of [Mazamua]	against Mannai
828	Ilu-mukîn-ahi	(governor) of	revolt
827	Shulman-asharidu (Shalmaneser)	king of Assyria	revolt
826	Dâian-Ashur	[field-marshal]	revolt
825	Ashur-bunâia-usur	[chief cup-bearer]	revolt
824	Iahallu	[abarakku]	revolt
823	Bêl-bunâia	[high chamberlain]	revolt
822	Shamshi-Adad	king of [Assyria	against Sikris]
821	Iahalu	[field-marshal	against Madai]
820	Bêl-dain	high chamberlain	against .... Shumme
819	Urta-upahhir	[abarakku	against Karne]
818	Shamash-ilia	[abarakku	against Karne]
817	Nergal-ilia	[(governor) of Arrapha	against Tille]
816	Ashur-bana-usur	[chief cup-bearer	against Tille]
815	Nishpatî-Bêl	(governor) of [Nasibina]	against Zarate
814	Bêl-balat	(governor) of [Calah] against Dêr	The great god went to Dêr
813	Mushiknish	(governor) of [Kirruri]	against Ahsana
812	Urta-asharid	(governor) of [Salmat]	against Chaldea
811	Shamash-kumua	(governor) of Arrapha	against Babylonia
810	Bêl-kâta-sabat	(governor) of Mazamua	in the land

809	Adad-nirâri	[king] of Assyria	against Madai
808	Nergal-ilia	field-marshal	against Guzana
807	Bêl-daiân	high chamberlain	against Mannai
806	Sil-bêl	chief cup-bearer	against Mannai
805	Ashur-taklak	abarakku	against Arpadda
804	[Shamash-ilia]	abarakku	against Hazazi
803	Nergal-êresh	(governor) of Rasappa	against Ba'li
802	Ashur-baltu-nishe	(governor) of Arrapha	against the seacoast. A plague
801	Urta-ilia	(governor) of Ahi-Suhina	against Hubushkia
800	Shêpâ-Ishtar	(governor) of Nasibina	against Madai
799	Marduk-ishme-ani (?)	(governor) of Amedi	against Madai
798	Mutakkil-Marduk	Rab-shakê	against Lusia
797	Bêl-tarsi-iluma	(governor) of Calah	against Namri
796	Ashur-bêl-usur	(governor) of Kirruri	against Mansuate
795	Marduk-shaddua	(governor) of Salmat	against Dêr
794	Kîn-abua	(governor) of Tushhan	against Dêr
793	Mannu-ki-Ashur	(governor) of Guzana	against Madai
792	Mushallim-Urta	(governor) of Tillê	against Madai
791	Bêl-ikîshani	(governor) of Mehi-nish (?)	against Hubushkia
790	Shêpâ-Shamash	(governor) of Isana	against Itu'a
789	Urta-mukîn-ahi	(governor) of Nineveh	against Madai
788	Adad-Mushammir	(governor) of Kakzi	against Madai
787	Sil-Ishtar	(governor) of [Arba-ilu?]	against Madai. Nabu entered the new temple
786	Balatu	(governor) of [Shiba-niba?]	
	Nabu-shar-usur	(governor) of [Rimusi]	against [Kishi]
785	Adad-uballit	(governor) of [Udnunna]	against Hubushkia. The great god went to Dêr
784	Marduk-shar-usur	(governor) of	against Hubushkia
783	Ninurta-nasir	(governor) of Mazamua	against Itu'
782	Nabu-li'	(governor) of Nasibina	against Itu'
781	Shulman-asharid (Shalmaneser)	king of Assyria	against Urarti
780	Shamshi-ilu	field-marshal	against Urarti
779	Marduk-rîmani	chief cup-bearer	against Urarti
778	Bêl-lishir	high chamberlain	against Urarti
777	Nabu-ishid-ukîn (var., Shamash-ishi-dia-ukîn)	abarakku	against Itu'
776	Pân-Ashur-lamur	shaknu	against Urarti
775	Nergal-êresh	(governor) of Rasappa	against Erini
774	Ishtar-d'uri	(governor) of Nasibina	against Urarti (and) Namri
773	Mannu-ki-Adad	(governor) of Salmat	against Damascus
772	Ashur-bêl-usur	(governor) of Calah	against Hatarika
771	Ashur-dân	king of Assyria	against Gananati
770	Shamshi-ilu	field-marshal	against Marrat
769	Bêl-ilia	(governor) of Arrapha	against Itu'
768	Aplia	(governor) of Mazamua	in the land
767	Kurdi-Ashur	(governor) of Ahi-Suhina	against Gananati
766	Mushallim-Urta	(governor) of Tillê	against Madai
765	Urta-mukîn-nishê	(governor) of Kirruri	against Hatarika. A plague
764	Sidki-ilu	(governor) of Tushhan	in the land
763	Bur (Ishdi)-Sagale	(governor) of Guzana	revolt in city of Ashur. In the month of *Simânu* an eclipse of the sun took place
762	Tâb-bêl	(governor) of Amedi	revolt in the city of Ashur
761	Nabu-mukîn-ahi	(governor) of Nineveh	revolt in the city of Arrapha

760	Lakipu	(governor) of Kakzi	revolt in the city of Arrapha
759	Pân-Ashur-lamur	(governor) of Arbailu	revolt in the city of Guzana. A plague
758	Bêl-taklak	(governor) of Isana	against Guzana. Peace in the land
757	Urta-iddina	(governor) of Kurban	in the land
756	Bêl-shadua	(governor) of Parnunna	in the land
755	Ikishu (var., Kîsu)	(governor) of Mehi-nish (?)	against Hatarika
754	Urta-shezibani	(governor) of Rimusi	against Arpadda. Return from the city of Ashur
753	Ashur-nirâri	king of Assyria	in the land
752	Shamshi-ilu	field-marshal	in the land
751	Marduk-shallimani	high chamberlain	in the land
750	Bêl-dân	chief cup-bearer	in the land
749	Shamash-kên-dugul	abarakku	against Namri
748	Adad-bêl-ukîn	shaknu	against Namri
747	Sin-shallimani	(governor) of Rasappa	in the land
746	Nergal-nâsir	(governor) of Nasibina	revolt in the city of Calah
745	Nabu-bêl-usur	(governor) of Arrapha	On the thirteenth day of the month of *Airu* Tiglath-Pileser took his seat on the throne. In the month of *Tashritu* he marched to the territory between the rivers
744	Bêl-dân	(governor) of Calah	against Namri
743	Tukulti-apal-esharra (Tiglath-Pileser)	king of Assyria	in the city of Arpadda. A massacre took place in the land of Urartu (Armenia)
742	Nabu-daninani	field-marshal	against Arpadda
741	Bêl-harran-bêl-usur	high chamberlain	against Arpadda. After three years it was conquered
740	Nabu-êtirani	chief cup-bearer	against Arpadda
739	Sin-taklak	abarakku	against Ulluba. The fortress was taken
738	Adad-bêl-ukîn	shaknu	Kulani was captured
737	Bêl-emurani	(governor) of Rasappa	against Madai
736	Urta-ilia	(governor) of Nasibina	to the foot of Mount Nâl
735	Ashur-shallimani	(governor) of Arrapha	against Urarti
734	Bêl-dân	(governor) of Calah	against Philistia
733	Ashur-daninani	(governor) of Mazamua	against the land of Damascus
732	Nabu-bêl-usur	(governor) of Si'mê	against the land of Damascus
731	Nergal-uballit	(governor) of Ahi-Suhina	against Sapia
730	Bêl-ludâlri	(governor) of Tillê	in the land
729	Naphar-ilu	(governor) of Kirruri	The king took the hand of Bêl
728	Dur-Ashur	(governor) of Tushhan	The king took the hand of Bêl
727	Bêl-harran-bêl-usur	(governor) of Guzana Shalmaneser	against Damascus took his seat on the throne
726	Marduk-bêl-usur	(governor) of Amedi	in the land
725	Mahdê	(governor) of Nineveh	against [Samaria]
724	Ashur-ishmeani	(governor) of [Kakzi]	against [Samaria]
723	Shalmaneser	king of Assyria	against [Samaria]
722	Urta-ilia	[field-marshal]	[The foundation of the temple of Nabu was torn up (for repairs)]
721	Nabutâris	[high chamberlain]	[Nabu entered the new temple]
720	Ashur-iska-danin	[field-marshal	against Tabala]
719	Sargon	king of [Assyria]	The foundation of the [temple of Nergal] was torn up (for repairs)

718	Zêr-ibni	(governor) of Ra..........	against Mannai
717	Tâb-shar-Ashur	[abarakku]	.... provinces were established
716	Tâb-sil-esharra	(governor) of Ashur	.... Musasir of Haldia
715	Taklak-ana-bêl	(governor) of Nasibina	great .... in Ellipa
714	Ishtar-duri	(governor) of Arrapha	Nergal entered the new temple
713	Ashur-bâni	(governor) of Calah	against Musasir
712	Sharru-êmurani	(governor) of Zamua	in the land
711	Urta-âlik-pâni	(governor) of Si'me	against Markasa
710	Shamash-bêl-usur	(governor) of [Arzu-hina]	against Bêt-zêrnâîd, the king of Kish ....
709	Mannu-ki-Ashur-li'	(governor) of Tillê	Sargon took the hand of Bêl
708	Shamash-upahhir	(governor) of Kirruri	Kumuha was captured. A governor was appointed
707	Sha-Ashur-dubbi	(governor) of Tushhan	The king returned from Babylon
706	Mutakkil-Ashur	(governor) of Guzana	.... from the city of Dur-Iakin brought out
705	Nashir-Bêl	(governor) of Amedi	The city of Dur-Iakin was destroyed
704	Nabu-dîn-epush	(governor) of Nineveh	The gods entered into their temples
703	Kannunnai	(governor) of Kakzi	[The nobles] were in Karalli
702	Nabu-li'	(governor) of Arbailu	
701	Hananai	(governor) of .... bi	
700	Metunu	(governor) of Isana	
699	Bêl-sharani	(governor) of [Kurban]	
698	Shulmu-shar	(governor) of	
697	Nabu-dur-usur	(governor) of	
696	Shulmu-bêl	(governor) of Rimusa	
695	Ashur-bêl-usur	(governor) of	
694	Ilu-ittia	(governor) of Damascus	
693	Nâdin-ahê	(governor) of	
692	Zazai	(governor) of Arpadda	
691	Bêl-êmurani	(governor) of Carchemish	
690	Nabu-mukin-ahi (var., Nabu-bêl-usur)	(governor) of Samaria	
689	Gilhilu	(governor) of Hatarika	
688	Nadin-ahê	(governor) of [Simirra]	
687	Sennacherib	king of Assyria	
686	Bêl-êmuranni	(governor) of Calah	
685	Ashur-daninanni	(governor) of ....ub	
684	Mannu-zirni (var., Man-zirnê	(governor) of Kullania	
683	Mannu-ki-Adad	(governor) of Supite	
682	Nabu-shar-usur	(governor) of Markasi	
681	Nabu-ah-êresh	(governor) of Samalli	
680	Dananu	(governor) of [Mansua]	
679	Iti-Adad-aninu	(governor) of Magidunu	
678	Nergal-shar-usur	chief cup-bearer	
677	Abi-rama	high minister	
676	Banbâ	second minister	
675	Nabu-ahi-iddina	chief governor	
674	Sharru-nuri	(governor) of Barhalzi	
673	Atar-ilu	(governor) of Lahiri	
672	Nabu-bêl-usur	(governor) of Dur-Shar-rukîn	
671	Kanunai	sar-tinu-official	
670	Shulmul-bêl-lashme	(governor) of Dêr	

669 Shamash-kâshid-aibi   (governor) of Ashdod
668 Mar-larim   field-marshal
667 Gabbar   (governor) of ....
666 Kanunai   (governor) of Bît-eshshi
665 Mannu-ki-sharri   prefect of the land
664 Sharru-ludâri   (governor) of Dur-shar-rukîn
663 Bêl-nâid   field-marshal
662 Tâb-shâr-Sin   (governor) of Rasappa
661 Arbailai
660 Gir-zapuna
659 Simil-Ashur
658 Sha-Nabu-shu
657 Lâbâsi
656 Milki-râmu
655 Amiânu
654 Ashur-nâsir
653 Ashur-ilai
652 Ashur-dur-usur
651 Sagabbu
650 Bêl-harrân-shadua
649 Ahu-ilai
648 Bêlshunu

THE RULERS OF BABYLON AND PERSIA ACCORDING TO THE CANON OF PTOLEMY

BABYLON

Ruler		Years	Years of the Nabonassar Era	Years of the Christian Era
Nabonassar	Nabonassaros	14	1– 14	747–734 B.C.
Nabu-nadinzir	Nadius	2	15– 16	733–732
Ukinzer, Pulu	Chinziros and Poros	5	17– 21	731–727
Ululai	Iloulaios	5	22– 26	726–722
Marduk-appal-iddin	Mardokempados	12	27– 38	721–710
Sargon	Arkeanos	5	39– 43	709–705
....	First Interregnum	2	44– 45	704–703
Bel-ibni	Belibos	3	46– 48	702–700
Ashur-nadin-shum	Aparanadios	6	49– 54	699–694
Nergal-ushezib	Regebelos	1	55	693
Mushezib-Marduk	Mesesimordakos	4	56– 59	692–689
....	Second Interregnum	8	60– 67	688–681
Ashur-akh-iddin	Asaridinos	13	68– 80	680–668
Shamash-shum-ukin	Saosdouchinos	20	81–100	667–648
Kandalanu	Kineladanos	22	101–122	647–626
Nabopolassar	Nabopolassaros	21	123–143	625–605
Nebuchadnezzar	Nabocolassaros	43	144–186	604–562
Amel-Marduk	Illaoroudamos	2	187–188	561-560
Nergal-shar-usur	Nerigasolassaros	4	189–192	559–556
Nabonidus	Nabonadios	17	193–209	555–539

PERSIA

Ruler	Years	Years of the Nabonassar Era	Years of the Christian Era
Cyrus	9	210–218	538–530 B.C.
Cambyses	8	219–226	529–522
Darius I	36	227–262	521–486
Xerxes	21	263–283	485–465
Artaxerxes I	41	284–324	464–424
Darius II	19	325–343	423–405

Ruler	Years	Years of the Nabonassar Era	Years of the Christian Era
Artaxerxes II	46	344–389	404–359
Ochus	21	390–410	358–338
Arses	2	411–412	337–336
Darius III	4	413–416	335–332

NOTE: The canon of Ptolemy is completely reliable. It was prepared primarily for astronomical purposes. It did not pretend to give a complete list of all the rulers of either Babylon or Persia, or the exact month or day of the beginning of their reigns, but it was a device that made possible the correct allocation into a broad chronological scheme of certain astronomical data that were then available. Kings whose reigns were less than a year and did not embrace the New Year's Day were not mentioned in the canon. The years are Egyptian years beginning with 1 Thoth 747 B.C., which that year fell on 27 February and which every four years thereafter came one day earlier, till in 332 it fell on 15 November.

ECLIPSES ESTABLISHING THE CHRONOLOGY OF THE ANCIENT NEAR EAST

Date		Eponymy	Year of King	Year of the Nabonassar Era
15 June	763	Bur-Sagale	10th year of Ashur-dan III	
19 March	721		1st year of Mardokempados	27
8 March	720		2d year of Mardokempados	28
1 Sept.	720		2d year of Mardokempados	28
22 April	621		5th year of Nabopolassar	127
4 July	568		37th year of Nebuchadnezzar	180
16 July	523		7th year of Cambyses	225
19 Nov.	502		20th year of Darius	246
25 April	491		31st year of Darius	257

Glossary of Basic Terms

accession year: The year in which a ruler begins to reign.

accession-year dating: The method employed for numbering the years of a king when the year in which he comes to the throne is termed his accession year, and his first official year is that which begins with the new year's day after his accession. Also called *postdating*.

actual years of reign: Years from a king's accession to his death.

antedating: See *nonaccession-year dating*.

Canon of Ptolemy: A document prepared by the famous Egyptian astronomer Ptolemy (A.D. 70–161) in which he enumerates the years of a consecutive series of rulers commencing with Nabonassar of Babylon in 747 B.C. as the first year, and continuing with the succeeding rulers of Babylon; then the rulers of Persia to Darius III, the last ruler of Persia when it was overthrown by Alexander the Great; next the Greek rulers of Egypt from Alexander and the Ptolemies to Cleopatra; and concluding with the Roman rulers of Egypt from Augustus to Antoninus Pius (A.D. 138–161). What makes Ptolemy's Canon of such immeasurable chronological value is the fact that in his *Almagest* Ptolemy has recorded over eighty solar, lunar, and planetary positions together with their dates, which may be coordinated with the years of the Nabonassar era beginning in 747 B.C., and thus securing a complete confirmation of this series of years.

chronology: The science that deals with time and assigns dates to the years involved.

coregency: A period of rulership when a son sits on the throne with his father.

double dating: A reign that is synchronized with another reign. For example (p. 55) in Egypt, the year 30 of Amenemhet I corresponds to the year 10 of Sesostris. In Israel, the accession of Joram occurred in the second year of Jehoram of Judah and the eighteenth year of Jehoshaphat.

double synchronism: See *double dating*.

dual dating: In an overlapping reign the datum for the length of reign includes both the period of overlap and the sole reign, but the synchronism of accession denotes the end of the period of overlap and the start of the sole reign (pp. 55, 106, 119–20).

eponym: An Assyrian official whose name was given to some particular year in his honor.

eponymy: An Assyrian year that was named after some officer of state.

interregnum: Vacant throne between two reigns. None occurs in Judah or Israel.

Julian year: A year that begins in January.

Nisan: A spring month with which religious or regnal years were sometimes begun.

nonaccession-year dating: The method of numbering the years of a ruler in which the year he comes to the throne is termed his first year, and his second official year begins with the new year's day following his accession. Also called *antedating*.

231

official first year: The year that was termed first year of a ruler's reign in the record of his reign.

official reign: The years of reign as officially counted. In the case of an overlapping reign this may include both the years of overlap and of sole reign, or it may include only the years of sole reign.

overlapping reign: Years when a king ruled at the same time as another ruler, either as coregent or rival.

postdating: See *accession-year dating.*

regency: The period of a ruler's reign.

regnal: Pertaining to the year of reign.

synchronism: The coordination of the year of a ruler in one nation with the same year of a ruler in another nation.

synchronistic: Taking place at the same time.

Tishri: A fall month with which religious or regnal years were sometimes begun.

Bibliography

PERIODICALS

Albright, William F. "The Chronology of the Divided Monarchy of Israel." *Bulletin of the American Schools of Oriental Research* 100 (1945): 16–22.

—————. "Further Light on Synchronisms Between Egypt and Asia in the Period 935–685 B.C." *Bulletin of the American Schools of Oriental Research* 141 (1956): 23–27.

—————. "King Joiachin in Exile." *Biblical Archaeologist* 5 (1942): 49–55.

—————. "Mélanges Isidore Lévy." *l'Annuaire de l'Institut de Philologie et d'Histoire Orientales et Slaves* 13 (1955): 1–9.

—————. "The Nebuchadnezzar and Neriglissar Chronicles." *Bulletin of the American Schools of Oriental Research* 143 (1956): 28–33.

—————. "The New Assyro-Tyrian Synchronism and the Chronology of Tyre." *l'Annuaire de l'Institut de Philologie et d'Histoire Orientales et Slaves* 13 (1953):1–9.

—————. "New Light from Egypt on the Chronology and History of Israel and Judah." *Bulletin of the American Schools of Oriental Research* 130 (1953): 4–11.

—————. "The Original Account of the Fall of Samaria in II Kings." *Bulletin of the American Schools of Oriental Research* 174 (1964): 66–67.

—————. "The Seal of Eliakim and the Latest Preëxilic History of Judah, With Some Observations on Ezekiel." *Journal of Biblical Literature* 51 (1932): 77–106.

—————. "The Son of Tabeel (Isaiah 7:6)." *Bulletin of the American Schools of Oriental Research* 140 (1955): 34–35.

Andersen, K. T. "Die Chronologie der Könige von Israel und Juda." *Studia Theologie* 23 (1969): 67–112.

Anderson, Robert T. "Was Isaiah a Scribe?" *Journal of Biblical Literature* 79 (1960): 57–58.

Auerbach, Elias. "Der Wechsel des Jahres-Anfangs in Juda im Lichte der neugefundenen babylonischen Chronik." *Vetus Testamentum* 9 (1959): 113–21.

Begrich, Joachim. "Jesaja 14, 28–32: Ein Beitrag zur Chronologie der israelitisch-judäischen Königzeit." *Zeitschrift der deutschen morgenländischen Gesellschaft* 86 (1932): 66–79.

—————. "Der syrisch-ephraimitische Kreig und seine weltpolitischen Zusammenhänge." *Zeitschrift der deutschen morgenländischen Gesellschaft* 83 (1929): 213–37.

Cazelles, Henri. "Une nouvelle stele d'Adad-nirari d'Assyrie et Joas d'Israel." *Comptes rendus de l'Académie des inscriptions et belles-lettres* (1969): 106–17.

Clines, D. J. A. "The Evidence for an Autumnal New Year in Pre-exilic Israel Reconsidered." *Journal of Biblical Literature* 93 (1974): 22–40.

_____. "Regnal Year Reckoning in the Last Years of the Kingdom of Judah." *Australian Journal of Biblical Archaeology* 5 (1972): 13–33.

Cody, Aelred. "A New Inscription from Tell āl-Rimah and King Jehoash of Israel." *Catholic Biblical Quarterly* 32 (1970): 325–40.

Cook, H. J. "Pekah." *Vetus Testamentum* 14 (1964): 121–35.

Dubberstein, Waldo H. "Assyrian-Babylonian Chronology (669–612 B.C.)." *Journal of Near Eastern Studies* 3 (1944): 38–42.

Eaton J. H. "The Origin of the Book of Isaiah." *Vetus Testamentum* 9 (1959): 138–57.

Forrer, Emil. "Zur Chronologie der neuassyrischen Zeit." *Mitteilungen der vorderasiatischen Gesellschaft* 20 (1915): 5ff.

Freedman, David Noel. "The Babylonian Chronicle." *The Biblical Archaeologist* 19 (1956): 50–60.

Gelb, I. J. "Two Assyrian King Lists." *Journal of Near Eastern Studies* 13 (1954): 209–30.

Goetze, Albrecht. "Additions to Parker and Dubberstein's *Babylonian Chronology*." *Journal of Near Eastern Studies* 3 (1944): 43–46.

Gooding, D. W. Book review of *Chronology and Recensional Development in the Greek Text of Kings* by J. D. Shenkel. *Journal of Theological Studies* 21 (1970): 118–31.

Green, Alberto R. "The Chronology of the Last Days of Judah: Two Apparent Discrepancies." *Journal of Biblical Literature* 101 (1982): 57–73.

Hallo, William W. "From Qarqar to Carcemish. Assyria and Israel in the Light of New Discoveries." *The Biblical Archaeologist* 23 (1960): 34–61.

Haydn, Howell M. "Azariah of Judah and Tiglath-Pileser III." *Journal of Biblical Literature* 28 (1909): 182–99.

Hontheim, Josef. "Die Chronologie des 3. und 4. Buches der Könige." *Zeitschrift für katholische Theologie* 42 (1918): 463–82, 687–718.

Horn, Seigfried H. "The Chronology of King Hezekiah's Reign." *Andrews University Seminary Studies* 2 (1964): 40–52.

_____. "From Bishop Ussher to Edwin R. Thiele." *Andrews University Seminary Studies* 18 (1980): 37–49.

Horn, Seigfried H., and Wood, Lynn H. "The Fifth-Century Jewish Calendar at Elephantine." *Journal of Near Eastern Studies* 13 (1954): 1–20.

Horner, Joseph. "Biblical Chronology." *Proceedings of the Society of Biblical Archaeology* 20 (1898): 237.

Hyatt, J. Philip. "New Light on Nebuchadrezzar and Judean History." *Journal of Biblical Literature* 75 (1956): 277–84.

Irwin, William A. "The Exposition of Isaiah 14:28–32." *American Journal of Semitic Languages and Literatures* 44 (1927–28): 73–87.

Jaubert, A. "Le calendrier des jubilés et la secte de Qumrân: ses origines bibliques." *Vetus Testamentum* 3 (1953): 250–64.

Jepsen, A. "Ein neuer Fixpunkt für die Chronologie der israelitischen Könige?" *Vetus Testamentum* 20 (1970): 359–61.

_____. "Israel und Damaskus." *Archiv für Orientforschung* 14 (1942): 153–72.

Kleber, Albert M. "The Chronology of 3 and 4 Kings and 2 Paralipomenon." *Biblica* 2 (1921): 3–29, 170–205.

Koenig, E. "Kalenderfragen im althebräischen Schrifttum." *Zeitschrift der deutschen morgenländischen Gesellschaft* 60 (1906): 605–44.

Kutsch, E. "Das Jahr der Katastrophe: 597 c. Chr." *Biblica* 55 (1974): 520–43.

───────. "Zur Chronologie der letzten judäischen Könige (Josia bis Zedekia)." *Zeitschrift für die Alttestamentliche Wissenschaft* 71 (1959): 270–74.

Langdon, Stephen. "Evidence for an Advance on Egypt by Sennacherib in the Campaign of 701–700 B.C." *Journal of the American Oriental Society* 24 (1903): 265–74.

Levine, Louis D. "Menahem and Tiglath-pileser: A New Synchronism." *Bulletin of the American Schools of Oriental Research* 206 (1972): 40–42.

───────. "Two Neo-Assyrian Stelae from Iran." *Occasional Paper 23*. Royal Ontario Museum, Toronto, 1972.

Lewy, H., and Lewy, J. "The Origin and Development of the Israelite Festivals." *Hebrew Union College Annual* 17 (1943): 106–46.

Lewy, Julius. "Forschungen zur alten Geschichte Vorderasiens." *Mitteilungen der vorderasiatischen Gesellschaft* 29 (1924): 25.

Lipinski, E. "The Assyrian Campaign to Manṣuate, in 796 B.C., and the Zakir Stele." *Annali dell' Instituto Orientale di Napoli* 30 (1970): 393–99.

Liver, J. "The Chronology of Tyre at the Beginning of the First Millennium B.C." *Israel Exploration Journal* 3 (1953): 113–20.

Löv, Gustav. "Das synchronistische System der Königsbücher." *Zeitschrift für wissenschaftliche Theologie* 43 (1900): 161–79.

Luckenbill, Daniel David. "Azariah of Judah." *American Journal of Semitic Languages and Literatures* 41 (1924–25): 217–32.

Malamat, A. "The Last Kings of Judah and the Fall of Jerusalem." *Israel Exploration Journal* 18 (1968): 135–56.

───────. "The Last Wars of the Kingdom of Judah." *Journal of Near Eastern Studies* 9 (1950): 218–27.

───────. "A New Record of Nebuchadrezzar's Palestinian Campaigns." *Israel Exploration Journal* 6 (1956): 246–56.

───────. "The Twilight of Judah: in the Egyptian-Babylonian Maelstrom." *Supplement to Vetus Testamentum* 28 (1974): 123–45.

McCarter, P. K. "'Yaw, Son of Omri': A Philological Note on Israelite Chronology." *Bulletin of the American Schools of Oriental Research* 216 (1974): 5–8.

McHugh, John. "The Date of Hezekiah's Birth." *Vetus Testamentum* 14 (1964): 446–53.

Millard, A. R. "Adad-nirari III, Aram, and Arpad." *Palestine Exploration Quarterly* 105 (1973): 161–64.

Millard, A. R., and Tadmor, H. "Adad-nirari III in Syria." *Iraq* 30 (1968): 148–49.

───────. "Adad-nirari III in Syria." *Iraq* 35 (1973): 57–64.

Morgenstern, Julian. "Supplementary Studies in the Calendars of Ancient Israel." *Hebrew Union College Annual* 10 (1935): 1–148.

Mowinckel, Sigmund. "Die Chronologie der israelitischen und judaische Könige." *Acta Orientalia* 10 (1932): 161–277.

───────. "Die israelitische-judaische Königschronologie." *Norsk Theologisk Tidsskrift* 56 (1955): 279–95.

Neugebauer, O. "Chronologie und babylonischer Kalendar." *Orientalische Literaturzeitung* 42 (1939): cols. 403–14.

Noth, Martin. "Die Einnahme von Jerusalem im Jahre 597 v. Chr." *Zeitschrift des deutschen Palästina-vereins* 74 (1958): 133–57.

Olmstead, A. T. "The Assyrian Chronicle." *Journal of the American Oriental Society* 34 (1915): 344–68.

_____. "Bruno Meissner." *Archiv für Orientforschung* 5 (1928–29): 30.

_____. "The Fall of Samaria." *American Journal of Semitic Languages and Literatures* 21 (1904–5): 179–82.

_____. "Shalmaneser III and the Establishment of the Assyrian Power." *Journal of the American Oriental Society* 41 (1921): 345–82.

_____. "The Text of Sargon's Annals." *American Journal of Semitic Languages and Literatures* 47 (1930–31): 259–80.

Page, Stephanie. "Adad-nirari III and Semiramis: the Stelae of Saba'a and Rimah." *Orientalia* 38 (1969): 457–58.

_____. "A Stela of Adad-nirari III and Nergal-eres from Tell al Rimah." *Iraq* 30 (1968): 139–53.

_____. "Joash and Samaria in a new Stela Excavated at Tell al Rimah, Iraq." *Vetus Testamentum* 19 (1969): 483–84.

Pavlovsky, V., and Vogt, E. "Die Jahre der Könige von Juda und Israel." *Biblica* 45 (1964): 321–47.

Poebel, Arno. "The Assyrian King List from Khorsabad," parts 1-3. *Journal of Near Eastern Studies* 1 (1942): 247–306, 460–92; 2 (1943): 56–90.

Rowton, M. B. "Jeremiah and the Death of Josiah." *Journal of Near Eastern Studies* 10 (1951): 128–30.

Rühl, Franz. "Chronologie der Könige von Israel and Juda." *Deutsche Zeitschrift für Geschichtsvissenschaft* 12 (1894–95):44ff.

Safar, Fuad. "A Further Text of Shalmaneser III from Assur." *Sumer* 7 (1951): 10–12.

Saggs, H. W. F. "The Nimrud Letters, 1952—Part II." *Iraq* 17 (1955): 126–60.

Schedl, Claus. "Nochmals das Jahr der Zerstörung Jerusalems, 587 oder 586 v. chr." *Zeitschrift für die Alttestamentliche Wissenschaft* 74 (1962): 209–13.

_____. "Textkritische Bemerkungen zu den Synchronismen der Könige von Israel und Juda." *Vetus Testamentum* 12 (1962): 88–119.

Segal, J. B. "Intercalation and the Hebrew Calendar." *Vetus Testamentum* 7 (1957): 250–307.

Shea, William H. "Adad-nirari III and Jehoash of Israel." *Journal of Cuneiform Studies* 30 (1978): 101–13.

_____. "Menahem and Tiglath-pileser III." *Journal of Near Eastern Studies* 37 (1978): 43–52.

_____. "The Date and Significance of the Samaria Ostraca." *Israel Exploration Journal* 27 (1977): 16–27.

Soggin, J. Alberto. "Ein Ausserbibliches Zeugnis für die Chronologie des Jᵉhô'āš/Jô'āš, König von Israel." *Vetus Testamentum* 20 (1970): 366–68.

Smith, W. Robertson. "The Chronology of the Book of Kings." *Journal of Philology* 10 (1882): 209–13.

Tadmor, Hayim. "Azriyau of Yaudi." *Studies in the Bible, Scripta Hierosolymitana* 8 (1961): 252–58.

_____. "The Campaigns of Sargon II of Asshur: A Chronological Study." *Journal of Cuneiform Studies* 12 (1958): 22–40, 77–100.

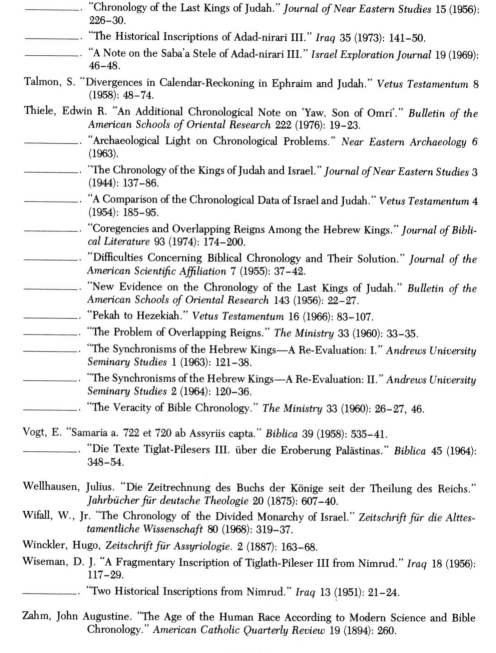

_____. "Chronology of the Last Kings of Judah." *Journal of Near Eastern Studies* 15 (1956): 226–30.

_____. "The Historical Inscriptions of Adad-nirari III." *Iraq* 35 (1973): 141–50.

_____. "A Note on the Saba'a Stele of Adad-nirari III." *Israel Exploration Journal* 19 (1969): 46–48.

Talmon, S. "Divergences in Calendar-Reckoning in Ephraim and Judah." *Vetus Testamentum* 8 (1958): 48–74.

Thiele, Edwin R. "An Additional Chronological Note on 'Yaw, Son of Omri'." *Bulletin of the American Schools of Oriental Research* 222 (1976): 19–23.

_____. "Archaeological Light on Chronological Problems." *Near Eastern Archaeology* 6 (1963).

_____. "The Chronology of the Kings of Judah and Israel." *Journal of Near Eastern Studies* 3 (1944): 137–86.

_____. "A Comparison of the Chronological Data of Israel and Judah." *Vetus Testamentum* 4 (1954): 185–95.

_____. "Coregencies and Overlapping Reigns Among the Hebrew Kings." *Journal of Biblical Literature* 93 (1974): 174–200.

_____. "Difficulties Concerning Biblical Chronology and Their Solution." *Journal of the American Scientific Affiliation* 7 (1955): 37–42.

_____. "New Evidence on the Chronology of the Last Kings of Judah." *Bulletin of the American Schools of Oriental Research* 143 (1956): 22–27.

_____. "Pekah to Hezekiah." *Vetus Testamentum* 16 (1966): 83–107.

_____. "The Problem of Overlapping Reigns." *The Ministry* 33 (1960): 33–35.

_____. "The Synchronisms of the Hebrew Kings—A Re-Evaluation: I." *Andrews University Seminary Studies* 1 (1963): 121–38.

_____. "The Synchronisms of the Hebrew Kings—A Re-Evaluation: II." *Andrews University Seminary Studies* 2 (1964): 120–36.

_____. "The Veracity of Bible Chronology." *The Ministry* 33 (1960): 26–27, 46.

Vogt, E. "Samaria a. 722 et 720 ab Assyriis capta." *Biblica* 39 (1958): 535–41.

_____. "Die Texte Tiglat-Pilesers III. über die Eroberung Palästinas." *Biblica* 45 (1964): 348–54.

Wellhausen, Julius. "Die Zeitrechnung des Buchs der Könige seit der Theilung des Reichs." *Jahrbücher für deutsche Theologie* 20 (1875): 607–40.

Wifall, W., Jr. "The Chronology of the Divided Monarchy of Israel." *Zeitschrift für die Alttestamentliche Wissenschaft* 80 (1968): 319–37.

Winckler, Hugo, *Zeitschrift für Assyriologie.* 2 (1887): 163–68.

Wiseman, D. J. "A Fragmentary Inscription of Tiglath-Pileser III from Nimrud." *Iraq* 18 (1956): 117–29.

_____. "Two Historical Inscriptions from Nimrud." *Iraq* 13 (1951): 21–24.

Zahm, John Augustine. "The Age of the Human Race According to Modern Science and Bible Chronology." *American Catholic Quarterly Review* 19 (1894): 260.

BOOKS

Anspacher, Abraham S. *Tiglath Pileser III.* New York, 1912.

Anstey, Martin. *The Romance of Bible Chronology.* 2 vols. London, 1913.

Auchincloss, William S. *Standard Chronology of the Holy Bible.* New York, 1924.

Babylonian Talmud. Tract Rosh Hashana.

Bähr, Karl Chr. W. G. *The Books of Kings.* Translated by Edwin Harwood and W. G. Sumner. Vol. 6. *Commentary on the Holy Scriptures.* Edited by J. P. Lange; translated by Philip Schaff. New York, 1915.

Barton, George A. *Archaeology and the Bible.* Philadelphia, 1937.

Beecher, Willis Judson. *The Dated Events of the Old Testament.* Philadelphia, 1907.

Begrich, Joachim. *Die Chronologie der Könige von Israel und Juda und die Quellen des Rahmens der Königsbücher.* Tübingen, 1929.

"Bible Chronology from Exodus to Exile." *The Seventh-day Adventist Bible Commentary.* Vol. 2. Washington D.C., 1954.

Bleek, Friedrich. *Einleitung in das Alte Testament.* 4th ed. Berlin, 1878.

Breasted, J. H. *History of Egypt.* New York, 1921.

Brown, Francis. *Assyriology: Its Use and Abuse in Old Testament Study.* New York, 1885.

Bright, John. *A History of Israel.* Philadelphia, 1959.

Burney, C. F. *Notes on the Hebrew Text of the Books of Kings.* Oxford: Clarendon, 1903.

Bury, J. B., Cook, S. A., and Adcock, F. E., eds. *The Cambridge Ancient History.* Vol. 2. New York, 1929.

Campbell, Edward F., Jr. "The Ancient Near East: Chronological Bibliography and Charts." *The Bible and the Ancient Near East.* Edited by G. Ernest Wright. New York, 1961.

Chapman, W. J. "The Problem of Inconsequent Postdating in II Kings XV. 13, 17 and 23." *Hebrew Union College Annual.* Vol. 2. 1925.

"Chronology." *Seventh-day Adventist Bible Dictionary.* Vol. 8. Commentary Reference Series. Washington, D.C., 1960.

Cook, Stanley A. "Chronology: II The Old Testament." *The Cambridge Ancient History.* Edited by J. B. Bury, S. A. Cook, and F. E. Adcock. Vol. 1 New York, 1928.

Coucke, V. "Chronologie biblique." *Supplément au Dictionnaire de la Bible.* Edited by L. Pirot. Vol. 1 Paris, 1928.

Curtis, E. L. "Chronology of the Old Testament." *A Dictionary of the Bible.* Edited by James Hastings. Vol. 1. New York, 1908.

Curtis, Edward Lewis, and Madsen, Albert Alonzo. *A Critical and Exegetical Commentary on the Books of Chronicles.* The International Critical Commentary. New York, 1910.

Deimel, Anton. *Veteris Testamenti chronologia monumentis babylonico-assyriis illustrata.* Rome, 1912.

De Vries, Simon J. "Chronology of the Old Testament." *The Interpreter's Dictionary of the Bible,* vol. 1. New York, 1962.

Donner, Herbert. "Adadnirari III. und die Vasallen des Westens." *Archäologie und Altes Testament. Festschrift für Kurt Galling,* 1970.

Driver, S. R., and Driver, G. R. "Bible, Old Testament, Chronology," *Encyclopaedia Britannica.* 14th ed. Vol. 3.

Ebeling, Erich, and Meisner, Bruno. *Reallexikon der Assyriologie.* Vol. 2, 1938.

Ewald, Heinrich. *The History of Israel.* Edited by R. Martineau. 4th ed. Vol. 1. London, 1883.

_____. *The History of Israel.* Edited by R. Martineau. 2nd ed. Vol. 2. London, 1869.

_____. *The History of Israel.* Edited by J. Estlin Carpenter. Vol. 4. London, 1878.

Finegan, Jack. *Handbook of Biblical Chronology.* Princeton, 1964.

Freedman, David Noel. "The Chronology of Israel and the Ancient Near East." *The Bible and the Ancient Near East.* Edited by G. Ernest Wright. New York, 1961.

Gadd, C. J. *The Fall of Nineveh.* London, 1923.

Ginzel, Friedrich Karl. *Handbuch der mathematischen und technischen Chronologie.* 3 vols. Leipzig, 1906–14.

――――――. *Spezieller Kanon der Sonnen und Mondfinsternisse.* Berlin, 1899.

Gordon, Cyrus H. *The World of the Old Testament.* New York, 1958.

Gray, John "Chronology of the Old Testament." *Dictionary of the Bible.* Edited by James Hastings, revised by Frederick C. Grant and H. H. Rowley. New York, 1963.

――――――. *I & II Kings, A Commentary.* Philadelphia, 1963.

Hales, William. *A New Analysis of Chronology and Geography, History and Prophecy.* 4 vols. London, 1830.

Hall, H. R. *The Ancient History of the Near East.* 9th ed. rev. London, 1936.

Hall, Harry R., and Smith, Sidney. "Chronology," *Encyclopaedia Britannica.* Vol. 5. 1961.

Herzog, Franz Alfred. *Die Chronologie der beiden Königsbucher.* Münster, 1909.

Hieronymus. *Traditio catholica.* Edited by J. P. Migne, vol. 1, Ep. 72. Paris, 1864. *Ad Vitalem. Patrologia Latina.* Vol. 22, col. 676.

Hommel, Fritz. *Abriss der babylonisch-assyrischen und israelitischen Geschichte von den ältesten Zeiten bis zur Zerstörung Babels, in Tabellenform.* Leipzig, 1880.

Honor, Leo L. *Sennacherib's Invasion of Palestine.* New York, 1926.

Horn, Seigfried H., and Wood, Lynn H. *The Chronology of Ezra 7.* Washington, D.C., 1953.

Howlett, J. A. "Chronology." *The Catholic Encyclopedia.* Vol. 3. 1908.

Ionides, M. G. *The Regime of the Rivers Euphrates and Tigris.* London, 1937.

Irwin, William A. *The Problem of Ezekiel.* Chicago, 1943.

Jepsen, A. *Die Quellen des Königsbuches.* Halle, 1956.

Jepsen, Alfred, and Hanhart, Robert. *Untersuchungen zur israelitisch-jüdischen Chronologie* (*Beihefte zur Zeitschrift für die Alttestamentliche Wissenschaft,* No. 88). Berlin, 1964.

Johns, C. H. W. *Assyrian Deeds and Documents.* Vol. 2. Cambridge, 1901.

Josephus. Translated by H. St. J. Thackeray and Ralph Marcus. *Against Apion.* Vol. 1. *Jewish Antiquities,* 5:5–8, *Jewish Antiquities,* 6:9–11. Cambridge, 1926, 1934, 1937.

Kamphausen, Adolf. *Die Chronologie der hebräischen Könige.* Bonn, 1883.

Keil, Karl Friedrich. *Commentary on the Books of Kings.* Vol. 2. Translated by James Murphy. Edinburgh, 1857.

Kent, Charles Foster. *A History of the Hebrew People.* Vol. 2. New York, 1904.

Kitchen, K. A., and Mitchell, T. C. "Chronology of the Old Testament." *The New Bible Dictionary.* Grand Rapids, 1962.

Kittel, Rudolf. *Die Bücher der Könige* ("Hand-Kommentar zum Alten Testament," edited by W. Nowak). Göttingen, 1900.

――――――. *Geschichte des Volkes Israel.* Vol. 3. Stuttgart, 1929.

――――――. *A History of the Hebrews.* Vol. 2. Translated by Hope W. Hogg and E. B. Speirs. London, 1896.

Kraeling, Emil G. H. *Aram and Israel.* New York, 1918.

Kugler, Franz Xaver. *Von Moses bis Paulus*. Münster, 1922.

_____. *Sternkunde und Sterndienst in Babel*. 3 vols. Münster, 1907–12.

Langsberger, Benno. *Sam'al: Studien zur Entdeckung der Ruinenstätte Karatepe*. Vol. 1. "Veröffentlichungen der Türkischen historischen Gesellschaft" 7. Ankara, Turkey, 1948.

Layard, Austen Henry. *Nineveh and Its Remains*. 2 vols. New York, 1850.

Lederer, Carl. *Die Biblische Zeitrechnung vom Auszufe aus Ägypten bis zum Beginne der babylonischen Gefangenschaft*. Speier, 1888.

Lewy, Julius. *Die Chronologie der Könige von Israel und Juda*. Giessen, 1927.

Lie, A. G. *The Inscriptions of Sargon II, King of Assyria*. Paris, 1929.

Luckenbill, Daniel David. *Ancient Records of Assyria and Babylonia*, 2 vols. Chicago: University of Chicago Press, 1926–27.

_____. *The Annals of Sennacherib*. Chicago, 1924.

MacDonald, Malcolm. *Harmony of Ancient History, and Chronology of the Egyptians and Jews*. Philadelphia, 1891.

Mahler, Eduard. *Handbuch der jüdischen Chronologie*. Leipzig, 1916.

Marti, Karl. "Chronology." *Encyclopedia Biblica*. Vol. 1. Edited by T. K. Cheyne and J. S. Black, 1899.

Martin, Thilo (Emil). *Die Chronologie des Alten Testaments*. Barmen, 1917.

Mauro, Philip. *The Chronology of the Bible*. Boston, 1922.

Meer, P. van der. *The Chronology of Ancient Western Asia and Egypt*. 2nd rev. ed. Documenta et Monumenta Orientis Antiqui. Vol. 2. Leiden, 1963.

Meissner, Bruno. *Babylonien und Assyrien*. Vol. 2. Heidelberg, 1925.

Mercer, Samuel A. B., ed. *Extra-Biblical Sources for Hebrew and Jewish History*. New York, 1913.

Meyer, Eduard. *Aegyptische Chronologie* ("Abhandlungen der Königlichen preussischen Akademie der Wissenschaften." Phil.-Hist. Klasse). Berlin, 1904.

_____. *Die ältere Chronologie Babyloniens, Assyriens und Ägyptens*. Stuttgart, 1931.

_____. *Geschichte des Altertums*. Stuttgart, 1926.

_____. *Nachträge zur ägyptischen Chronologie* ("Abhandlungen der Königlichen preussischen Akademie der Wissenschaften." Phil-Hist. Klasse). Berlin, 1907.

Montgomery, James A. *A Critical and Exegetical Commentary on the Books of Kings*. The International Critical Commentary. Edited by Henry Snyder Gehman. New York, 1951.

Morgenstern, Julian. "The New Year for Kings." *Occident and Orient: Gaster Anniversary Volume*. London, 1936.

_____. *Amos Studies*. Cincinnati, 1941.

Neugebauer, Paul V., and Weidner, Ernst F. "Ein astronomischer Beobachtungstext aus dem 37. Jahre Nebukadnezars II (567/66)." *Berichte über die Verhandlungen der Könige. Sächsischen Gesellschaft der Wissenschaften zu Leipzig*. Phil.-Hist. Klasse, 67, 1915, part 2.

Newton, Isaac. *The Chronology of Ancient Kingdoms Amended*. London, 1728.

Niebuhr. *Die Chronologie der Geschichte Israels, Aegyptens, Babyloniens und Assyriens*. Leipzig, 1896.

Nilsson, Martin P. *Primitive Time Reckoning*. Lund, 1920.

Noth, Martin. *Geschichte Israels*. Göttingen, 1950.

_____. *The History of Israel*. Translated by S. Godman. New York, 1958.

Oesterley, W. O. E., and Robinson, Theodore H. *A History of Israel.* 2 vols. Oxford, 1934.

Olmstead, A. T. *Assyrian Historiography.* Columbia, Mo., 1916.

_____. *History of Assyria.* New York, 1923.

_____. *History of Palestine and Syria.* New York, 1931.

_____. *Western Asia in the Days of Sargon of Assyria, 722–705 B.C..* New York, 1908.

Oppert, Jules, McCurdy, J. Frederic, and Jacobs, Joseph. "Chronology." *Jewish Encyclopedia.* Vol. 4. 1903.

Oppolzer, Theodor von. *Canon der Finsternisse.* "Denkschriften der kaiserlichen Akademie der Wissenschaften," Math-Naturwissensch. Klasse, LII. Vienna, 1887.

Otero, Antonio Lopez. *Cronologia e Historia de los Reinos Hebreos (1028–587 a. C.)* Lugo, 1963.

Parker, Richard A., and Dubberstein, W. H. *Babylonian Chronology, 626 B.C.–A.D. 75.* Providence, 1956.

_____. *The Calendars of Ancient Egypt.* Studies in Ancient Oriental Civilization No. 26. Chicago: University of Chicago Press, 1950.

Pfeiffer, Robert H. *Introduction to the Old Testament.* New York, 1941.

Pritchard, James B., ed. *Ancient Near East Texts Relating to the Old Testament.* 2nd ed. Princeton, 1955.

Ptolemy (Claudius Ptolemaeus). *The Almagest.* Translated by R. Catesby Taliaferro. "Great Books of the Western World." Vol. 16. *Ptolemy, Copernicus, Kepler.* Edited by John Maynard Hutchins and Mortimer J. Alder. Chicago, 1952.

Rawlinson, George. *Introduction to the Books of Kings.*

Ricciotti, Giuseppi. *The History of Israel.* Vol. 1. Translated by C. D. Penta and R. T. A. Murphy. Milwaukee, 1955.

Robinson, Theodore H. *A History of Israel.* Oxford, 1934.

Rogers, Robert William. *Cuneiform Parallels to the Old Testament.* 2nd ed. New York, 1926.

Rost, P., ed. *Die Keilschrifttexte Tiglat-Pilesers III.* Vol. 1. Leipzig, 1893.

_____. *Mitteilungen der vorderasiatischen Gesellschaft.* Vol. 2. 1897.

Rowley, H. H. *Hezekiah's Reform and Rebellion.* Manchester, 1962.

Schmidtke, Friedrich. *Der Aufbau der babylonischen Chronologie.* Münster, 1952.

Schofield, J. N. *The Historical Background of the Bible.* London, 1938.

Schrader, Eberhard. *The Cuneiform Inscriptions and the Old Testament.* 2 vols. Translated by Owen C. Whitehouse. London: William and Norgate, 1885, 1888.

Sellin, E. *Geschichte des israelitisch-judischen Volkes.* Vol. 1. Leipzig, 1935.

Shenkel, James Donald. *Chronology and Recensional Development in the Greek Text of Kings.* Cambridge: Harvard University Press, 1968.

Smith, George. *The Assyrian Eponym Canon.* London, 1875.

Smith, Sidney. *Cambridge Ancient History.* Cambridge, 1929.

Smith, W. Robertson. "Kings." *Encyclopaedia Britannica.* 9th ed. Vol. 14.

Smith, W. Robertson, and Kautzsch, E. "Kings." *Encyclopaedia Biblica.* Vol. 2. Edited by T. K. Cheyne and J. Sutherland Black. New York, 1903.

Stade, Bernhard. *Geschichte des Volkes Israel.* Vol. 1. Berlin, 1887–88.

Steuernagel, D. Carl. *Lehrbuch der Einleitung in das Alte Testament.* Tübingen, 1912.

Stiles, Mervin. *Shofar Synchronizing Hebrew Originals.* Vol. 1–18. Aptos, California, 1972–1982.

Tadmor, Hayim. *Problems in Biblical Chronology.* Jerusalem, 1955.

Thiele, Edwin R. *A Chronology of the Hebrew Kings.* Grand Rapids: Zondervan, 1977.

_____. *The Mysterious Numbers of the Hebrew Kings.* Chicago: University of Chicago Press, 1955.

_____. "The Question of Coregencies among the Hebrew Kings." *A Stubborn Faith.* Edited by Edward C. Hobbs. Dallas, 1956.

Thomas, D. Winton, ed. *Documents from Old Testament Times.* London, 1958.

Unger, Merrill F. *Israel and the Aramaeans of Damascus.* London: Clarke, 1957.

Ungnad, Arthur. "Eponymen." *Reallexikon der Assyriologie.* Edited by Erich Ebeling and Bruno Meissner. Vol. 2. Berlin, 1938.

Ussher, James. *Annales Veteris et Novi Testamenti.* Genevae, 1722.

_____. *The Annals of the World.* London, 1658.

_____. *Annales Veteris Testamenti.* Londini, 1650.

Vaux, Roland de. *Ancient Israel—Its Life and Institutions.* New York: McGraw-Hill, 1961.

_____. *Les livres des rois.* Paris, 1949.

Vogelstein, Max. *Biblical Chronology,* part 1. Cincinnati, 1944.

_____. *Jeroboam II—The Rise and Fall of His Empire.* Cincinnati, 1945.

Wade-Gery, H. T. "Chronological Notes." Part 3. *The Cambridge Ancient History.* Vol. 3. Edited by J. B. Bury, S. A. Cook, and F. E. Adcock. Cambridge, 1929.

Weidner, Ernst F. "Joiachin, Koenig von Juda, in babylonischen Keilschrifttexten." *Mélanges syriens offerts à Monsieur Réné Dussanud.* Vol. 1. Paris, 1939.

Wellhausen, Julius. *Prolegomena to the History of Israel.* Translated by J. Sutherland Black and Allan Menzies. Edinburgh, 1885.

Winckler, Hugo. *Die Keilschrifttexte Sargons.* Leipzig, 1889.

Wiseman, D. J. *Chronicles of Chaldaean Kings (626–556 B.C.) in the British Museum.* London: British Museum, 1956.

Zöckler, Otto. *The Books of the Chronicles.* Translated by James G. Murphy. Vol. 7. *A Commentary on the Holy Scriptures: Critical, Doctrinal, and Homiletical.* Edited by John Peter Lange; English edition edited by Philip Schaff. New York, 1877.

SUBJECT AND PERSON INDEX

Prepared by James F. Scott

AUTHOR INDEX

SCRIPTURE INDEX

Prepared by James F. Scott

249